Pocket Guide
to the
Common Birds of Ireland

Author
ERIC DEMPSEY

Artist
MICHAEL O'CLERY

GILL & MACMILLAN

Gill & Macmillan Ltd
Hume Avenue
Park West
Dublin 12
with associated companies throughout the world
www.gillmacmillan.ie

© text Eric Dempsey 1993, 1995
© artwork Michael O'Clery 1993, 1995

ISBN-13: 978 07171 2296 7
ISBN-10: 0 7171 2296 4

Print origination by Typeform Repro Ltd, Dublin
Printed in Malaysia

*The paper used in this book is made from the wood pulp of
managed forests. For every tree felled, at least one tree
is planted, thereby renewing natural resources.*

A catalogue record is available for this book
from the British Library.

6 8 10 9 7

Contents

How to use this book

This book consists of two sections:

- Introduction
- Species accounts

Introduction

This section gives a brief history of Irish ornithology. It discusses the importance of Ireland for birds and introduces various Irish habitats.

Species Accounts

This section describes the 210 species most frequently recorded in Ireland. Each description is accompanied by an illustration showing the main identification features. The written description includes separate sections on the voice and diet of each species, as well as its habitat and status in Ireland.

Understanding the maps

The maps are in three colours:

- Red shows the summer distribution.
- Blue shows the winter distribution.
- Green shows resident distribution.

Bird topography

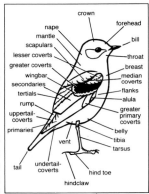

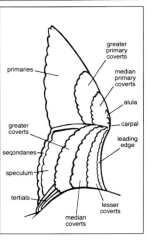

Winter distribution of Merlin

Summer distribution of Merlin

Resident distribution of Red Grouse

Solid colour shows where species are generally considered common within suitable habitat.

Hatched colour shows where species are considered uncommon to rare.

Introduction

A History of Irish Birdwatching

Until relatively recently, birds were considered only for their food value, the sport which they provided, or as vermin to be eliminated. The concept of sharing our world with other species of mammals and birds came much later to Ireland than to other countries.

While little is known of the birdlife of the past, an examination of Irish literature and poetry reveals references to Bitterns, Cranes and other species which are now no longer a part of Irish avifauna. Birds such as the Wild Swans of Lir have passed into Irish folklore, while other species like the Wren hold an important part in rural customs.

On St Stephen's Day, in many parts of the country, the 'Wran Boys' can still be heard singing the ancient rhyme:

The Wran, the Wran, king of all birds,
On St Stephen's Day he got caught in the furze,
Up with the kettle and down with the pan,
A penny or tuppence to bury the Wran.

The hunting of the Wren is an ancient Irish tradition which dates back to pre-Christian times. At the winter solstice, the king decreed that, for just one day, the roles of everyone would be inverted. The king would therefore become the pauper, and the Wren, the smallest of the birds, would become the king for one day. However, on this day, the Wren had to be hunted and killed, or everyone would remain in this inverted state. Thankfully, Wrens are no longer killed during such festivities.

Further evidence of past birdlife is the fact that many species which are now rare or extinct in Ireland have old Irish names. This suggests a familiarity with the species and may indicate that these birds were quite numerous in the past.

Discoveries of ancient Irish dwellings in caves and on island crannógs have produced bones of Irish birds such as geese, ducks, crows and finches, as well as those of eagles and cranes. Even bones of the extinct Great Auk have been identified at old coastal dwellings.

Introduction

The first written record of Irish birdlife can be traced back to the twelfth century when a Welsh monk, Giraldus Cambrensis, wrote a *History and Topography of Ireland.* While many observations made at the time were unreliable, he did describe species such as Ospreys, Peregrines and Dippers, and commented on the lack of Nightingales, Magpies and gamebirds like Pheasant and Partridge in Ireland.

Up to the early nineteenth century, most written work referred to gamebirds. However, it was with the increased interest in the world of science which occurred in the early part of that century that the first real studies began. The first book on the birds of Ireland was written by William Thompson. It appeared as three volumes between 1849 and 1851. During the latter half of that century, and in the early years of the twentieth century, many new and young ornithologists came to prominence. Of these, R. J. Ussher was among the most influential. In 1900, he and R. Warren published the *Birds of Ireland.* The work described the distribution and status of Irish birds. Also in 1900, another important book, *The Migration of Birds as observed at Irish Lighthouses and Lightships,* was published by R. M. Barrington. This was an extremely important account of the movements of birds off our coasts; in many ways, it was the first coastal bird observatory report.

In 1904, an important step towards bird conservation was taken with the formation of the Irish Society for the Protection of Birds. In 1921, the Ulster Society for the Protection of Birds was formed. Together, these two organisations purchased land in Mayo to protect breeding Red-necked Phalaropes. The threats to birds during the first half of this century included egg-collectors and shooting, and these societies were instrumental in the introduction of protective legislation.

Among the best known ornithologists of this period was George Humphreys who produced the *List of Irish Birds* in 1937. In 1950, the Irish Ornithologists Club was founded; in 1954, it produced the first *Irish Bird Report.* Also in 1954, three of the foremost Irish ornithologists, Major R. F. Ruttledge, Rev. P. G. Kennedy S. J., and Col. C. F. Scroope published the *Birds of Ireland.*

Introduction

Another important development during this period was the establishment of bird observatories, a direct result of the interest taken in bird migration by this time. Migration was studied on the Great Saltee in Wexford; on Copeland Island, Co. Down; on Malin Head and Tory Island in Donegal; and on Cape Clear Island in Cork. Many of today's prominent ornithologists learned their trade at these observatories. The sightings from these locations formed the basis of the *Irish Bird Report* and, in 1966, a systematic list, *Ireland's Birds,* was produced by Major Ruttledge.

A new era dawned in 1968 when the Irish Wildfowl Conservancy, the Irish Society for the Protection of Birds and the Irish Ornithologists Club amalgamated to form the Irish Wildbird Conservancy (IWC). This new society led the way in bird and habitat protection, scientific research and long-term studies carried out by amateur birdwatchers, including the Breeding and the Wintering Atlases.

The IWC still fulfils this role. It is now the largest conservation body in Ireland and has produced many publications, including the annual *Irish Birds.* This journal, while publishing scientific papers, also incorporates the *Irish Bird Report.*

Probably due to a greater awareness of the environment, the number of active amateur birdwatchers grew during the 1970s and early 1980s. Gordon D'Arcy produced *The Guide to the Birds of Ireland* during this period, while Clive Hutchinson published a book on the best birdwatching sites in Ireland. This latter book not only described the species which could be found at each site, but also provided details on the best routes to take, along with an Ordnance Survey map of each location.

With an increase in the observers, the availability of improved optical equipment and the great advances made in identification criteria, new and exciting discoveries were made. New species for Ireland were found on headlands and estuaries, while pelagic (deep water) trips off south-western Ireland found large concentrations of seabirds including the occasional Wilson's Petrel.

Introduction

Reports of rare birds are now submitted to the Irish Rare Bird Committee both for acceptance and for publication in the Irish Bird Reports. In 1989, a new *Birds in Ireland* was written by Clive Hutchinson. This work detailed all bird records up to December 1986.

The interest in migration, as well as the occurrence and identification of rare and unusual species in Ireland, continued to grow. As a result of this, the Birds of Ireland News Service (BINS) was formed in 1990. BINS not only provides an information service on the sightings of unusual species found in Ireland, but also produces a new quarterly journal, *Irish Birding News.*

In recent years, new areas have been discovered as migration watchpoints. Work at Loop Head in Co. Clare and Dunquin in Co. Kerry has proved worthwhile. Firkeel, Mizen Head and Garinish Point in Co. Cork are also being watched on a regular basis each autumn, and this has produced many spectacular species, including Ireland's first Northern Parula. Islands such as Dursey in Cork and Tory in Donegal are again being manned in the autumn. There are undoubtedly many other areas awaiting discovery.

As concern for the environment continues to grow, the future of birds in Ireland looks good. Societies like the Irish Wildbird Conservancy continue to increase their membership. By doing so, they gain the political strength needed to ensure the protection of Irish habitats and of the birds which depend on them. Each year, more people are discovering the wealth of birdlife around them.

Youngsters who are now only learning the joy and skills of birdwatching are the prominent ornithologists of the future. It is up to us to teach them well.

Irish Breeding Birds

By comparison to Great Britain, Ireland has considerably fewer breeding species. While many of these are migratory, there are also many resident species which, while common in Britain, are rare or unusual visitors to Ireland. There are several reasons and theories why this should be.

Introduction

First, Ireland has been isolated as an island for approximately 8000 years. As a result, many sedentary species including Nuthatches, Willow Tits and Tawny Owls, which do not move great distances, have not managed to cross the Irish Sea. Of other common British breeding species, Ireland has recorded Marsh Tit on only one occasion, while Green Woodpeckers are exceptionally rare visitors. Great Spotted Woodpeckers do occur more regularly, but it is believed that these birds occur during hard weather movements or irruptions from Continental Europe.

Second, migrants are at a disadvantage to resident birds. Due to mild Irish winters, its resident species generally suffer a lower mortality rate. This allows them to commence breeding in the best habitats before many migrants have even arrived. With the best nesting territories and the most productive feeding areas already occupied, Ireland has fewer available niches for migratory species.

Lastly, and importantly, Ireland has fewer habitat types than Britain. Ireland contains less deciduous woodlands and Caledonian Scots pine forests, while habitats such as heaths, chalk downland and very high mountain ranges are totally absent. Such habitats attract a specialised selection of species, which explains why birds like Hobby, Woodlark, Dartford Warbler, Crested Tit and Ptarmigan do not breed in Ireland.

Although Ireland has generally fewer breeding birds than other European countries, it does hold important numbers of some species which are showing a serious decline elsewhere. While seabird colonies include the largest breeding numbers of Storm Petrels in the world, Ireland also holds good breeding tern colonies. These include Arctic, Common, Sandwich and Little Terns.

More importantly, Ireland holds important numbers of the rare Roseate Tern. This species has shown a serious population decrease throughout Europe and North America. However, Ireland has several colonies of these terns. Due to proper management and wardening of these important colonies, along with the discovery that Roseate Terns will readily breed in special nest boxes, numbers appear to be increasing at locations such as Lady's Island Lake in Wexford and on Rockabill Island in Dublin.

Introduction

Ireland is also home to one of the largest populations of Chough to be found in Europe. While this species is relatively rare in Britain, Choughs can still be found in good numbers in northern, western and southern counties.

Of all the species which breed in Ireland, the Corncrake is the most threatened. Ireland now holds one of the largest concentrations of Corncrakes in western Europe. Despite exhaustive work, this species may now be sliding towards extinction. Declines in Ireland were first noted around the turn of the century. Although populations continued to decrease throughout the country, a survey carried out between 1968 and 1972 showed that Corncrakes were still present in all counties. However, work done in 1978 showed that the species was absent from many of its former breeding strongholds. It was estimated that approximately 1200 to 1500 pairs were present in Ireland. By 1988, the Irish breeding population was estimated to be fewer that 1000 birds. By 1992, it was considered that fewer than 400 pairs of Corncrakes were left. Studies of Corncrakes on the Shannon Callows (flood plains) involved radio-tracking individual birds. Early results from such work have shown that calling males do not necessarily mean that a pair is established in a territory. As early survey work regarded each calling male as representing a pair, it now seems that Ireland has even fewer breeding pairs than once believed.

The main reason for the decline of the Corncrake is recent changes in farming practices, in particular the cutting of silage. This requires the grass meadows to be cut earlier in the year than was formerly the practice when farmers engaged in haymaking. As a result, eggs and nests are destroyed. Very often, chicks and females, reluctant to leave the nest, are killed.

With a species such as the Corncrake on the edge of extinction, the small breeding territories which Ireland still offers are of international importance. Ireland also holds the most southern-breeding Red-necked Phalaropes in the world. This elegant species breeds occasionally at a site in Co. Mayo. At the beginning of the century, this site held up to fifty pairs. In recent years, however, only one or two birds are found annually and breeding does not always take place.

There are several other species which are declining as breeding birds in Ireland. These include Corn Bunting, Yellowhammer, Nightjar, Grey Partridge, Twite, Red Grouse, Merlin and Hen Harrier. Most of these declines are related to changes in habitat management.

There is some good news, however, and it seems that certain species are now increasing their breeding numbers in Ireland. For example, Reed Warblers, once a very rare breeding bird, are now present in good numbers in reed-beds along southern, eastern and north-eastern counties. Breeding populations of Wood Warblers and Buzzards are also increasing, while Peregrine Falcons are now back to their former numbers. Very small numbers of Garganey now also breed on a regular basis in suitable Irish wetlands.

There are also other potential breeding species. Of these, the Lesser Whitethroat, formerly a rare vagrant, is now occurring on a regular basis in spring and autumn. Several reports refer to males singing and holding territory at suitable breeding locations. In 1989, a male was heard in song at a location in the south-east. The following year, Lesser Whitethroats bred for the first time in Ireland at this site.

In 1992, Whooper Swans bred for the first time in Co. Donegal. A gull which may also possibly breed in the future is the Ring-billed Gull. First recorded in Ireland in 1979, this North American species is now frequently found among gull flocks around Ireland.

Such colonisations are usually the result of a range expansion by a species. The best example of such expansion is the Collared Dove. This Asian species began to spread across Europe during the first half of the twentieth century. It was first recorded in Ireland in 1959 and slowly began to extend its Irish range. Now, Collared Doves breed in all counties. Such sudden range expansions can be difficult to predict. Perhaps in the next ten years, a species which is now considered rare will become a common Irish breeding bird.

Looking to the future, it seems obvious that only proper conservation actions and management policies will slow the decline of those breeding

Introduction

birds which are now under threat. It will be a great tragedy if, in the future, the sounds of Corncrakes and Corn Buntings are not heard in our countryside, or if the graceful Roseate Tern is no longer seen off our coasts.

Irish Races

Ireland has fewer breeding bird species than its nearest neighbours. The island has been isolated for up to 8000 years, and this has prevented many species from reaching Ireland's shores. The diversity of bird species changes from season to season. Migrants arrive each summer and winter. Even birds which are generally considered to be resident can engage in movements between countries.

However, some of our species rarely leave Ireland. In effect, these species have been isolated from their main European populations for thousands of years. They have gradually adapted to their Irish habitats and now appear significantly different from their British and European counterparts. As a result, they are considered as distinct Irish races.

Ireland has four such species. They are Coal Tit, Dipper, Jay and Red Grouse.

Coal Tit

Parus ater

Irish Coal Tits, *P. a. hibernicus,* differ from birds of the British race, *P. a. britannicus,* and the Continental race, *P. a. ater,* by showing a different plumage tone. Irish birds also show a larger bill, although this feature is impossible to discern in the field.

Irish Coal Tits are best recognised by the strong sulphur-yellow tones on the cheeks, breast and belly. Both British and Continental races show white cheeks and underparts. British birds lack the buffish tinge on the greyish-green upperparts as seen on the Irish race, while Continental birds show pure grey upperparts.

Irish Coal Tits also tend to show buff tips to the uppertail-coverts. This can give them a slight pale-rumped appearance. On British birds, this feature is much duller, while Continental birds do not have any suggestion of a paler rump.

While these differences appear subtle, and variations can occur, the classic Irish race of Coal Tit is very distinctive. Equally distinctive is the Continental race, and birds showing features of this race have occurred in Ireland on coastal islands in the autumn. Birds showing some or all of the characteristics of the British race are frequently recorded in Ireland, often associating with Irish birds.

Dipper
Cinclus cinclus

The Irish race, *C. c. hibernicus,* and the British race, *C. c. gularis,* of Dipper are very similar. They both show a chestnut band on the lower breast forming a border to the white gorget. This feature alone easily distinguishes them from the Continental race, *C. c. cinclus,* which shows a black lower breast and belly.

Top: Typical Coal Tit of the Irish race.
Centre: Typical Coal Tit of the British race.
Bottom: Typical Coal Tit of the Continental race.

However, the Irish race does show subtle differences from the British race. The best feature is the extent and brightness of the chestnut band on the lower breast. Irish birds tend to show a narrower and duller band. Irish Dippers also show slightly darker upperparts.

9

Introduction

It appears that Dippers showing the features of the Irish race are also resident and breeding in parts of western Scotland.

Birds of the Black-bellied Continental race have occurred in Ireland on two occasions. One was present on the River Tolka, Dublin, during the winter of 1956, and one was found on Tory Island, Donegal, in the autumn of 1962.

Jay
Garrulus glandarius

The Irish race of Jay, *G. g. hibernicus,* appears generally darker and duller than both the British race, *G. g. rufitergum,* and the Continental race, *G. g. glandarius.*

In comparison to the British race, *hibernicus* shows darker ear-coverts, sides of the head and mantle, while the underparts of the British race are slightly paler, especially towards the vent area. The dark crown streaking on the British race tends to be thinner with broader white edges. This

Top: Typical Dipper of the Irish race.
Centre: Typical Dipper of the British race.
Bottom: Typical Dipper of the Continental race, known as the 'Black-bellied Dipper'.

can give the crown a whiter appearance than seen on Irish birds. British Jays also show whiter throats and have a tendency to show a white area immediately below the eye which is rarely seen on birds of the Irish race.

Introduction

The Continental race shows greyish to greyish-brown upperparts, while the underparts appear even paler than those of the British race. The dark Irish race therefore differs significantly from the Continental race.

Red Grouse
Lagopus lagopus
The Irish race of Red Grouse, *L. l. hibernicus,* shows very subtle differences compared to the British race, *L. l. scoticus.* Irish birds are generally paler than British birds.

Females especially appear paler and more yellowish, and show paler, more finely barred underparts. The differences between males of the two races are less significant, but again, Irish birds tend to show a paler plumage and paler, finer barring.

It is believed that the paler plumage of Irish birds is an adaptation to their heather habitat which tends to have a higher content of grasses and sedges. This allows for potentially better camouflage.

Top: Typical Jay of the Irish race.
Centre: Typical Jay of the British race.
Bottom: Typical Jay of the Continental race.

Equally, the darker birds of Britain are best suited to their darker heather habitat which contains a lower grass and sedge content.

Introduction

As these differences are very subtle, some believe that both the Irish and British birds belong to the same race, *L. l. scoticus.*

Red Grouse itself is a race of the Willow Grouse which shows extensive white on the underparts and wings. In winter, Willow Grouse show an almost wholly white plumage. Willow Grouse occur in Scandinavia and northern Europe.

The Importance of Irish Seabird Colonies

Surrounded by food-rich waters, Ireland plays host each summer to thousands of seabirds which breed on naturally rocky islands and steep cliffs. Few European countries can surpass Ireland for the sheer numbers and variety of seabird species found along Irish coastlines.

Top: Typical Red Grouse of the Irish race.
Bottom: Typical Red Grouse of the British race.

The geographical location of these sites is extremely important, dictating the numbers and the species which are found in each. Seabirds which feed far out on open, exposed seas tend to breed on the Atlantic shoreline. Those which feed on shallower, inshore waters are usually found close to the Irish Sea.

Up to nine Irish seabird colonies contain over 10,000 pairs. Of these, six lie on the Atlantic. They are the Skellig Islands, the Blasket Islands and Puffin Island in Co. Kerry; Inishglora and Illaunmaistir in Co. Mayo;

and Horn Head in Co. Donegal. The three large eastern seaboard colonies are on Rathlin Island, Co. Antrim; Lambay Island, Co. Dublin; and Great Saltee, Co. Wexford.

The largest breeding colonies of Storm Petrels in the world are found on the small, remote, rugged islands off Kerry. These islands also hold tens of thousands of Puffins and Manx Shearwaters. The rare Leach's Petrel also breeds in very small numbers on the remote islands off Co. Mayo. It is suspected that Leach's Petrels may also breed off Kerry and Donegal.

One of the most dramatic seabird colonies in Ireland is the isolated Little Skellig Island which is home to over 20,000 pairs of Gannets. Other Gannet colonies can be found on the Bull Rock, Co. Cork; Clare Island, Co. Mayo; and on the Great Saltee Island, Co. Wexford, where two separate colonies are now established. In recent years, a new and successful colony has started on the stacks off Ireland's Eye, Co. Dublin.

Fulmars, Cormorants, Shags, Kittiwakes, Greater and Lesser Black-backed Gulls and Herring Gulls breed in large numbers at suitable sites along most coastal counties. Colonies of Guillemots and Razorbills are also present in most coastal regions, but the largest numbers occur in the north and north-west. The Black Guillemot is found in small numbers in most coastal regions.

Irish seabirds face many dangers. They are particularly vulnerable to pollution and oil spillages, while thousands drown in the miles of almost invisible gill nets which are laid around the coasts each year. However, the presence of such a variety and number of breeding seabirds serves as a constant reminder of the rich, clean waters which surround Ireland.

Migration

Ireland experiences vast movements of birds to and from its shores each year. In autumn, wintering waders and wildfowl arrive from their northern breeding grounds, while our summer visitors are beginning their return journey south. Other species, such as Little Stints and Curlew Sandpipers, simply use Ireland as a stopping-off point on their long flights.

Introduction

In spring, this situation is reversed, with birds arriving from Africa to spend the summer here. Most people are aware of this annual spectacle and letters appear annually in the newspapers about sighting the first Swallow or hearing the first Cuckoo. All birdwatchers will admit to a feeling of great excitement on seeing the first migrants of the year flying in off the sea or feeding on a coastal headland.

Due to Ireland's westerly location, many species do not reach its shores. Some birds which are common in Europe are relatively rare in Ireland. In autumn and spring, rarer vagrants from Europe and Siberia do not occur here in the same numbers in which they are found in Britain.

However, Ireland's geographical location is extremely important for the occurrence of other long-distance migrants. Being on the western edge of Europe, Ireland is often the first landfall for North American species. Irish coasts also experience dramatic seabird movements which make it the envy of many European neighbours.

American Vagrants

Over two thousand miles of open ocean lie between Ireland and the North American continent, a seemingly unsurmountable obstacle to the occurrence of North American species in Ireland. However, North American waders, gulls and passerines are found every autumn. In winter, North American ducks are also frequently found associating with commoner duck species.

Most of the waders which occur breed on the tundras of Arctic Canada. Each autumn, they begin their long southward migration to Central or South America. Many fly over the open Atlantic, performing long-distance, non-stop flights. It is during such flights that birds can get lost or caught in strong weather fronts. Such fronts can sometimes cross the Atlantic rapidly, depositing weary travellers on Irish shores. It is interesting to note that most American waders which occur here are immature birds which are making the journey for the first time.

Most of these vagrants simply begin feeding and will often associate with other wader species. Among the more common American waders are Pectoral, Baird's, White-rumped and Buff-breasted Sandpipers.

Introduction

Long-billed Dowitchers and Wilson's Phalaropes are frequent visitors, as are American Golden Plovers. Ireland has also recorded some of Europe's rarest wader visitors, including Short-billed Dowitcher and Western Sandpiper.

Weather also plays a vital role in the arrival of North American passerines to Ireland. Most of these birds winter or migrate through the Gulf regions of Central America. Autumn is, of course, the hurricane season in these parts. Occasionally these hurricanes move north-eastwards across the Atlantic. Travelling at great speeds, they usually arrive on Irish shores as severe storms. Small and light passerines which are caught in such storms are carried helplessly with them. Many must die out at sea, but occasionally a tiny proportion survive the ordeal and reach Irish coastal headlands and islands.

At migration watchpoints in the south-west, these birds are often found following such storms. Among the most frequently seen are Red-eyed Vireos and Rose-breasted Grosbeaks. Ireland has been graced by some of the rarest North American passerines ever to be recorded in Europe, including Philadelphia Vireo, Ovenbird, Indigo Bunting and Gray Catbird. Some birds, like Yellow-billed Cuckoos, are usually exhausted when they are found and most are discovered dead or dying. Ireland has even recorded a North American woodpecker in the shape of a Yellow-bellied Sapsucker. Belted Kingfishers have also occurred on three occasions although, regrettably, the first two birds were shot.

Ireland is also famous for the occurrence of North American gulls. Each autumn, Sabine's Gulls are seen during seawatches, while Ring-billed Gulls can occur in good numbers and at all times of the year. Other rarer gull species recorded in Ireland are Bonaparte's and Laughing Gulls. North American terns have also been found, and there are now several records of Forster's Terns, usually seen during the winter months. However, the most dramatic find was an Elegant Tern which spent almost two weeks at a tern colony in Greencastle, Co. Down, in 1982. It was also seen later that summer in Cork. This species is found on the Pacific coast of North America and this record was one of the first for the Western Palearctic.

Introduction

In winter, many American ducks are found within flocks of more common species. At sea, Surf Scoters occur with the large Common Scoter flocks. On Irish estuaries, Green and Blue-winged Teals and American Wigeons are frequently found feeding alongside their European counterparts. On lakes, diving ducks such as Ring-necked Ducks can associate with Pochard and Tufted Ducks. One of the rarest species to be found in recent years is a drake Lesser Scaup which has now wintered for several years on the inland lakes of Northern Ireland.

Snow and Canada Geese can often be found among the flocks of geese which winter in Ireland each year. Some birds return to winter in the same areas year after year. Vagrants can even be found with swans, and there are now several records of Whistling Swans, the North American race of Bewick's Swan.

It is possible for any North American migrant to land in Ireland. Even the unexpected can occur, as was proved by the finding of an American Coot in Cork in 1981.

Considering the thousands of miles these birds have travelled to reach Ireland, the fact that some survive the journey at all is testament to the strength and endurance of long-distance migrants.

Seabird Migration

While Ireland's westerly location is a disadvantage to the occurrence of European passerines, its geographical position is ideal for witnessing spectacular seabird movements in the autumn.

Many of the species, which pass in tens of thousands off south-western and western headlands and islands, are birds which breed in Ireland. These include Gannets, Fulmars, Kittiwakes, Manx Shearwaters, Storm Petrels and auks. Many of these also come from colonies in other countries. However, the most spectacular seabird movements off the Irish coasts involve not only breeding species, but also shearwaters from the South Atlantic, gulls from North America and skuas from northern breeding grounds.

Introduction

Studies have indicated that such movements can often be anticipated by watching the changing weather patterns. Birds which feed out at sea or which migrate south are often blown to inshore waters by strong winds or bad weather. Strong south-westerly winds with rain, usually associated with a rapidly moving weather front, can result in a large passage of common species as well as Sooty, Mediterranean, Great and Cory's Shearwaters; Great, Pomarine and Arctic Skuas; Grey Phalaropes and Sabine's Gulls. During such conditions, islands and headlands like Cape Clear and the Old Head of Kinsale, both in Cork, have proved to be the best locations.

Should such weather conditions result in strong north-westerly winds, headlands in the north and west can provide the best seawatching. Of these, the Bridges of Ross near Loop Head in Co. Clare has gained an international reputation for the birds which pass in such conditions. While thousands of commoner seabirds are seen, species such as Long-tailed Skua and Leach's Petrel pass in unprecedented numbers. Also recorded are Sabine's Gulls. Seawatches in the winter have resulted in the largest recorded movements of Little Auks off Ireland. The rare and elusive Wilson's Petrel has even been recorded off the Bridges of Ross.

In spring, while seabird passage is not spectacular, observations indicate that a good northerly movement of Pomarine Skuas takes place off southern and western coasts. Seawatching off extreme western locations has revealed that Long-tailed Skuas also move north off Irish coasts each spring.

With a greater understanding of the feeding patterns of seabirds, pelagic trips off western and south-western coasts have been organised in recent years in an effort to locate them. The best feeding areas are where warm and cool waters mix, and where cool upwelling currents bring nutrients to the surface to promote the growth of plankton. This in turn supports the various fish species on which seabirds feed. Waters over the Continental Shelf provide such ideal conditions.

Pelagic trips also attempt to attract feeding seabirds by spreading chum (an extremely strong-smelling mixture of fish oil and offal) on the surface of the sea. Such tactics have been successful on many occasions, with

Introduction

species such as Wilson's Petrel giving tantalising close-up views. Other species seen on the trips include Long-tailed Skuas, Sabine's Gulls, Grey Phalaropes and a variety of shearwaters.

The variety and numbers of seabirds present off Ireland each year provide birdwatchers with an opportunity to witness some of the best seabird movements in Europe. Any seabird species can conceivably pass the coastline, with extraordinary sightings including Little Shearwaters, Magnificent Frigatebirds and Black-browed Albatrosses.

New discoveries are constantly being made. In recent years, the first Soft-plumaged Petrel was recorded off Ireland. This was quickly followed by several records in successive years. An increased awareness of these and other species provides an opportunity to discover more about the exciting seabirds which can pass Irish headlands and islands. Seawatching requires skill and patience. Those who possess such qualities are usually rewarded.

The Importance of Ireland in Winter

The Irish climate, with comparatively few hard winters, allows resident birds to enjoy a relatively low winter mortality rate. Mild winters are also important for providing the rich, soft feeding necessary for waders. The wet climate creates the suitable wetlands for wildfowl, and the relatively snow-free weather provides ideal winter feeding grounds for thousands of thrushes and finches.

Lying on the western edge of Europe, Ireland is ideally located to attract wintering wildfowl, waders and passerines from breeding grounds in Arctic Canada, Greenland, Iceland, northern Europe and Siberia.

Up to eighteen coastal and fourteen inland Irish wetland sites have now been recognised as holding internationally important populations of wildfowl and waders. Of the coastal areas, Lough Foyle, Co. Derry; Strangford Lough, Co. Down; the Shannon Estuary of Kerry, Clare and Limerick; Cork Harbour; Dundalk Bay, Co. Louth; and the North Bull Island, Co. Dublin, usually attract over 20,000 waders each winter. Irish estuaries also hold most of the Icelandic breeding population of

Black-tailed Godwits; areas such as Ballymacoda in Co. Cork hold internationally important numbers of this species.

The sight of thousands of waders feeding or flying in large, dense flocks is a spectacular winter experience not to be forgotten. Equally exciting is the sight and sound of skeins of geese arriving in Ireland each winter. Some coastal locations have attained international recognition purely based on the wintering populations of pale-bellied Brent Geese, while Lissadell in Sligo has been recognised as holding important numbers of Barnacle Geese. On the Wexford Wildfowl Reserve, up to half the world's population of Greenland White-fronted Geese can be found. The reserve also attracts large numbers of Bewick's Swans, Bar-tailed Godwits and ducks annually.

Ireland's inland wetlands provide a secure and food-rich winter haven for Whooper and Bewick's Swans, Greylag Geese, many species of duck, and waders such as Curlew, Lapwing and Golden Plover.

Of the large inland lakes, Loughs Neagh and Beg of Antrim, Armagh, Derry and Tyrone hold the largest numbers of Goldeneye, Pochard and Tufted Duck to be found anywhere in Europe. Lough Neagh also attracts the largest European inland population of Scaup. Lough Corrib in Co. Galway holds an important wintering population of Pochard as well as large numbers of Coot. Other larger and deeper inland lakes do not have a significantly large wildfowl population, while smaller lakes like Lough Iron, Owel and Derravaragh are known to attract significant wildfowl numbers.

Flooded callows and marshes are important wetland areas which hold large wintering populations of waders and wildfowl. Of these, the Shannon Callows between Portumna and Athlone, the Little Brosna in Offaly and Tipperary, and the callows of the River Suck in Galway and Roscommon hold important wintering populations of Wigeon, Whooper Swans and, at some locations, Greenland White-fronted Geese. On the fringes of these wetlands, Golden Plover, Lapwing, Curlew, Black-tailed Godwit and Snipe occur in large numbers.

Off Ireland's coasts each winter, sea-duck such as Common Scoters are found in large flocks, while species such as Velvet Scoters and

Introduction

Long-tailed Ducks occur in smaller numbers. Other wintering species include Red-throated and Great Northern Divers, Great-crested Grebes and, in some traditional locations, Slavonian and Black-necked Grebes. Iceland and Glaucous Gulls also occur annually, usually at fishing ports, harbours or on rubbish tips.

Ireland's mild climate, with comparatively few hard winters, is a great attraction to thousands of winter thrushes. On still November nights, the thin, high-pitched calls of Redwings and Fieldfares can often be heard as the birds arrive overnight. Large, mixed flocks of these thrushes are a common winter sight in open country. They will also occasionally visit gardens in towns and cities. Colourful Bramblings can also occur with finch flocks while, along some coasts, tame and charming Snow Buntings are annual visitors.

Ireland is also an important refuge for many thousands of birds which arrive here during extremely cold weather on the Continent or in Britain. When this occurs, normal wintering numbers are swollen considerably, but the rich winter food resources can cope adequately with such influxes. Occasionally, Ireland is graced with large numbers of Waxwings which irrupt from northern Europe. These tame berry-eaters are the most colourful and exotic species which occur in winter.

By early spring, thousands of winter visitors will have begun the long journey north to their breeding grounds. There, they will spend the brief northern summer before returning in autumn to the safe, food-rich winter haven that awaits them in Ireland.

Bird Habitats in Ireland

Ireland has a wide variety of different habitats ranging from mountains and moorland to coastal estuaries and islands. Each habitat is unique, holding specific species of birds at different times of the year. It is important to know how to birdwatch in each of these areas without causing disturbance, especially to breeding species. Equally, it is very useful to know when to visit each habitat and to know what birds to expect.

Introduction

This section will examine nine different habitats in Ireland. It will suggest how and when to birdwatch in them and will indicate which species can be expected in each.

Mountains and Moorlands

Ireland is a reasonably flat country, with only 25% of the total land mass over 150m. Yet the mountains and moorlands not only provide spectacular scenery, but are also home to many species of birds. Irish mountain ranges are mostly situated around the edges of the island and as such do not suffer the harsh winter snowfalls of similar ranges in Britain and Continental Europe. However, in winter, Irish mountains and moorlands are relatively bleak, with most species moving to lower or coastal regions.

In spring, Stonechats, Wheatears, Meadow Pipits and Skylarks are found in abundance on the moorlands, while Cuckoos are reasonably common. The rocky, upland scree slopes provide an ideal habitat for Ring Ouzels, while cliff faces provide suitable breeding sites for Ravens, Kestrels and Peregrine Falcons. On moorlands, the small, agile Merlin nests in small numbers. In the north and west, a small breeding population of Golden Plovers is present. Red Grouse are also found on the mountainous moorlands, although populations appear to have declined in recent years.

Much of Ireland's moorlands are being lost to conifer plantations. However, young plantations provide an ideal breeding habitat for Hen Harriers. Whinchats too can occur in such areas. In some of the lower stretches of moorland, the reeling of Grasshopper Warblers can often be heard. These birds are difficult to see, and are best listened for at dusk or dawn.

Birdwatching in the mountains and moorlands, although rewarding, can also be difficult. The methods employed depend on the species one wants to see and, more importantly, on one's level of fitness. Watching from a suitable vantage point can be productive and causes the least disturbance. Patient observations can result in stunning views of a variety of birds, including raptors, warblers, Ring Ouzels and Ravens. However,

Introduction

climbing and walking the moorlands is usually the only way of seeing Red Grouse. Along mountain tops and moorland, species including Skylarks and Meadow Pipits can be found in large numbers. In winter, Snow Buntings can occur in small flocks on higher ground.

Coniferous Forests

More and more of Ireland's mountainous regions are being covered by coniferous plantations. These mostly consist of Sitka Spruce and Lodgepole Pine, as well as some Larch, Norway Spruce, and Douglas and Noble Firs. While young plantations do offer breeding sites for Hen Harriers and Whinchats, the more mature forests, with trees closely planted side by side, provide little in the way of suitable habitat for many species. With careful searching, some specialised species can be found. The one advantage about coniferous forests is that, being mostly state-owned, access is easy. There are usually good pathways, and an effortless stroll can bring a birdwatcher into the heart of the forest. Such habitat is ideal for Siskins and Redpolls, while Goldcrests and Coal Tits are common. Sparrowhawks too can be found in such areas.

The coniferous forest is home to one of the most unusual species found in Ireland, the Crossbill. These birds are found in areas where trees are heavy with cones. Their especially adapted bills, with crossed mandibles, prise open the cones and extract the seeds inside. In some years, Crossbills can occur in large flocks. They are often found perched on the tops of the trees. They are also very vocal and their distinctive, loud *chip* calls can be the first indication of their presence.

At night, Woodcocks and Long-eared Owls can be found. These are best looked for by standing still, in cover, and watching over an open space. In some coniferous forests, the rare Nightjar also occurs. The far-carrying churring song of the male is perhaps one of the most dramatic songs to be heard in Ireland. Nightjars require more mature forests, usually those with large open tracts. They can also occur in forests close to open moorland and bogs.

Birdwatching in coniferous forests is best done by slowly walking the pathways, listening as well as looking. Another method is to view the forest from a height. This method is often rewarded by views of Sparrowhawks or perched Crossbills.

Deciduous Forests

Deciduous forests represent a sadly small proportion of Ireland's woodland areas. There are now few true Oak woodlands left. Many deciduous forests comprise a mixture of Oak, Ash, Hazel, Birch and smaller numbers of Yew and Elm. While not plentiful, such forests provide excellent birdwatching, particularly in summer.

Among the many species found in deciduous woodlands are resident birds like Treecreepers, Long-tailed, Great, Coal and Blue Tits, and Jays. Sparrowhawks may also find suitable nesting sites in the quieter, less disturbed parts of the woodland.

In summer, Spotted Flycatchers, Willow Warblers and Chiffchaffs are among the commoner migrants. Blackcaps can also be found, but only if there is suitable dense undergrowth. Some of the more mature woodlands are graced by the songs of the rare Wood Warbler and Redstart.

Birdwatching is at its best early in the morning when the birds are active and singing. If the weather is bad, with heavy rain, deciduous forests can seem barren and empty as birds tend to keep low and seek shelter in such conditions.

In winter, deciduous woodlands tend to be much quieter. While resident species are still present, winter visitors can include Bramblings which are particularly partial to Beech mast. Flocks of Siskins are also frequently encountered feeding in Birches and Alders. Mixed roving tit flocks are a familiar winter sight.

Birdwatching in deciduous woodlands is best done by walking slowly and quietly. Many of the birds which are found in these woodlands are usually heard first. It is therefore advisable not just to look for birds, but to listen carefully.

Searching for nocturnal species like Long-eared Owl and Woodcock requires patience and silence. Stand in cover overlooking open tracts of

Introduction

woodland. Listen especially for the muffled *oo* of adult Long-eared Owls or the low, guttural song of roding Woodcocks.

Freshwater Rivers

Ireland's landscape contains an intricate maze of freshwater river systems. All have their beginnings in the mountain ranges. As these ranges are usually close to the sea, rivers in Ireland consist of two main types. Those that run from the seaward side of the high ground are fast-flowing and quickly make their way to the coast. These differ from the river systems that run from the landward side which tend to be slow-flowing and meandering.

On the faster uphill river stretches, species such as Dippers and Grey Wagtails can be found feeding. Dippers walk or swim under the surface of the water in search of a variety of aquatic invertebrates. Grey Wagtails are usually seen searching for insects along the banks, although they may also be found perched on small rocks in the middle of fast-flowing water. Both species can also occur on lower stretches of such rivers. Along the rocky edges of upland streams and rivers, Common Sandpipers occur in summer.

The slower rivers usually allow dense vegetation to grow along their banks. These provide ideal breeding habitats for species such as Moorhens, Reed Buntings and, in suitable areas of rushes and reeds, Sedge Warblers. Mallard also breed in the dense cover afforded by such vegetation, while Mute Swans are a common sight on these slow, wide, food-rich water systems.

Along the quieter stretches of rivers, one may be lucky to glimpse the bright turquoise shock of a Kingfisher in flight. The speed and small size of this magnificent bird often come as a surprise to many. Kingfishers prefer slow, undisturbed stretches and tend to fish from favourite perches. In discovering such a perch, patience and silence will be rewarded with excellent views. Kingfishers breed in holes which are excavated in river banks. These nesting burrows can be unobtrusive and difficult to see. Not hard to notice, however, are Sand Martins which also nest in holes on river banks. These birds are usually found in small colonies and their noisy comings and goings make them difficult to overlook.

The shallower river stretches are favourite hunting grounds for Grey Herons. These birds stand motionless, waiting patiently before stabbing at prey with their long, dagger-like bills. Heronries are often found in stands of trees along such rivers and streams.

Closer to the coast, a variety of species can be found frequenting the river systems as they reach their final destination. These include ducks, gulls and waders. In summer, terns can also feed along rivers; many inland colonies are based along such courses. On quieter coastal streams, Green Sandpipers may even be encountered. In winter, Dippers, Grey Wagtails and Kingfishers sometimes find the coastal stretches more suitable.

Birdwatching methods along rivers vary according to the type of river and its location. Slow-moving rivers are best watched by walking the banks. Many species like Mute Swans and Mallards are easy to see. Others like Kingfishers can often give just a tantalising flight view. Faster, uphill river stretches are a little more difficult to watch. Check for shallow, fast-flowing water with suitable rocks on which birds may perch. Here, Dippers and Grey Wagtails are best found by watching from a vantage point and searching long stretches of river. At the coast, many species can be watched easily as they feed where rivers meet the sea.

Freshwater Lakes, Marshes and Reed-beds

These are among the richest birdwatching habitats in Ireland. Frequently found side by side, they provide an excellent selection of bird species at all times of the year.

Open freshwater areas vary greatly in size, from the enormous Lough Neagh to smaller, insignificant lakes. Marshland occurs where water just covers the surface. Here, feeding on the rich nutrients, grow a selection of plants including rushes, reeds and sedges. Some of these reed-beds can become quite extensive.

Introduction

Lakes are best visited in the winter when large flocks of diving ducks such as Pochard and Tufted Duck are found. Dabbling duck like Gadwall, Teal, Mallard and Wigeon also occur. In winter, ducks are shot and are usually extremely wary as a result. Care must therefore be taken not to cause further disturbance. Appearing suddenly on a lake shore or breaking the horizon usually results in absolute panic amongst the ducks. Watching wildfowl is best done from a hide or even a car.

In summer, lakes hold a wide variety of breeding species, especially if there are some small islets. Common and Arctic Terns may occur, sometimes in large numbers if the habitat is close to the coast. Such tern colonies may even contain breeding pairs of the rare Roseate Tern. Common and Black-headed Gulls also breed on lake islands. Common Sandpipers are another familiar species along lake shores in summer.

Swallows, Sand Martins and Swifts can be seen over lakes on balmy summer evenings. Large flocks of these agile, aerial hunters can give terrific views as they feed on the swarms of flying insects.

Birdwatching can be more difficult in marshes. These wet habitats are ideal for breeding Snipe, Redshank and Lapwing. While Redshank move to more coastal locations in winter, Snipe numbers usually increase. Occasionally the smaller Jack Snipe may occur. Such wet marshes usually contain dense vegetation where species like Mute Swans, Coots and Moorhens find suitable breeding sites. Such areas may also attract duck; the rare Garganey which now breeds in small numbers in Ireland favours the fringes of reed-beds and vegetation.

Reed-beds offer an opportunity to see and hear some specialised bird species. In the summer, a variety of migrants can be found, including Sedge, Grasshopper and, more recently, Reed Warblers. Cuckoos are also attracted to these areas in search of suitable nests in which to lay their eggs. Other species include Reed Buntings, Coots, Moorhens and, in the evenings, Swallows and Swifts. Raptors also hunt over reed-beds and in recent years Marsh Harriers have become annual passage migrants. It may not be too long before this powerful bird becomes a regular breeding species.

Introduction

In winter, reed-beds hold a large number and variety of wildfowl, Coots and Moorhens which, in turn, attract wintering Hen Harriers and Sparrowhawks. In some extensive stretches, enormous winter roosts of Starlings can be found. Reed-beds also serve as roosts for Swallows and martins in the autumn.

Reed-beds often cover large areas and can prove difficult to watch. Birds are frequently heard but not seen and this is particularly true of the Water Rail. Their high-pitched, pig-like squealing call is probably the most distinctive sound of this habitat.

At all times of the year, reed-beds are best viewed from a suitable vantage point. Patience is required but it is usually rewarded.

Farmland

Ireland is an agricultural land, with approximately 70% of the countryside consisting of farmland. Such habitat is ideal for the variety of wildlife that lives along hedgerows. Unlike many other countries, hedgerows still act as natural borders to land, and Ireland still provides some of the best examples of such habitat to be found anywhere in Europe. Among the commonest plants found in hedgerow systems are Hawthorn, Blackthorn, Gorse, Brambles and Dog Roses. Other climbing species can also be found, including Ivy and Woodbine.

In summer, breeding birds include Chiffchaffs, Willow Warblers, Whitethroats, Blackbirds, Song Thrushes, Greenfinches, Bullfinches and Chaffinches. The rich songs of these species are familiar features of the farmland habitat, as is the far-carrying call of the Cuckoo. Farmyards also provide suitable breeding habitat for Swallows, tits and, occasionally, Spotted Flycatchers. In cereal-growing areas, species such as Quail and Grey Partridge can occur in summer. In some regions in the midlands, west and north-west, Corncrakes can still be heard in the hay meadows. Unfortunately, this striking call, once a common sound of the Irish countryside, is now little more than a memory in most parts.

In winter, large flocks of Redwings and Fieldfares are found on open fields and along hedgerows. Skylarks and Meadow Pipits are found in

Introduction

abundance, while Lapwings, Golden Plovers, Curlews and Black-headed Gulls also feed in open tracts of land. Farmyards in winter can attract large mixed flocks of Greenfinches, Chaffinches and House Sparrows. Occasionally, Bramblings and Tree Sparrows can associate with these flocks.

Woodpigeons are a common sight on farmland at all times of the year, but the shyer Stock Dove can only be found in reasonably large flocks in winter.

Farmlands also provide good hunting grounds for raptors. Kestrels and Sparrowhawks are common throughout the year. Hen Harriers are occasionally found quartering over the fields in winter, taking advantage of the abundance of prey this habitat provides. Farmlands are also important for Barn Owls, providing safe nesting sites and rich food sources.

Birdwatching in farmland areas can be difficult. In summer, a walk along the hedgerows is the best method. In winter, however, it is often best to view feeding flocks of thrushes, plovers, waders and gulls from a distance. It is vital to remember that farmlands are usually privately owned, and permission should always be sought before entering any land.

Finally, it is worth noting that extraordinary species can occasionally be found on farmland. In the past, these have included Hoopoes, Cattle Egrets and even a Bald Eagle.

Estuaries

Less than 15% of the Irish coastline falls into this category. Yet coastal estuaries and mudflats are without a doubt among the most rewarding and productive habitats in Ireland. Mudflats contain countless numbers of invertebrates which provide a rich source of food for many shorebirds. An abundance of plant life can also be found on the mudflats and saltmarshes, and these attract feeding ducks and geese.

As most of the birds which feed on estuaries and mudflats are winter visitors, the best time to visit such a habitat is between late autumn and early spring when a wealth of waders including Dunlin, Knot, Bar and

Black-tailed Godwit, Redshank, Curlew and Oystercatcher occur in their thousands. Golden, Grey and Ringed Plovers also occur, while ducks include Pintail, Wigeon, Teal, Shoveler, Mallard and Shelduck. Large flocks of Brent Geese also graze on these estuaries; as the winter progresses, they can become exceptionally tame.

When visiting estuaries and mudflats, the fundamental rule which will allow for the best viewing is to arrive when the tide is either coming in, or just going out. If the tide is fully in, the birds could be roosting in an inaccessible area. Likewise, if the tide is too far out, the birds will be too far away and will not give good views. The best time is approximately one hour before high tide. Get into position and wait. As the water rises, the waders will be pushed closer and closer to the shore. They will usually be too busy feeding to notice anyone watching them. Waders, ducks and geese can be easily disturbed. Do not walk out onto the mudflat. A car is perhaps one of the best birdwatching hides for this habitat. Telescopes are a great advantage on estuaries and will allow excellent birdwatching from a safe distance.

In winter, coastal estuaries and mudflats play host to a variety of raptors which prey on the large numbers of wintering birds. A close watch should always be kept for Peregrine Falcons, Merlins or even Hen Harriers. On the saltmarshes, Short-eared Owls can occasionally be found hunting during the day. Also on the marshes, Snipe and the smaller Jack Snipe can frequent the pools, while Skylarks, Meadow Pipits, finches and buntings are usually found in reasonably large numbers.

In summer, estuaries and mudflats are much quieter, less productive areas, although Shelducks, Redshanks, Curlews and some Lapwings can usually be found. Other species which occur in summer may include Common and Arctic Terns which sometimes feed over estuaries at high tide.

Rocky Shores and Cliffs
Shaped by the power of the sea, the rugged Irish coastline consists mostly of rocky shores and cliffs. Such habitats vary from the low, rocky, coastal shorelines of the east coast, to the high cliffs of the headlands and islands

Introduction

of southern and western regions. Over 85% of the coastline consists of such habitat.

In winter, rocky shores provide suitable feeding areas for mixed flocks of Turnstones and Purple Sandpipers. These birds are ideally suited to such habitats and seem to blend perfectly into their surroundings. Along the lower shingle shores in winter, Linnets, Twite, Meadow Pipits and, occasionally, Snow Buntings are found. In summer, these shingle areas attract a variety of breeding birds like Ringed Plovers and Oystercatchers. A small proportion of such stretches may also contain a breeding colony of Little Terns. Because these species lay their well-camouflaged eggs in shallow scrapes on the ground, they are particularly vulnerable to disturbance. Care must be taken when birdwatching in these areas, as the eggs and nests are almost invisible against the stony background.

Sea cliffs in summer are the most exciting and noisy places to visit. They are similar in many ways to high-rise apartment blocks. During the breeding season, thousands of Guillemots, Razorbills and Kittiwakes cram onto the narrow ledges to nest. On wider ledges, Cormorants and Shags can be found, while Fulmars tend to nest on the higher parts of the cliffs. Gulls also breed on the cliffs and on the slopes above. Care should be taken not to wander into gull colonies. Some of the larger species, like Great Black-backed Gulls, can be quite aggressive.

On some islands and headlands, Puffins can be seen on the slopes. These charming auks nest in burrows. During the height of the breeding season, they can sometimes be seen returning from fishing trips with several sand-eels draped in their large, colourful bills.

On the more remote islands, Manx Shearwaters and Storm Petrels occur. These birds usually return to their nesting areas at night, and their strange, eerie calls add to the unforgettable experience of nights spent on such islands. Gannets also tend to breed on these islands, nesting on rocky ledges in large, extremely busy and noisy colonies. With an abundance of breeding species, such cliffs also attract Peregrine Falcons which nest on inaccessible ledges. Along the Atlantic shoreline, cliffs are also the main breeding sites for Choughs and Rock Doves.

By late summer and early autumn, most of the breeding birds have dispersed out to sea, and the cliffs are strangely silent.

Of all the habitats which birdwatchers visit, sea cliffs are the most dangerous. Extreme care must always be taken. Nesting seabird colonies are best visited from early spring to late summer. Viewing is best from a distance, and warning signs and notices should be heeded.

Towns, Parks and Gardens

While they may not appear to be the most attractive habitats at first glance, towns, parks and gardens do hold a surprisingly large number of bird species. In busy towns, Feral Pigeons, House Sparrows and Starlings are plentiful, as are Rooks, Jackdaws and Magpies. In summer, Swifts can be seen feeding high over busy areas, while Kestrels and Peregrine Falcons can occasionally find suitable breeding sites on high-rise or derelict buildings. Grey Wagtails, normally associated with uphill rivers and streams, are also found in Irish towns and cities in winter. In summer, this species even breeds near park ponds and streams in the heart of busy cities. Pied Wagtails also occur and can form very large winter roosts.

Parklands are like green oases in the midst of cities and towns. Breeding species include Great, Blue and Coal Tits, Dunnocks, Robins, Blackbirds, and Mistle and Song Thrushes. In more mature parks, Treecreepers or Jays may occur, while Sparrowhawks are not uncommon. In summer, Chiffchaffs may be heard singing over the noise of city traffic. In winter, parks provide ideal habitats for Redwings and Fieldfares.

Parks which have ponds usually contain resident Moorhens and Mallards, while Tufted Ducks and Coots will also take advantage of the generous food supply given by humans at these traditional, decorative ponds. Such a reliable food supply is vital for the survival of these species. Many gull species also occur on these ponds, including Herring and Black-headed Gulls. In winter, it is possible to encounter a Glaucous or Iceland Gull.

Introduction

Of all the birdwatching habitats that can be visited, the favourite is undoubtedly one's own garden. In the summer, Blackbirds and Dunnocks breed in hedgerows and trees. House Sparrows and Starlings are common while, under the eaves of our roofs, House Martins build their nests. In some areas, Swifts can also be found nesting under the eaves.

Robins can breed in a variety of locations around the garden. Occasionally, Spotted Flycatchers may choose to nest in the most unlikely sites such as hanging flower baskets. In dense bushes and ivy, Wrens may be found building their complicated, rounded nests. Nest boxes are one of the best ways of attracting breeding Blue or Great Tits. Such boxes should be erected early in the year if they are to be successful.

Song Thrushes are another familiar garden breeding bird. Many gardeners welcome this species as they can keep an area clear of snails and slugs. Watch for broken shells near a stone in the garden. Song Thrushes use favourite stones as anvils to break open snail shells.

In many ways, people have become the guardians of their breeding birds. Such species as Magpies, which fulfil a vital natural role in keeping small bird populations in check, are often discouraged.

In winter, gardens become a hive of activity. Nut-feeders attract tits, Greenfinches, Siskins and, occasionally, Redpolls. In recent years, House Sparrows and Chaffinches have learned to use these hanging feeders. Robins, Dunnocks and Blackbirds feed either on the ground or on bird tables. Berry bushes attract wintering Redwings and even Fieldfares. In some years, gardens are graced by the exotic Waxwing which feeds both on berries and, occasionally, fruit. Apples strategically placed on branches of trees provide food for Blackbirds, tits and finches. Apples also attract Blackcaps. These shy birds are one of only two warblers which winter in Ireland. The other species, Chiffchaff, seldom visits gardens. During the winter, roving tit flocks may move through gardens and these may include Long-tailed Tits.

It is extremely important to remember that birds also need water in winter. They can often survive longer without food than without water.

Introduction

They need to wash and preen to keep their feathers in good shape in order to provide the warmth and insulation needed to survive cold spells. It is also vital to remember that, once you start feeding birds, they depend on that food supply for the winter. Once you start, don't stop until early April, although this will depend on weather conditions.

Birdwatching in the garden is so easy. Feeders can be gradually moved closer to windows and, before long, many birds will become extremely tame. There is nothing quite like birdwatching from the warmth and comfort of home!

Divers

Great Northern Diver 69–81cm
Gavia immer   Lóma mór

A large, thick-necked, black and white diver. Shows a long flat crown, a steep forehead, a distinctive bump where the crown meets the forehead and a long, heavy, pale grey bill. **In summer**, shows a completely black head, with black and white striped patches on the sides of the neck and throat. Black upperparts show a white chequered pattern. **In winter**, the head and nape are black, contrasting strongly with the white on the throat, neck and breast. A black half collar extends from the nape onto the neck. Upperparts black. **Immatures** similar, but show pale fringes to the upperpart feathers. Deep red eye appears blackish at a distance. Flies with neck extended.

Voice and Diet   Although usually quiet, birds returning in autumn can give a far-carrying, wailing, gull-like call. Dives for fish and marine invertebrates. Can stay submerged for long periods, covering good distances under water. On occasions, this can make them difficult to relocate.

Habitat and Status   A common winter visitor to Ireland from breeding grounds in Greenland and Iceland. Found on open seas, bays and harbours in all coastal counties. Can also occur on inland lakes and reservoirs. Arrives in Ireland in late autumn, with most birds departing by April. In early spring, some can show full summer plumage.

Black-throated Diver 55–68cm
Gavia arctica

An elegant species with a slender, straight bill. **In summer**, shows a matt greyish head and nape with a black chin and throat. Black and white stripes extend from the sides of the neck onto the white breast. Belly white. Black upperparts show a white chequered pattern. **In winter**, the black crown extends down to eye. The blackish-grey nape extends well onto the sides of the neck, and is strongly demarcated from the white throat. Underparts white. Shows a gently angled forehead and a slightly rounded crown. Upperparts blackish. **Immatures** show pale fringes to upperpart feathers. Often shows a prominent white patch on the rear flanks. Eyes deep red.

Voice and Diet   Although normally quiet in Ireland, autumn birds can give a croaking-type call of a plaintive, wailing *arru-uuh*. Feeds by diving for fish and a variety of marine invertebrates. Capable of lengthy dives, moving reasonable distances when submerged.

Habitat and Status   A rare but regular winter visitor to Irish coastlines. In recent years, good numbers have been recorded annually in western, north-western and northern coastal regions. In spring, frequently reported off south-eastern counties. Usually found on open coastal waters, bays and, occasionally, harbours. Can occur on inland freshwater lakes.

Great Northern Diver

Winter

thick, heavy bill

Adult (summer)

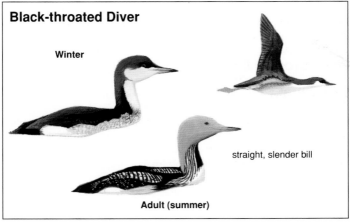

Black-throated Diver

Winter

straight, slender bill

Adult (summer)

Great Northern Diver

Black-throated Diver

35

Divers and Grebes

Red-throated Diver 53–60cm
Gavia stellata   Lóma rua

A small diver with a narrow, uptilted, pale greyish bill giving a distinctive head-in-the-air profile. **In summer**, shows a pale greyish head and a narrow red throat patch. Black and white stripes extend from the neck onto the sides of the breast. Upperparts brownish with small, faint, pale spots. **In winter**, appears very pale, with a grey, rounded crown and nape lacking a strong contrast with the whitish throat and breast. Upperparts show pale feather edges. Can show a white flank patch but is not usually as contrasting as on Black-throated. **Immatures** appear dirtier, and show a small, dull red throat patch. Dark red eye conspicuous in a plain face.

Voice and Diet   Gives a quacking *kruuk* call and a loud, wailing *ruu-aruu*. These calls are usually heard on the breeding grounds although can often be heard in very early autumn. Dives for fish and marine invertebrates. Can move considerable distances under water.

Habitat and Status   A rare Irish breeding bird found nesting on small islets on loughs or lakes. The main Irish breeding populations are based in north-western regions. A common winter visitor to all coastal counties. Found on open coastal waters, bays and harbours.

Great Crested Grebe 46–52cm
Podiceps cristatus   Foitheach mór

Large, elegant, slender-necked grebe with a long, pointed, pink bill. **In summer**, shows a black crown which extends back to form a double crest. Long rufous and black feathers from the rear of crown to the throat form a frill which is used during elaborate courtship displays. Dark line extends from base of bill to eye. Diagnostic white supercilium extends from the bill over the eye and blends with the white cheeks. Throat and breast whitish. Nape and upperparts plain brown. Shaggy, pale greyish flanks can show a rufous wash. **In winter**, the head frill and long double crest are lost. Eye red. In flight, shows white patches on forewing and secondaries.

Voice and Diet   On the breeding grounds gives a variety of harsh, croaking *kar-rraar* calls and whirring notes. An active diver, feeding on fish, insects and aquatic invertebrates.

Habitat and Status   A common Irish breeding bird found on inland lakes throughout the year. Builds a large floating nest among reeds and sedges, or hidden by tree branches. In winter, common in harbours and on open coastal waters in most regions. Tends to be scarce in some south-western areas. Breeding populations are highest in more northern regions of the country.

Red-throated Diver

Winter

thin, uptilted bill

Adult (summer)

Great Crested Grebe

Winter

pink bill

Adult (summer)

Red-throated Diver **Great Crested Grebe**

Grebes

Slavonian Grebe 32–37cm
Podiceps auritus   Foitheach cluasach

Small, solid, flat-crowned grebe with a stubby, pale-tipped black bill. **Summer adults** show a black crown separated from black cheeks and chin by golden horns extending from base of bill, through eye, and forming a crest on the rear of crown. Nape and upperparts blackish. Neck, upper breast and flanks chestnut-red. **In winter**, is strikingly black and white. Crown black, extending down to the red eye and sharply demarcated from the white cheeks. Also shows a thin stripe from eye to bill, and a pale loral spot. Nape and upperparts black, contrasting with the white breast and neck. Flanks greyish. Shows white secondaries and small white wedge on forewing in flight.

Voice and Diet   A silent species in Ireland. Slavonian Grebes are active feeders, sometimes jumping clear of the water when diving. Feeds primarily on small fish, insects and other small aquatic invertebrates.

Habitat and Status   An uncommon winter visitor from their breeding grounds in Iceland and Scandinavia. Found in coastal bays and harbours, often associating in small groups. Occasionally recorded on inland lakes and reservoirs, particularly in northern counties.

Little Grebe 24–29cm
Tachybaptus ruficollis   Spágaire tonn

Tiny, short-necked, stubby-billed grebe with a fluffed-up, short-bodied appearance. **Summer adults** show a black crown, nape and upper breast. Black on crown extends down to the eye. Cheeks, chin, throat and sides of neck deep chestnut-red. Also shows a pale yellow spot at the base of the bill. Upperparts blackish. Breast and flanks dark brownish-black, often fluffed. Sometimes shows rufous patches on rump. **In winter**, shows a dark brown crown, nape and upperparts, and greyish flanks. Cheeks, throat and neck pale buff-brown with a paler breast. **Immatures** similar to winter adults, but show a dark mark below the eye. In flight shows a completely plain wing.

Voice and Diet   On the breeding grounds can give a high-pitched, rattling call. Also gives a sharp *pit-pit* or *wit-wit* call when alarmed. An active, buoyant feeder, sometimes jumping clear of the water when diving for small insects and molluscs.

Habitat and Status   A common breeding bird found on ponds, lakes, reservoirs and marshes. Builds a floating nest among reeds and sedges. In winter, common on ponds, lakes and reservoirs. Uncommon, although occasionally seen, on estuary channels and in harbours. Rarely seen on open coastal water.

Slavonian Grebe

neat black crown, white cheeks

Winter

stubby dark bill with pale tip

Adult (summer)

Little Grebe

Adult (winter)

small, compact, stubby bill, often looks 'fluffed up'

Adult (summer)

Slavonian Grebe

Little Grebe

Gannet and Fulmar

Gannet 85–95cm
Sula bassana Gainéad

A large seabird with long narrow wings, a pointed tail and a spear-like bill. **Adults** are white with striking black wing tips, a creamy yellow head and black lores. Pointed bill bluish-grey with dark lines. Forward-facing eyes show a pale iris. Legs and feet greyish. **Juveniles** blackish-brown with pale speckling on upperparts and head, a paler lower breast and belly, and pale uppertail-coverts. Bill and legs dark. As birds mature, the plumage becomes gradually whiter, so that **3rd year birds** are very similar to adults but show some dark feathering on the inner wings, and can show a dark centre to the tail. Flight is graceful, with strong wing beats interspersed with long, easy glides.

Voice and Diet Noisy on the breeding colonies with birds giving loud, barking *arrah* calls. Usually silent at sea. Feeds on a wide variety of fish which are caught by dramatic plunges into the water, sometimes from substantial heights. When a shoal of fish is located, large numbers of Gannets can be seen diving together.

Habitat and Status A common bird of open sea found off the Irish coastline throughout the year. Breeds at colonies on Little Skellig in Co. Kerry, on the Bull Rock in Co. Cork, at two colonies on the Saltees in Co. Wexford, and on Clare Island in Co. Mayo. In recent years a colony has become established on a sea stack off Ireland's Eye, Co. Dublin. Nests on steep, rocky cliffs.

Fulmar 45–51cm
Fulmarus glacialis Fulmaire

A rather gull-like species with a thickset neck and long, narrow, stiff wings. **Adults** and **immatures** similar, showing a thick, tube-nosed, yellowish bill with a green or bluish-green base. Head and neck white with conspicuous black patches in front of eyes. Back and upperwings bluish-grey with pale inner primary patches. Underwings white with dusky edges. Tail and rump pale greyish. Flight strong with long glides and rapid, stiff wing beats. Soars over breeding cliffs with skilful twists and turns. When alarmed can spurt an oily substance which is foul-smelling and repulsive. The northern phase, known as **Blue Fulmar**, shows a smoky-grey head, neck and underparts.

Voice and Diet On the nest, gives a cackling, grunting, repeated *urg-urg-urg* call. Can also give a warning, growling call before spurting oil. Feeds on a wide range of marine fish, molluscs and crustaceans. Will also take fish offal from trawlers and can occasionally feed on carrion found at sea.

Habitat and Status Although Fulmars first bred in Ireland as recently as 1911, they are now a widespread breeding species found nesting in most coastal counties. Found throughout the year, Fulmars are strictly pelagic, rarely venturing inland. Observations in the south-west show that Fulmar numbers reach their peak in early April and early August. Good movements also occur in December and January. Nests in small colonies on coastal cliffs. Blue Fulmars are recorded annually in small numbers.

Gannet

long, black-tipped wings

Juvenile

Adult

2nd year

3rd year

Fulmar

stiff-winged flight

pale wing flashes

Gannet

Fulmar

Shearwaters

Sooty Shearwater 38–44cm
Puffinus griseus

A distinctive, stocky bird, showing an all-dark body plumage and long, narrow wings. Head, upperparts, upperwings and tail sooty-brown. Underparts can appear slightly paler or greyish-brown. In flight, the conspicuous silvery centre to the underwing contrasts strongly with the dark plumage. Bill dark. Flies with long, angled-back wings, gliding in arcs over the water. On the water, appears wholly dark and could be mistaken for a dark-phase Arctic Skua at a distance. Could also be mistaken for Mediterranean Shearwater but the all-dark underparts, the angled-back wings, larger size and flight are diagnostic.

Voice and Diet Silent away from the breeding grounds and at sea. Feeds on a wide range of marine life, taking small fish, squid and crustaceans.

Habitat and Status A bird of open oceans and seas, Sooty Shearwaters are regular late summer and autumn visitors from breeding grounds in the southern hemisphere. Usually seen off seawatching points in most coastal counties, with the largest movements recorded in the south and south-west. The peak passage is normally between late August and mid-September. Also encountered on oceanic pelagic trips.

Great Shearwater 42–50cm
Puffinus gravis

A large shearwater which glides effortlessly on bowed wings, or flies with stiff, fast wing beats. **Adults** and **immatures** similar, showing a black bill, a dark brownish cap which contrasts strongly with a white throat, and a whitish collar which almost extends around the nape. Underparts white with diagnostic dark brownish patches on the sides of the breast, and a dark belly patch. Mantle and rump greyish-brown. Wings show greyish-brown coverts and contrasting blackish wing tips and secondaries. Whitish underwings show black edges, and black markings on the coverts and axillaries. White tips to the uppertail-coverts form a narrow horseshoe patch above the dark tail.

Voice and Diet If close to a feeding flock of Great Shearwaters, a raucous, gull-like call can occasionally be heard. Feeds on a wide range of small fish, squid and offal from trawlers. Can be attracted to trawlers at sea.

Habitat and Status An annual autumn visitor to Irish waters, with most records occurring between July and October. Breeds in the South Atlantic. Most are recorded from seawatching sites in the south-west or on open seas during pelagic trips. However, occasional sightings have been recorded off southern, south-eastern, eastern, north-western and western counties.

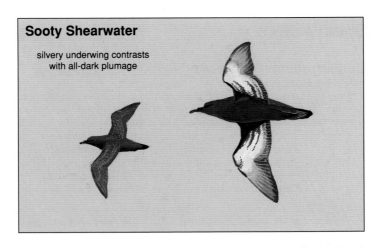

Sooty Shearwater

silvery underwing contrasts
with all-dark plumage

Great Shearwater

dark cap,
thin white rump

brown on breast-
sides and belly

Sooty Shearwater **Great Shearwater**

Shearwaters

Mediterranean Shearwater 32–38cm
Puffinus mauretanicus

A brown and white shearwater, slightly bulkier and larger than Manx Shearwater, with a shortish tail and long, narrow, pointed wings. Upperparts brown, with a slightly darker brown cap fading into a paler throat. Underparts pale whitish-brown, but can show very dark underparts with a pale belly. Underwing whitish with a thick, dark border. The underwing can appear quite greyish or silvery. Bill dark. Legs pinkish. In bad light can appear all-dark, and could be confused with Sooty Shearwater. However, Mediterranean is smaller with shorter, less angled wings. Glides and shears like Manx Shearwater, but flight tends to appear more fluttery with rapid stiff wing beats.

Voice and Diet   Being silent at sea, Mediterranean Shearwaters are rarely heard in Irish waters. Feeds on a wide range of small fish and molluscs. Like other shearwaters, can also be attracted to offal from trawlers.

Habitat and Status   A scarce but annual late summer and early autumn visitor from breeding grounds in the western regions of the Mediterranean. Has also been recorded in winter and spring. Most sightings are from seawatching points in the south and south-west, with occasional reports from other coastal regions. Most birds are seen flying, feeding and generally associating with flocks of Manx Shearwaters at sea.

Manx Shearwater 30–35cm
Puffinus puffinus   Cánóg dhubh

A slender, black and white shearwater with long, narrow, pointed wings. Upperparts black. Crown black, extending below eye. Underparts white. Underwing white with a black border and extensive dark wing tips. Bill dark. Legs pinkish. Very distinctive in flight, with quick, stiff wing beats followed by long gliding, shearing and banking low over the waves. This flight gives contrasting flashes of the black upperparts, followed by the white underparts. In very calm weather, can fly with rapid wing beats and very little gliding, leading to confusion with Little Shearwater. However, size, long, slender wings and black crown to below eye are diagnostic.

Voice and Diet   Silent at sea. At the breeding grounds, however, Manx Shearwaters can be heard to give a range of weird, wild, crooning and crowing calls. These raucous calls are given both in flight and in the burrows. Returns to the nesting burrows at night, adding to the eeriness of the calls. Feeds on a wide range of small fish and molluscs. Will also be attracted to offal from trawlers.

Habitat and Status   A very common, numerous breeding seabird found off all coastal counties on passage and in summer. Winters far out into the Atlantic Ocean. Found breeding at many sites on quiet islands and headlands, with the largest concentrations in the south-west. Can pass seawatching locations in very large numbers in late summer and early autumn. Found on open sea and oceans, with occasional inland records usually referring to large inland lakes.

Mediterranean Shearwater

similar to Manx
Shearwater but browner
overall

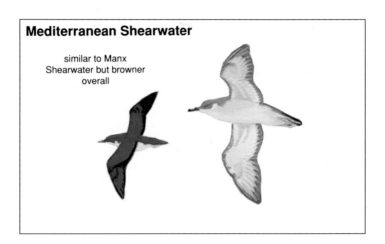

Manx Shearwater

strikingly black and white

white underparts

Mediterranean Shearwater　　　　**Manx Shearwater**

Petrels

Storm Petrel 13–16cm
Hydrobates pelagicus   Guairdeall

A small, dark petrel with a square tail, a white rump and short, rounded wings. **Adults** and **immatures** show a sooty-black head, underparts, mantle and upperwing, contrasting strongly with a square, white rump which extends onto the lower flanks. Tail dark. Upperwing plain, lacking any pale covert panel as seen on other petrel species. However, the underwing does show a striking white line on the coverts. Legs dark and short, not extending beyond tail. Bill small and dark. Flight is fluttery and bat-like, with fast wing beats interspersed with glides. When feeding, can paddle the feet in the water as it moves back and forth on raised wings.

Voice and Diet   Silent at sea. At night, around the breeding colonies, gives a variety of repeated, squeaking and growling *tur-wik* and *pee* calls. At the nest, gives a purring call which ends in a distinctive hiccup-type note. Feeds on a variety of marine food items, including small fish and plankton. Can also be attracted to trawlers, readily feeding on scraps.

Habitat and Status   A common bird of open sea and ocean, breeding in colonies on small, undisturbed islands. Ireland holds the world's largest breeding population of this species, with most colonies concentrated in north-western, western and south-western counties. Nests in crevices in walls, under rocks and in burrows. Following breeding, disperses to open seas, with large numbers often recorded off seawatching sites in the south-west. Birds can occasionally be found inland after storms.

Leach's Petrel 19–23cm
Oceanodroma leucorhoa

A dark petrel, larger and paler than Storm Petrel, and showing long, pointed wings, a forked tail and a white rump. **Adults** and **immatures** show a dark blackish-brown head, mantle and underparts. Upperwing dark with a distinctive greyish band across the coverts. Underwing wholly dark. Narrow rump can show a dark central line, a feature only obvious at very close range. Tail dark and forked. Bill and legs dark. In flight, shows long, pointed wings which are swept back at the carpals. Flight appears easy, with slow wing beats and glides. Moves back and forth across the water when feeding, pattering the feet in the water while holding the wings flat or slightly bowed.

Voice and Diet   Silent at sea. At breeding sites at night, gives a variety of chatters and screeches. At the nest, gives purring-type calls and a distinctive, wheezing *wick* call. Like Storm Petrel, feeds on a wide variety of marine food items, including small fish, plankton and occasionally trawler offal and scraps.

Habitat and Status   An uncommon petrel, with a very small Irish breeding population based on small, remote islands off western counties. May also be breeding on islands in the north. Nests under rocks or boulders, or in burrows. Regularly reported off western and northern coasts in autumn. Disperses to open seas and oceans in winter. Following storms, birds are occasionally wrecked by being blown close offshore.

Storm Petrel

tiny size

white rump

white line on underwing

Leach's Petrel

small size

dark underwing, pale
wingbar on upperwing

long, pointed wings

Storm Petrel

Leach's Petrel

Cormorant and Shag

Cormorant 83–97cm
Phalacrocorax carbo   Broigheal

A stockier, thicker-necked bird than Shag, with a heavier bill, a large area of bare skin on the lores, face and chin, and a slanted forehead. **Summer adults** show yellow around eye, a white throat and check patch, white head and neck feathers, a blue gloss on head and underparts, and white thigh patches. Upperparts show a bronzy gloss. **Winter adults** lack thigh patches, are less glossy, and show dark mottling on the white face patch. Eyes green. **Immatures** show a yellow or orange face, a blackish-brown plumage, mottled or whitish underparts, and brownish eyes. Legs dark. In flight, appears heavy and goose-like. Swims low in the water. Often seen perched on rocks or buoys, drying open wings.

Voice and Diet   On the breeding cliffs can give low, guttural *rr-rah* calls. Rarely heard away from the breeding areas. Feeds by diving, jumping clear of the water. Takes a wide variety of fish.

Habitat and Status   A common breeding species found nesting in colonies on cliffs and islands along most coastal counties. Also breeds on large inland lakes, nesting on islands and in trees. In winter, Cormorants are common and can be found on estuaries, open offshore waters, and on inland lakes, rivers and canals.

Shag 72–80cm
Phalacrocorax aristotelis   Seaga

A smaller, thinner-necked bird than Cormorant, with a steep forehead and a slim bill. **Summer adults** show a dark bill with a yellow gape line, an upcurved forehead crest, and a dark, glossy-green head, neck and underparts. Upperparts dark with a purple gloss. **In winter**, shows a pale throat, a duller plumage and no crest. Eyes green. Legs dark. Brownish **immatures** show pale wing coverts, yellowish eyes and a pale brown throat and breast. Belly can also be pale. Underparts rarely as white as immature Cormorant. Legs yellow-brown. In flight, appears light, with pointed wings. Tends to fly low over the water. Swims higher on the water than Cormorant. Often seen perched, drying open wings.

Voice and Diet   On the breeding cliffs can be heard to give a range of croaks, grunts and hisses. Rarely heard away from the nest. Feeds on a wide variety of small fish and some crustaceans. Jumps clear of the water when diving.

Habitat and Status   A common breeding species found nesting in colonies on rocky cliffs and islands off most coastal counties. Shags are more maritime than Cormorants, and are rarely found inland. In winter, occurs on open coastal waters and harbours. Found less frequently in estuaries.

Cormorant

heavy build, striking white facial and thigh patches, yellow around eye

Adult (summer)

Shag

forehead crest, dark around eye

Young Cormorant & Young Shag

Adult (summer)

Cormorant

Shag

Little Egret and Spoonbill

Little Egret 55–64cm
Egretta garzetta

This elegant, thin-necked, all-white heron, with a long dagger-like bill, is unlikely to be confused with any other species. Plumage all white. **Summer adults** show two long white plumes on the head and long aigrettes (back and mantle plumes). The bare skin on the lores is yellowish in summer, being a greyish-blue out of breeding plumage. **In winter**, the head plumes are lost and the aigrettes are reduced. The long, pointed, dagger-like bill is blackish. The legs are black, with contrasting yellow feet, this being difficult to observe if the bird is feeding in water. In flight, withdraws the neck and shows white, rounded wings and long, trailing legs.

Voice and Diet   Usually silent in Ireland, can give a croaking *arrk* call on occasions. Feeds actively in shallow water, catching fish, insects or frogs with quick stabs of the bill.

Habitat and Status   A rare bird from Europe, Little Egrets can occur at any time of the year, with most records referring to spring when small influxes have been noted. Can occasionally over-winter. Usually found in marshes, lakes and estuaries where they feed in the channels at low tide. Sometimes roosts in trees. Once hunted extensively for its plumes to serve the fashion industry.

Spoonbill 81–90cm
Platalea leucorodia   Leitheadach

An unmistakable, white, heron-like bird with a long neck and legs and a distinctive long, spatulate bill. **Adults** show an all-white plumage with a yellow throat, a black, yellow-tipped bill and black legs. Shows yellowish neck plumes and a yellow ring around the base of the neck in summer. In flight, shows an outstretched neck and trailing legs. Flies with fast wing beats, interspersed with short glides. **Immature** birds are similar to adults, but show a pinkish throat and bill, as well as black tips to the wings, obvious in flight. **Immatures** also show pinkish legs. Feeds with diagnostic, side-to-side sweeps of the bill.

Voice and Diet   Although usually silent in Ireland, can occasionally give grunting-type calls. An active feeder, taking fish, molluscs and insects from shallow water by side-to-side sweeps of the sensitive bill.

Habitat and Status   A rare visitor from Europe, Spoonbills can occur at any time of the year, with some birds over-wintering. Feeds in shallow water and can be found on marshes or lakes. Often found on estuaries feeding in shallow channels at low tide.

Little Egret

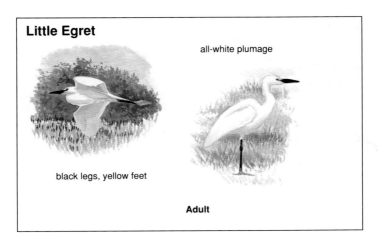

all-white plumage

black legs, yellow feet

Adult

Spoonbill

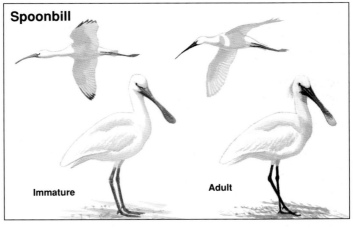

Immature

Adult

Little Egret

Spoonbill

Grey Heron and Mute Swan

Grey Heron 90–100cm
Ardea cinerea   Corr réisc

Large, long-necked bird with a long, stout, pointed bill. **Adults** show a white head and neck with a black crown-stripe which forms a loose crest. Black stripes obvious on foreneck extending onto loose, shaggy breast. Upperparts blue-grey with a black shoulder patch and pale, elongated scapulars forming plumes. Black on sides of breast continues down as flank stripe, meeting on the ventral area. Flanks and belly white. Bill orange-yellow. Flies on bowed wings, showing contrasting grey wing coverts and blackish primaries and secondaries. Flies with neck retracted, and trailing, dull-greenish legs. **Immatures** show a dark crown, greyish sides to neck and a duller bill.

Voice and Diet   Gives a harsh, grumpy *krarnk* call, especially when disturbed. Feeds by standing patiently, watching for prey items which are caught with a fast, sudden stab of the dagger-like bill. Takes fish, insects, frogs and small mammals.

Habitat and Status   A common resident species found throughout the country. Breeds in colonies known as heronries, building nests on tops of trees and bushes. In winter, populations may increase with the arrival of birds from Scandinavia and Britain. Found on lakes, rivers, canals, marshes and estuaries.

Mute Swan 144–160cm
Cygnus olor   Eala bhalbh

Their all-white plumage, long, curved neck and their elegance in the water, often with the wings arched back, make this species easy to identify. The long, pointed tail is another useful feature, especially when birds are up-ending. **Male** (the cob) and **female** (the pen) are identical in plumage and both have orange bills with black edges and a black base which continues up to meet the dark eye. The sexes can easily be distinguished by the size of the knob on the top of the bill, which is larger and more obvious on the cob. Legs black. **Immatures** are brownish-grey in colour, with pinkish bills, and lacking the bill knob of adults.

Voice and Diet   Despite their name, Mute Swans can be surprisingly vocal. When threatened or when aggressive, they make a hissing sound. They also give a muffled 'nasal' grunt. In flight, they do not call, but the wings make a whistling, throbbing sound. Feeds on various water plants which are pulled from lake and river bottoms while up-ending. Also feeds on grasslands and cereal crops.

Habitat and Status   A common bird found on lakes, rivers and canals throughout Ireland. A resident bird which only rarely makes long-distance movements. Gathers in large, sociable herds in winter at traditional sites. In summer, however, quite territorial and aggressive towards other pairs. Nests are enormous, round constructions found by rivers, canals and lakes, often hidden in reeds.

Grey Heron

Immature

long, white neck and long pointed bill

Adult

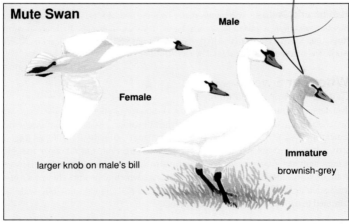

Mute Swan

Male

Female

larger knob on male's bill

Immature
brownish-grey

Grey Heron

Mute Swan

Swans

Bewick's Swan 116–129cm
Cygnus columbianus   Eala Bhewick

The smallest swan to occur in Ireland, Bewick's is more likely to be confused with Whooper than Mute. Both sexes are identical with an all-white plumage, often with pale brown staining on the head, a short, straight, thick neck and a short black and yellow bill. The combination of size and body proportions give Bewick's Swan an almost goose-like appearance. The black on the bill is more extensive than on Whooper, with the rounded, rather than wedge-shaped, yellow area being confined to the base of the bill. **Juvenile** birds have a pale greyish plumage and a pale creamy-pink bill, with the black confined to the edges and extreme tip of the bill. The **North American race**, Whistling Swan, shows a tiny yellow spot on the all-dark bill.

Voice and Diet   A quieter species than Whooper, giving a goose-like honking call. When in herds, can often give more melodic 'babbling' calls. Feeds on grass, roots and water plants, usually in large flocks, often alongside Whoopers and Mutes.

Habitat and Status   A common winter visitor to Ireland's lakes and marshes, they can also be found in large mixed flocks grazing on fields and sloblands. Breeding in northern Russia and Siberia, they arrive in Ireland in late autumn/early winter and leave by March or April. The North American race, known as Whistling Swan, is a rare winter visitor.

Whooper Swan 145–160cm
Cygnus cygnus   Eala ghlórach

The larger of the two migratory swans, Whooper is slightly smaller than Mute. Separated from Mute by the short tail and the bill colour, it is easily confused with the smaller Bewick's. Best identified by the long, slender, straight neck, sloped forehead, size, and by the extent and shape of yellow on the larger bill. On Whooper, the yellow is large and triangular, with the black confined to the lower edge and tip. Like Bewick's, both sexes are identical, with an all-white plumage which sometimes shows pale brown head staining. Legs blackish. **Immatures** show a pale creamy-pink bill, with black confined to the tip, and a pale greyish plumage.

Voice and Diet   Often heard before they are seen, a loud honking-type call is delivered in flight. When displaying, a loud, excitable, trumpeting call is given. In threat displays, this trumpeting is equivalent to the aggressive hissing and arched wing display of Mute Swan. Feeds on grasses, roots and water plants, often alongside other species of swan.

Habitat and Status   A common winter visitor to lakes and marshes. Like Bewick's Swan, can also be found in large mixed flocks grazing on fields and sloblands. Breeding in Iceland and northern Europe, Whooper Swans arrive in Ireland in late autumn, and leave by mid-April, although a few may remain throughout the summer. Whooper Swans were first recorded breeding in Ireland in 1992. A pair nested and successfully reared one fledgling at an undisclosed site in the north-west.

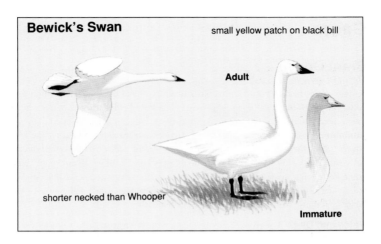

Bewick's Swan

small yellow patch on black bill

Adult

shorter necked than Whooper

Immature

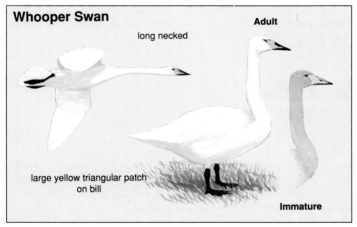

Whooper Swan

long necked

Adult

large yellow triangular patch
on bill

Immature

Bewick's Swan

Whooper Swan

Geese

Brent Goose 56–61cm
Branta bernicla   Cadhan

A small, short-necked goose with a black head, neck and breast, a small white neck collar, and dark blackish-brown upperparts. The **Pale-bellied race** shows a whitish lower breast and belly, and dark barring along whitish flanks. Undertail white. **Immatures** similar, but show a thinner neck collar and broad white edges to the wing coverts. The **Dark-bellied** eastern race is a rare visitor and shows a blackish breast, belly and flanks which do not contrast with the upper breast. **Black Brant** show a large white neck collar, dark belly and white flanks. In flight, shows a darkish upper- and underwing, the pale belly contrasting with the underwings. Black tail contrasts with white uppertail-coverts. Short dark bill. Legs blackish.

Voice and Diet   A noisy species which calls both in flight and also when in feeding parties. The call is a nasal *rronk*. Grazes on coastal grasslands, on estuaries and mudflats, taking a wide variety of plant material, especially eel grass.

Habitat and Status   A common winter visitor from the breeding grounds in Arctic Greenland and Canada. Found on coastal estuaries and mudflats, usually in noisy flocks. Can be very tame and approachable. The Dark-bellied race breeds in Arctic Siberia, and is a rare winter visitor. The North American Black Brant is a very rare vagrant.

Barnacle Goose 59–69cm
Branta leucopsis   Gé ghiúrainn

A small, distinctive goose with a black crown, neck and breast and a contrasting creamy-white face which shows a black line from the dark eye to the bill. The upperparts are pale grey with broad, black, white-tipped barring. The underparts are whitish with pale grey barring on the flanks and a pure white undertail. **Immatures** similar, but show duller plumage and black speckling on the white face. In flight, the pale grey underwing with darker flight feathers distinguishes this species from Brent Goose. The upperwing is greyish with black barring. The rump and tail are black with a contrasting, broad white crescent formed by white uppertail-coverts. Legs blackish.

Voice and Diet   In flight, Barnacle Geese flocks give very distinctive, short, repeated, barking calls which may recall a pack of yelping dogs. When feeding gives a chattering *hugug, hugug* call. Feeds on grass, rushes and other plant material.

Habitat and Status   A winter visitor from breeding grounds in north-east Greenland. The main population is almost exclusively on the west coast. Also occurs along the east coast where small flocks winter on offshore islands. Found on quiet, undisturbed grazing areas, especially favouring uninhabited islands. Also found on grass and sloblands.

Brent Goose

Immature

Black Brant

Adult

Dark-bellied Brent

Barnacle Goose

dark neck,
striking whitish face

Brent Goose

Barnacle Goose

Geese

Canada Goose 55–110cm
Branta canadensis

A long-necked goose with a black head and neck, and a diagnostic white throat and cheek patch. The upperparts are brownish with pale fringes to the feathers. Underparts show a pale creamy breast and a brownish belly and flanks with narrow creamy barring. Undertail white. **Immatures** show a slightly duller plumage, with a brownish wash occasionally visible on throat patch. In flight, the black head and neck, the white face patch, the pale breast and dark underwing are obvious. The rump and tail are black with a contrasting, narrow white crescent formed by white uppertail-coverts. Bill and legs are blackish. There are up to ten different races, each varying in size and colour tones.

Voice and Diet   Gives a loud, trumpeting *ah-honk* call with the second note higher pitched. Feeds on grass, aquatic plants, grain and other plant matter.

Habitat and Status   Feral populations have now established themselves in many parts of the country, having originally escaped from wildfowl collections. However, a small number of genuine birds from breeding grounds in Arctic Canada do occur. These are sometimes found grazing on open pastures and sloblands with Greenland White-fronted Geese.

Greylag Goose 76–90cm
Anser anser   Gé ghlas

A large, thick-necked, heavy goose with a broad orange bill and pinkish legs. The head and neck are greyish-brown with dark neck streaking. Breast and belly slightly paler with variable amounts of black spotting on belly. Flanks show dark centres to the feathers with pale, greyish-brown edges. Undertail white. Upperparts pale greyish-brown with paler grey fringes to the feathers. **Immatures** similar but lack black belly spots. In flight, shows a strikingly pale grey forewing and pale grey underwing coverts. The rump is greyish. The uppertail-coverts are white and form a narrow white crescent which does not contrast strongly with the rump. Tail dark with white border.

Voice and Diet   As Greylag Geese are the original farmyard goose, the cackling, hoinking *aahng-unng-ung* call may be familiar to many. Feeds on grass, grain, roots and other plant matter.

Habitat and Status   A locally common winter visitor from breeding grounds in Iceland. Populations are concentrated along the northern, eastern and south-eastern counties, with smaller numbers in the south-west. In many parts of Ireland, small pockets of feral birds are present, these having escaped from wildfowl collections or even farmyards. Found on open grasslands, arable fields, marshes and lakes.

Canada Goose

long, black neck, white throat and cheek patch

Greylag Goose

large build, heavy orange bill

grey forewing

pink legs

Canada Goose

Greylag Goose

Geese

White-fronted Goose 66–76cm
Anser albifrons   Gé bhánéadanach

A thick-necked, greyish-brown goose with a striking white patch around the base of the bill. Head and neck brown, with thin black streaking on the sides of the neck. Upperparts greyish-brown with narrow, pale fringes. Underparts greyish-brown with black patches on the belly and flanks, and a thin white line along upper flanks. Undertail white. **Immatures** similar, but lack belly patches and white base to the bill. The **Greenland race** shows an orange bill and legs. The **Siberian race**, which is occasionally seen in Ireland, has a pinkish bill. In flight, shows pale coverts on a plain upperwing. Underwing dark. Rump and tail dark, with a white tail band and white uppertail-coverts.

Voice and Diet   Gives a loud, melodious, high-pitched *kow-lyok* call in flight. These calls are far-carrying, and White-fronted Geese are occasionally heard before they are seen. Feeds on grass, grain, fodder, beet and other plant material.

Habitat and Status   Ireland holds approximately half of the world's wintering population of the Greenland race. The main population is concentrated in the south-east, with smaller numbers present in the midlands, the west and north-west. Found on open grasslands, sloblands, marshland areas and loughs. At coastal localities, can roost on estuaries or sandbanks. The Siberian race is a rare winter visitor.

Pink-footed Goose 60–74cm
Anser brachyrhynchus   Gé ghobghearr

A small, short-necked, greyish-brown goose with a small, round-headed appearance. Head and neck dark chocolate-brown, contrasting with a pale, fawn breast. Darker rear flanks show a narrow white upperflank line. Undertail white. Upperparts pale, frosted, greyish-brown with pale greyish fringes to the feathers. Short, stubby bill is black with a pink subterminal band. Bill can sometimes show a white base. Legs deep pink. **Immatures** similar, but show a duller and browner plumage, lacking greyish tones to upperparts. In flight, shows a contrasting pale grey forewing, a darkish underwing and a white-bordered dark tail. Uppertail-coverts white.

Voice and Diet   Gives a loud, repeated *wink-wink* or *wink-wink-wink* call, which is shriller and more high-pitched than other species of grey geese. Also gives an *ang-unk* call. Feeds on grass, grain, potatoes, fodder and other plants and roots.

Habitat and Status   An uncommon but regular winter visitor from breeding grounds in Iceland and Greenland. Found on open grassland, stubble fields, sloblands, lakes and wetlands. Freely associates with other goose species.

White-fronted Goose

white base to bill

orange bill and legs,
dark belly markings

Immature

Adult

Pink-footed Goose

dark head, pink on dark bill

pink legs

White-fronted Goose

Pink-footed Goose

Ducks

Shelduck 57–64cm
Tadorna tadorna   Seil-lacha

A large duck with a bright red bill and pinkish legs. **Males** show a large bill knob, a blackish-green head and neck, and a white lower neck and upper breast. A broad, chestnut band extends from mantle onto breast. Underparts white with a black belly stripe from breast to vent. Undertail-coverts chestnut. Upperparts white with a black scapular stripe, chestnut-coloured tertials, dark green secondaries and black primaries. Bill knob reduced in winter. **Females** show no bill knob, white mottling around base of bill and duller plumage. **Immatures** blackish-grey on head and upperparts, and white below. In flight, shows a striking black and white plumage, a white rump and a white, dark-tipped tail.

Voice and Diet   Relatively noisy in the breeding season, with males giving melodious whistling calls. Females, however, give a repeated *ag-ag-ag-ag* call. Feeds on small molluscs, crustaceans and insects. Feeds by sifting in mud or by up-ending in deeper water.

Habitat and Status   A common resident breeding species found in all coastal counties. Nests in old rabbit burrows and other holes. In July, most adults depart to moult their feathers, leaving the immatures in large crèches, usually attended by a small number of adult birds. Moulting takes place on sandbanks off north-west Germany with birds returning in early winter. Feeds on estuaries and mudflats. Nests in sand-dune systems.

Shoveler 47–54cm
Anas clypeata   Spadalach

A large spatulate bill gives Shoveler a striking profile. **Males** show a black bill, a glossy, dark green head and white breast. A chestnut belly contrasts with a white ventral spot and a black undertail. Upperparts white with a dark central stripe. Long black scapulars show white edges. Forewing pale blue. Shows white tips to greater coverts, a green speculum in flight, blackish primaries, a black rump and white sides to a black tail. **Female** pale brown with dark spotting, best recognised by the large bill which shows an orange cutting edge. In flight, females show a grey-blue forewing and dull green speculum. Legs and feet orange. Eye yellowish on male, duller on female.

Voice and Diet   A relatively quiet species, males can give a hollow *tunk-tunk* call, while females give quacking-type calls. Feeds by sifting the surface of the water with the large bill or by up-ending. Takes molluscs, insects, crustaceans, seeds and water plants.

Habitat and Status   A common wintering species from Iceland, Scandinavia and northern Russia. Found on freshwater lakes and marshes, as well as estuaries and mudflats. Shoveler are a rare breeding species, nesting in grass or rushes close to water. The main breeding populations are concentrated in the midlands and north-east.

Shelduck

Female

large knob on male's forehead

Immature

striking white, chestnut and dark green plumage

Male

Shoveler

Male

large bill, chestnut flanks

blue forewing

Female

Shelduck

Shoveler

Ducks

Ruddy Duck 36–42cm
Oxyura jamaicensis

A small, dumpy, diving species with a large, broad bill and a stiff tail, which, on occasions, can be held upright. **Summer males** show a striking black crown and nape, with a pure white face and a bright blue bill. Breast, flanks and upperparts rich chestnut with white belly and undertail. Wings and tail brownish. **Winter males** show a mottled grey-brown breast and flanks, and brownish upperparts. The crown and nape are dark brown in winter with a clean whitish face and a duller bill. **Females** similar to winter males but show a dark line from base of bill onto cheeks. Females show a dull grey-blue bill. In flight, shows a plain brown upperwing and a whitish underwing panel.

Voice and Diet Usually a quiet species, males can give low, belching calls and bill slaps and rattles. Females can also give bill slaps and rattles as well as a low hissing call. Feeds by diving for insect larvae. Also takes aquatic plant seeds.

Habitat and Status An uncommon species which occurs in small numbers on reservoirs and lakes. A North American species, Ruddy Duck were introduced into Britain in the 1960s and since then have become established in Ireland. The main population is based on the lakes of Northern Ireland where the species is now breeding. Nests in reeds and rushes.

Goldeneye 41–48cm
Bucephala clangula   Órshúileach

A small diving duck with a peaked head, pale yellow eyes, orange-yellow legs and a blunt bill. **Males** show a dark, green-glossed head and a white spot on face at the base of the dark grey bill. Neck, breast, flanks and belly white. Upperparts black with a white, black-striped wing patch formed by white secondaries and coverts, and black scapulars. Tail greyish. Undertail-coverts black. In flight, shows a striking black and white wing pattern. Duller **females** show a reddish-brown head, a whitish neck collar, dark upperparts with grey mottling, and greyish breast and flanks. Belly white. The dark grey bill shows an orange-yellow tip. Also shows white wing patches in flight.

Voice and Diet Usually a silent species, males can give whistling-type calls associated with dramatic courtship displays. These displays can be seen from late winter into spring. Dives for insects, molluscs and crustaceans.

Habitat and Status A common wintering species from northern Europe and Russia. Small numbers have been seen on occasions in summer on lakes in Northern Ireland, making Goldeneye a potential Irish breeding species. Found on coasts, bays, reservoirs and lakes.

Ruddy Duck

Male

large-headed, blue bill, white cheeks

Female

dark stripe on pale cheek

Goldeneye

striking white spot on cheek

Male

Female

reddish-brown head

Ruddy Duck   **Goldeneye**

Ducks

Tufted Duck 41–46cm
Aythya fuligula   Lacha bhadánach

A small, tufted, diving duck with yellow eyes. **Males** show a black head, breast, ventral area, tail and upperparts. Head shows a purple-blue sheen and a long crest. Belly and flanks white. **Females** are brownish on the head, upperparts, breast and tail. Flanks pale brown. Belly pale. The crest is short on females and sometimes difficult to see. **Females** can also show an area of white around the base of the bill which could lead to confusion with female Scaup. Tufted, however, lack the full-bodied, round-headed shape of Scaup and show a neater bill. **Females** can also show a whitish undertail. In flight, shows a long, broad, white wing stripe and a whitish underwing. Bill pale grey with a black tip.

Voice and Diet   Usually a silent species, males can give low whistling calls during breeding displays, females giving growling-type calls. Feeds by diving for marine invertebrates. Also feeds on aquatic plants.

Habitat and Status   A common winter visitor and breeding species, found on freshwater lakes, reservoirs and small ponds. Breeds on lakes in the midlands and the north, with smaller populations in the south-east, south and west. Nests in thick cover close to water. In winter, numbers are increased with the arrival of birds from Scotland, Iceland and Europe.

Scaup 46–52cm
Aythya marila   Lacha iascán

A large, full-bodied, round-headed, diving duck with pale yellow eyes. **Males** show a black head and breast, with a green sheen to head. Belly and flanks white. Tail and undertail blackish. Mantle pale greyish with dark, narrow barring on the lower mantle. Rump black. Wing coverts blackish-grey. **Females** show a brownish head and breast, and an extensive white patch at base of bill, larger than that of female Tufted. In spring, can show a whitish ear-covert patch. Upperparts greyish-brown. Flanks pale grey-brown, appearing broadly barred. Belly whitish. Tail and undertail brownish. In flight, shows a long, broad, white wing stripe. Broad bluish-grey bill shows a black nail.

Voice and Diet   Usually a silent species in Ireland. Females, if flushed, can give a gruff *karr* call. Dives for molluscs and crustaceans, as well as feeding on marine plants.

Habitat and Status   A common winter visitor from breeding grounds in Iceland and Scandinavia. Found on open coastal waters, bays and also on freshwater lakes close to coastal localities.

Tufted Duck

Male

black and white, tuft at rear of head

Female

brown, can show some white at base of bill

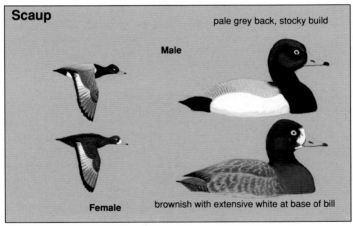

Scaup

Male

pale grey back, stocky build

Female

brownish with extensive white at base of bill

Tufted Duck

Scaup

Ducks

Teal 34–39cm
Anas crecca   Praslacha

A small duck. **Males** show a chestnut head with a buff border to green head band. Breast buff with dark spotting. Flanks grey, finely vermiculated. Yellow, black-bordered undertail patches obvious. Upperparts grey with fine vermiculations, and black and white scapular stripes. Bill dark. **Females** greyish-brown with heavy mottling, and show a dark eye-stripe on a plain face, a diagnostic white undertail-covert stripe and a pale base to bill. In flight, black and green speculum shows broad white upper border and a thin, white trailing edge. **Males** of North American race, known as **Green-winged Teal**, show a white breast stripe, a finer buff edge to head band and no white scapular stripe.

Voice and Diet   Males give a very distinctive, bell-like *prrip* call, while females give a sharp, Mallard-like *quack*. Feeds by up-ending in shallow water or by dabbling on the surface. Takes aquatic plants, seeds and aquatic invertebrates.

Habitat and Status   An uncommon breeding species, found nesting on small lakes, pools and on rivers. In winter, is very common, with birds from Scandinavia, Britain and Iceland wintering on lakes, marshes and on estuaries. The North American race, Green-winged Teal, is a very rare winter visitor.

Garganey 37–42cm
Anas querquedula

A small duck which holds the rear end of the body high out of the water. **Males** show a rich brown head with a striking white stripe from above eye onto nape. A brown breast shows dark mottling. Flanks pale grey. Brown undertail shows dark spotting. Upperparts dark. Elongated scapulars show white edges. **Females** greyish-brown with broad dark mottling. Head shows a whitish supercilium contrasting with a dark crown and eye-stripe, a whitish loral patch and throat, and a dark green stripe. In flight, males show a grey-blue forewing, a green and black speculum, and even white upper and trailing edges. Females show duller forewing, a white trailing edge and a thin white upper edge.

Voice and Diet   Males give a distinctive, croaking, rattling call, while females give a short *quack*. Feeds on aquatic plants, seeds and invertebrates. Dabbles and immerses head in water, but rarely up-ends like Teal.

Habitat and Status   An uncommon spring and autumn visitor. A very rare breeding species, with breeding records from the north and south-east. Found on freshwater lakes, pools and marshes with good reed and plant cover. Nests in dense vegetation close to water. Usually seen feeding on water along fringes of reeds and sedges.

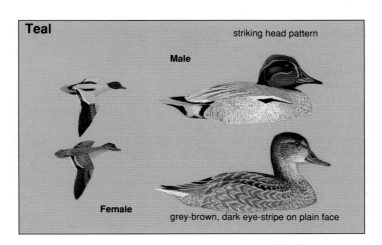

Teal

striking head pattern

Male

Female

grey-brown, dark eye-stripe on plain face

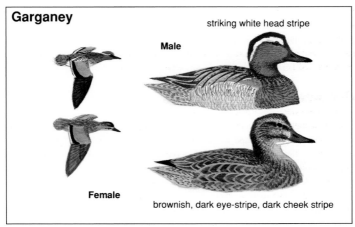

Garganey

striking white head stripe

Male

Female

brownish, dark eye-stripe, dark cheek stripe

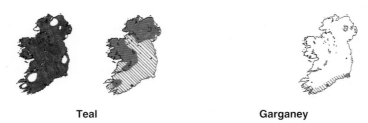

Teal   Garganey

Ducks

Mallard 55–62cm
Anas platyrhynchos   Mallard

A very familiar, large duck with a broad bill and orange-yellow legs. **Males** show a dark, glossy, green head, a white neck collar and purple-brown breast. Central tail feathers black and curled, contrasting with white outer-tail. Flanks greyish with fine vermiculations. Black undertail shows white edges. Back blackish. Upperparts greyish with fine vermiculations. Wing coverts brownish. Rump black. Bill olive-yellow with black nail. **Females** buff-brown with coarse, dark mottling. Face shows a pale supercilium and throat, and a dark eye-stripe. Bill grey with orange at base and tip. In flight, shows a black-bordered blue speculum with even, white trailing and upper edges.

Voice and Diet   The familiar, laughing *quack, quack, quack* call is given by females only. Males give soft, weak *kairp* calls, as well as grunts and whistles. Feeds by dabbling or up-ending, taking aquatic plants, seeds and invertebrates. Will also graze on crops and stubble.

Habitat and Status   An extremely common and widespread breeding species. In winter, populations increase with the arrival of birds from northern Europe. Found on lakes, ponds, marshes and estuaries. This species is widely reared and released for shooting.

Gadwall 48–53cm
Anas strepera   Gadual

A slender duck with a steep forehead and yellowish-orange legs. **Males** greyish on head, with crown and nape streaking. Breast and flanks grey with vermiculations heaviest on breast. Stern black. Upperparts vermiculated grey with elongated buff-edged scapulars and paler grey tertials. Bill dark. **Females** show dark scalloping on brownish-grey upper and underparts. Head pale buffish-grey with dark crown and eye-stripe. Bill dark with clear-cut yellowish edges. In flight, males show a black and white speculum, a chestnut median covert panel and white trailing edge to secondaries. Females show a whitish speculum on inner secondaries and a thin white trailing edge.

Voice and Diet   Relatively silent, although males give whistling calls. Females give a high-pitched, repeated *quack* in flight and when disturbed. Feeds by up-ending or dabbling, taking aquatic plants and seeds. Occasionally feeds on stubble and crops.

Habitat and Status   A scarce breeding species, with very small populations in the south-west, west, north and south-east. Breeds on freshwater lakes with good vegetation, suitable for cover when nesting. Uncommon in winter, despite the arrival of birds from Iceland, Britain and Europe. Winters on open freshwater lakes and marshes.

Mallard

glossy green head, purple-brown breast

Male

Female

brown, orange and grey bill

Gadwall

black stern, dark bill

Male

black and
white
speculum

Female

brownish-grey, dark bill with yellow edges

Mallard

Gadwall

Ducks

Wigeon 43–49cm
Anas penelope   Lacha rua

A short-necked duck with a black-tipped, blue-grey bill. **Males** show a chestnut head, a creamy-yellow forehead and crown, a greyish-pink breast, grey, vermiculated flanks, a white ventral patch and black undertail. Belly white. Grey and white vermiculated upperparts show black- and white-edged tertials and white coverts. In flight, shows a white covert patch and a black-bordered, dark green speculum. **Females** grey-brown on head with a dull, warm brown breast and flanks, a white belly and a spotted, whitish undertail. Brownish upperparts show pale fringes and white-edged tertials. In flight, shows a greyish forewing. Blackish-green speculum shows a white upper edge and a pale trailing edge.

Voice and Diet   Males give a very distinctive, whistling *wheeoo* call, while females give a growling *krrr*. Feeds on a wide variety of aquatic plants and seeds. Will also graze on grasslands. Feeds on eel-grass at coastal locations in winter.

Habitat and Status   A very common winter visitor from Iceland, Scandinavia and Siberia. Very small numbers may spend the summer in Ireland, with breeding being recorded on only a few occasions in northern counties. Found on coastal estuaries, lagoons, freshwater lakes, marshes and grassland close to water.

Pintail 53–59cm
Anas acuta   Biorearrach

A long-necked, elegant duck. **Males** show a chocolate-brown head and throat, with a thin white stripe meeting a white neck and breast. Belly white. Creamy ventral patch contrasts with black undertail. Fine grey vermiculations on upperparts and flanks. Tertials and elongated scapulars black with white and grey edges. White-edged black tail shows long central feathers. Bill dark grey with blue-grey edges. In flight, shows a chestnut covert panel, and a dark green and black speculum with a white trailing edge. **Females** show a plain, buff-brown head, a coarsely marked, pale grey-brown body and a longish, pointed tail. Shows a dark speculum with a white trailing edge. Bill dark greyish.

Voice and Diet   A relatively quiet species, males can give a Teal-like *krrip* call and low, whistling calls. Females give a repeated, weak, Mallard-like *quack*. Feeds by dabbling, up-ending or grazing on land. Takes a wide variety of aquatic plants, seeds and other plant material. Will also take aquatic invertebrates.

Habitat and Status   An extremely rare breeding species, with records from the midlands and north. A scarce winter visitor from Iceland and continental Europe. Breeds on wet meadows and lakes, nesting in short vegetation. In winter, is found on open freshwater lakes, coastal lagoons and estuaries.

Wigeon

creamy-yellow forehead, chestnut head

Male

Female

grey-brown head, brownish breast and flanks

Pintail

long tail, chocolate-brown head

Male

Female

bill dark grey, pale head and neck

Wigeon

Pintail

Ducks

Common Scoter 46–52cm
Melanitta nigra   Scótar

A distinctive sea duck with a square head, a long neck and a longish tail. **Males** are totally black. Black bill shows a small knob and a yellow central patch. **Females** dark brown, with contrasting pale brown cheeks and throat. Can sometimes show pale barring on breast and flanks. Bill dark grey. **Immature males** also show a dark brown plumage with pale face patches on some birds. The longish tail can be held cocked, especially at rest. Usually dives with wings closed. In flight, appears uniformly blackish or dark brownish, with a slight contrast between the darker wing coverts and the flight feathers. When wing flapping, droops the neck and head in a distinctive S-shape.

Voice and Diet   Normally a silent species, males on the breeding grounds give high, piping, whistling calls. Females give harsh, grating calls. Feeds by diving for crustaceans, cockles, mussels, larvae and worms. Occasionally takes seeds.

Habitat and Status   A rare breeding species found in small numbers on large inland lakes in the west. Common in winter, with the arrival of birds from Iceland and northern Europe. Found on open coastal waters, often in very large flocks, the largest of which occur on the east, north-west and west coasts.

Velvet Scoter 53–60cm
Melanitta fusca

A large, thick-necked, bulky sea duck with a wedge-shaped head. **Males** all black, with a small white crescent below the whitish eye and pure white secondaries. The large bill is orange-yellow with a black basal knob. **Females** appear dark brown, with white secondaries and pale, oval face patches on the loral area and towards the rear of the cheek. Females also show a dark eye and a greyish bill. **Immature males** lack the white eye crescent and show a duller bill. Legs orange-red. In flight, the white wing patches are striking. However, on the water, the white secondaries are not always obvious and may appear as a small white crescent towards the rear of the wing. Tends to open wings when diving.

Voice and Diet   Relatively silent when found in Ireland, although males can give a piping call in flight. Females can give a harsher *garr* call in flight. Feeds by diving for mussels, worms, crabs, shrimps and cockles.

Habitat and Status   An uncommon but regular winter visitor from northern Europe. Found on open coastal waters, usually associating with flocks of Common Scoters. Most sightings occur off the eastern coastal counties, with birds also seen off the south-west, west and north-west.

Common Scoter

Male

all dark, yellow on bill

Female

dark brown, pale cheeks and throat

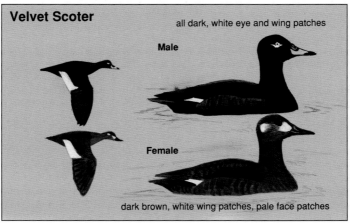

Velvet Scoter

Male

all dark, white eye and wing patches

Female

dark brown, white wing patches, pale face patches

Common Scoter   **Velvet Scoter**

75

Ducks

Pochard 44–48cm
Aythya ferina   Póiseard

A diving duck with a high, domed crown and a long bill. **Males** show a rich chestnut head, a black breast, tail and undertail, and whitish-grey flanks. Upperparts pale grey. Eye reddish. Bill black with a grey central patch. **Females** show brownish crown, with paler lores and throat. Eye dark, with thin pale orbital ring which can extend back as line over ear-coverts. Breast brownish with pale barring. **In summer**, upperparts brownish with grey scalloping. Flanks warm brown with buff scalloping. Upperparts and flanks show pale grey scalloping in winter. Tail and undertail brown. Bill dark with pale subterminal band sometimes present. In flight, Pochard shows a broad, greyish wing stripe.

Voice and Diet   Usually silent, except during the breeding season when males can give a wheezing-type call. Females can give a growling call in flight. An active diving species which feeds on aquatic invertebrates and water plants.

Habitat and Status   A common winter visitor from Europe, with a very small breeding population concentrated in the midlands and north. In winter, the largest concentration occurs on Lough Neagh, with smaller numbers found throughout the country. Occurs on freshwater lakes, ponds and reservoirs.

Smew 36–42cm
Mergus albellus   Síolta gheal

An attractive, compact diving duck with a steep forehead and a short crest. **Males** are unmistakable, with a striking black and white plumage. Head white with a large black patch around eye, a black line along rear crown, and a short crest. Breast white, with two narrow black lines on breast sides. Flanks greyish with fine vermiculations. Upperparts black and white. In flight, shows black wings with a broad white wing patch. **Females** show a reddish-brown crown and nape, with a slightly darker brown patch around the eye and a bold white cheek patch. Upperparts dark greyish with paler grey underparts. In flight, shows a whitish wing patch and a dark grey rump and tail.

Voice and Diet   Rarely heard in Ireland. An active feeder, Smew dive for small fish and invertebrates.

Habitat and Status   A rare winter visitor from breeding grounds in northern Europe. Found on lakes, reservoirs and occasionally on estuaries. Smew now occur annually on inland lakes and reservoirs in northern counties.

Pochard

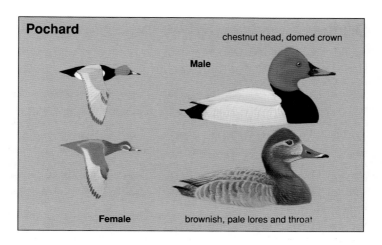

chestnut head, domed crown

Male

Female

brownish, pale lores and throat

Smew

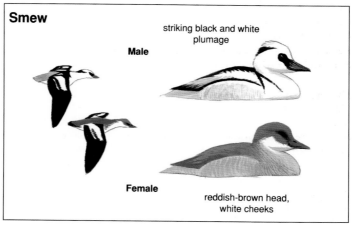

striking black and white plumage

Male

Female

reddish-brown head, white cheeks

Pochard

Smew

Ducks

Red-breasted Merganser 52–61cm
Mergus serrator Síolta rua

A slender, thin-necked duck with a long, slightly up-curved, thin bill. **Males** show a blackish-green head with long, wispy head crests, a white lower neck and a spotted, reddish-buff breast. Vermiculated greyish flanks contrast with black and white breast sides. Mantle black. In flight, shows a white inner wing, broken by two black bars. Outer wing and leading edge black. Rump and tail greyish. Eye and bill bright red. **Females** rufous-brown on head with wispy crests, a whitish loral stripe and a whitish throat. Head colour merges into pale breast. Flanks greyish-brown. Upperparts mottled brownish-grey. In flight, shows a broken, white wing patch on the inner rear wing. Eye brownish. Bill dull red.

Voice and Diet   Usually a quiet species, males can give low, purring calls during elaborate courtship displays. Females give harsher, grating calls. Feeds by diving for fish and invertebrates.

Habitat and Status   A common resident species breeding on inland lakes and large river systems in most regions except the south and east. A small breeding population is also present in the south-east. In autumn, large flocks of moulting birds can occasionally be seen at coastal locations. A common coastal duck in winter, found in harbours, bays and estuaries.

Goosander 57–69cm
Mergus merganser Síolta mhór

A slender duck, very similar to Red-breasted Merganser. **Males** show a dark blackish-green head with a full, bulging rear head crest. White breast and flanks can show a pink wash. Upperparts black and white. Eye dark. Bill red. In flight, shows an unbroken, white inner wing, a black leading edge and outer wing, and a greyish rump and tail. **Females** show a dark rufous-brown head, a bulging rear head crest and a clear-cut white throat patch. Rich head colour is sharply demarcated from the pale breast. Flanks and upperparts greyish. Red bill is broader-based and shorter than on Red-breasted Merganser. In flight, females show a broken white patch on the rear inner wing.

Voice and Diet   Usually silent in Ireland. On the breeding grounds, males can give strange, twanging-type calls. Females give harsher *karr* calls. Feeds by diving for fish, also taking invertebrates.

Habitat and Status   A very rare breeding species, with a small population concentrated in the north-west. Uncommon in winter, Goosanders are more likely to be found in the north where they are now regular annual winter visitors. Found on reservoirs, inland lakes and occasionally on estuaries.

Red-breasted Merganser

blackish-green head, thin red bill

Male

long crest

Female

rufous-brown head merging into pale breast

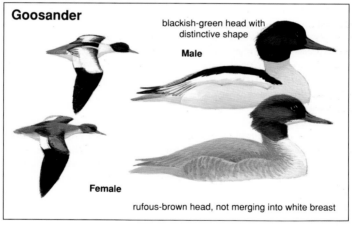

Goosander

blackish-green head with distinctive shape

Male

Female

rufous-brown head, not merging into white breast

Red-breasted Merganser   **Goosander**

Ducks

Eider 55–65cm
Somateria mollissima

A stocky duck with a diagnostic wedge-shaped head. **Males** black on forehead and crown, with white stripes through pale green nape and neck patches. Face and neck white. Breast tinged pink. Belly, flanks and undertail black with white ventral patch. Upperparts black and white. Bill olive-green. In flight, black primaries and secondaries contrast with white forewing and back. **Immature males** show a dark head, mottled brown underparts and whitish upperparts. **Females** greyish-brown with heavy barring and mottling. Best told by the large, stocky size, and the wedge-shaped head profile. In flight, plain wing shows a thin white covert bar and trailing edge to secondaries.

Voice and Diet   Very vocal in late winter and early spring when males give a cooing *oo-oh-wah,* the emphasis being on the second section of the call. Females give a growling *krrr* call. Feeds by diving for mussels and other molluscs. Will also take invertebrates.

Habitat and Status   A common sea duck along the northern coastline. Scarce elsewhere, with birds occasionally wintering on the east, south-east, south-west and west coasts. Found along rocky coasts and offshore islands. Nests in down-lined hollows on short grass, bracken or heather close to water.

Long-tailed Duck 41–46cm
Clangula hyemalis

A small sea duck, most likely to be seen in winter plumage when **males** show a white head, a pale pink-brown eye patch and a dark lower ear-covert patch. Breast, mantle and centre of upperparts blackish. Wings blackish with white scapulars. Tail shows elongated black central feathers. Belly, flanks and undertail white. In flight, shows dark wings. **Females** whitish on face and neck, with a dark crown and ear-covert patch. Breast and upperparts brownish-grey. Underparts white. **Summer females** similar, but show a dark head with a pale eye patch. **Summer males** show a pale grey eye patch on a dark head, neck and breast. Bill dark grey with broad, pinkish, central band on males.

Voice and Diet   Rarely heard in Ireland. Males can occasionally give a yodelling *aw-awlee* call in spring. Females give low quacking calls. Dives for a wide variety of molluscs, crustaceans and invertebrates.

Habitat and Status   A scarce winter visitor from northern Europe and Greenland. The largest wintering populations are based on the north and west coasts. Found on open coastal waters and bays. May be more numerous than expected, with birds wintering far offshore.

Eider

striking black and white plumage, green on nape

Male

Female

greyish-brown with wedge-shaped head

Long-tailed Duck

long tail, striking black and white plumage

Male

Female

Summer Male and Female

pale head, dark crown and cheek patches

Eider

Long-tailed Duck

Birds of Prey

Hen Harrier 43–52cm
Circus cyaneus   Cromán na gcearc

A slim, narrow-winged raptor. **Adult males** show whitish underparts, a white rump, a pale grey head, breast, tail and upperwing with black tips and a dark trailing edge. Underwing paler. **Females** brown above with a pale upperwing covert panel, a large white rump and barring on a brown tail. Owl-like face streaked brown, showing a dark crescent on rear cheeks. Underparts pale with brown streaking on neck, breast and flanks. Underwing shows mottled brown coverts, barred flight feathers and a dark trailing edge. **Immatures** buffier on underparts. Legs and cere yellowish. Flies with fast wing beats and short glides. Soars on raised wings. Rounded wings show four- or five-fingered primaries.

Voice and Diet   Males at the breeding sites give chattering *tchuc-uc-uc* calls. Females give high-pitched *ke-ke-ke* and whistling-type calls. Feeds on a wide variety of small birds and rodents. Hunts by gliding low over an area before swooping down on prey.

Habitat and Status   A scarce breeding species with small numbers present in the midlands, eastern, south-western, western and northern regions. In summer, found on mountains and moorlands, nesting on the ground. Also nests in young conifer plantations. Breeding numbers appear to be declining. In winter, birds can be found in most parts of Ireland with some hunting over coastal areas. Hen Harriers can roost communally in winter. A small spring and autumn passage is noted annually in the south-west.

Marsh Harrier 49–56cm
Circus aeruginosus   Cromán móna

A broad-winged, heavy raptor. **Adult males** show a dark brown mantle and wing coverts, a pale head, black wing tips, and pale grey flight feathers. Underwing shows brown coverts, pale flight feathers and a dark trailing edge. Underparts streaked brown. Tail grey. **Adult females** are larger and show a dark brown plumage, a dark eye-stripe, and a creamy-yellow crown and throat. Underparts brown with a paler breast. Wings dark brown with creamy-yellow forewing patches on the upperwing. Tail brown. **Immatures** similar but lack forewing patches. **Immature males** show greyish inner primaries. Cere and legs yellowish. Flight heavy with deep wing beats. Glides with wings raised in a shallow V.

Voice and Diet   Usually silent on passage, with males giving shrill *key-eoo* calls only at the nesting site. Feeds on a wide range of marshland birds, mammals and frogs. Will also take eggs, nestlings and carrion.

Habitat and Status   A scarce but regular spring and autumn passage migrant from Europe. Formerly a widespread breeding species, but numbers declined during the last century. In recent years, Marsh Harriers have been recorded more often and it is expected that breeding may again take place in the near future. Most reports refer to eastern, south-eastern and south-western counties. Found over large reed-beds and marshes.

Hen Harrier

Female

broad white rump

Young Male

Male

grey, black wing tips

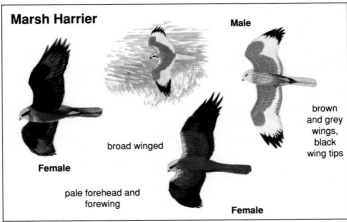

Marsh Harrier

Male

broad winged

Female

pale forehead and
forewing

Female

brown
and grey
wings,
black
wing tips

Hen Harrier

Marsh Harrier

Birds of Prey

Osprey 51–60cm
Pandion haliaetus   Coirneach

A large raptor with a contrasting plumage. When perched, shows dark brown upperparts, a crested white crown and a striking black eye-stripe which extends down side of neck. Underparts white with a brownish breast band. Hooked bill pale with a dark tip. Legs greyish. In flight, a pale underwing shows a blackish carpal patch, a black covert bar and dark wing tips. Shortish tail is pale below, dark above, and shows narrow barring. **Immatures** show pale tips to underwing coverts. Flies with strong, shallow wing beats on long, narrow wings. Soars on bowed wings. In the air can look gull-like. Hunts by hovering or gliding with legs dangling before plunging feet-first into the water. Shakes water from the plumage when rising.

Voice and Diet   Although seldom heard in Ireland, Osprey can give loud, repeated, whistling-type calls. Feeds exclusively on large fish which are caught from spectacular dives. Catches fish with specially adapted talons before flying off with fish held in both feet.

Habitat and Status   An uncommon spring and autumn passage migrant from Europe, occurring on an almost annual basis. In recent years, birds have been reported present in suitable breeding areas in spring and late summer and it is hoped that breeding may take place in the near future. Found on large lakes and rivers, often with suitable perches such as dead trees. Also reported on passage at coastal sites. Has been seen out at sea. Can be attracted to fish farms.

Buzzard 50–57cm
Buteo buteo   Clamhán

A large, stocky, short-necked raptor with broad wings and a shortish tail. Plumage can vary greatly, but most show a dark brown head, breast and upperparts with brown mottling on underparts. Lower breast can be paler, appearing as a pale crescent. Shortish tail pale brown below, darker above, with narrow barring. Upperwing plain, dark brown. Underwing shows dark brown coverts, dark carpal patches, blackish wing tips, pale base to primaries and a dark trailing edge. **Immatures** lack dark trailing edge to wings. Bill dark with a yellowish cere. Legs yellowish. Soars with wings held in a shallow V. When gliding, the wings can be held flat or just slightly raised.

Voice and Diet   Gives a distinctive, high-pitched, drawn-out, mewing *pee-oo* call. Feeds on a wide range of prey, including rats, rabbits, frogs, insects, worms, young birds and carrion and some may die due to feeding on poison-baited carcasses.

Habitat and Status   An uncommon breeding species but with a healthy population in Co. Antrim. Smaller numbers also breed in other northern counties. Recently, birds have also been seen during the breeding season in north-western and eastern counties; successful breeding may occasionally take place in these areas. Found in a wide range of habitats, including undisturbed coasts and islands, farmlands, mountains, moorlands and in wooded demesnes. Nests in trees or on cliffs.

Osprey

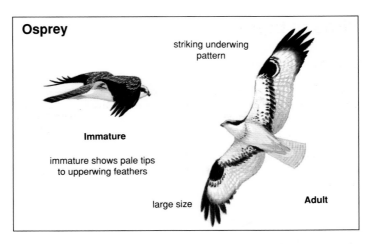

striking underwing
pattern

Immature

immature shows pale tips
to upperwing feathers

large size

Adult

Buzzard

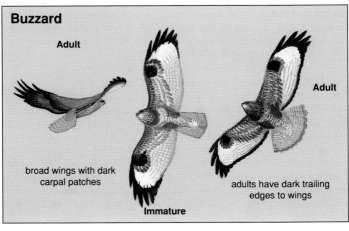

Adult

Adult

broad wings with dark
carpal patches

adults have dark trailing
edges to wings

Immature

Osprey

Buzzard

85

Birds of prey

Sparrowhawk 28–37cm
Accipiter nisus   Spioróg

A small raptor with yellow eyes. In flight, shows rounded wings and a long, square-ended tail. **Adult males** blue-grey on crown and upperparts, and show a white supercilium and rufous cheeks. White underparts show orange-red barring extending onto underwing coverts. Underwing flight feathers barred. Undertail shows dark bars. **Females** larger, with a grey-brown crown and upperparts, a white supercilium, and brown barring on white underparts and on underwing coverts and flight feathers. Tail shows dark bars. Bill dark. Legs and cere yellow. **Immatures** similar to females, but show pale edges to upperpart feathers and brown barring on buffish underparts.

Voice and Diet   Gives a loud, shrill, repeated *kek-kek-kek,* when agitated or when close to the nest. Also gives rattling calls during a slow-flapping display flight. Feeds by gliding low over the ground, along hedgerows or through trees, surprising small birds and mammals. Will also chase prey into thick cover. Will take large insects.

Habitat and Status   A resident breeding species found in all counties, frequents coniferous and mixed woodland, open farmland with scattered trees and hedgerows, parks and, especially in winter, suburban gardens. Nests high in trees, usually close to the main trunk. In autumn, found on coastal islands and headlands.

Peregrine Falcon 38–49cm
Falco peregrinus   Fabhcún gorm

A powerful, stocky, heavy-chested falcon with broad, pointed wings. **Adults** show a thick, blackish moustachial stripe, a dark crown, and a white face and throat. Upperparts bluish-grey. Darker tail shows dark bars. Underparts white with fine, delicate barring. In flight, underwing shows heavy barring on flight feathers and coverts. Undertail pale with dark bars. Cere and legs yellow. **Females** larger. **Immatures** show pale-fringed, brownish upperparts, a dark moustachial stripe, and heavy streaking on creamy underparts. Dark uppertail shows pale bars. Undertail as adult. Underwing heavily barred. Cere bluish. Legs yellow. Soars on stiff, slightly bowed wings.

Voice and Diet   At the nest, gives loud, repeated, chattering *keyak-keyak-keyak* calls. In winter, can occasionally give a harsh *arrk* call. Hunts by climbing to a great height and circling before diving at enormous speeds with wings held tight into the body. Snatches birds up to the size of pigeons from the air, but will also swoop through wader and duck flocks. Also takes rabbits and other smaller mammals.

Habitat and Status   A widespread resident breeding species found in all counties. Numbers declined dramatically in the 1950s and 1960s due to the effects of poisoning by pesticides. However, this powerful falcon can now be found in most of its former haunts. Frequents coastal and mountainous regions, nesting on cliff edges. Also found close to human habitation. In winter, most leave upland breeding areas, moving to coastal regions.

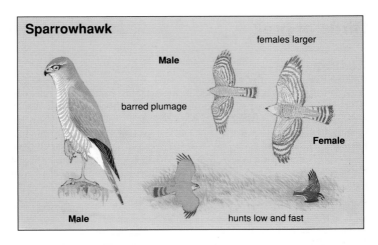

Sparrowhawk

females larger

Male

barred plumage

Female

Male

hunts low and fast

Peregrine Falcon

Immature

faintly barred underparts, bluish upperparts

powerful build

Adult

Immature

Sparrowhawk

Peregrine Falcon

Birds of prey

Kestrel 33–37cm
Falco tinnunculus   Pocaire gaoithe

A long-tailed falcon with pointed wings, often seen hovering in mid-air. **Adult males** show a blue-grey crown and nape, a dark moustachial stripe, black spotting on chestnut upperparts, and a black band and white tip to a grey tail. Creamy underparts show dark spotting. In flight, shows dark wing tips and dark spots on underwing coverts. Adult **females** and **immatures** show a streaked brown head, a dark moustachial stripe and heavy, dark barring on rufous upperparts. Brown tail shows dark bars and a white tip. Creamy-buff underparts and underwing coverts show heavy streaking. Shows dark tips to upperwing and barred underwing flight feathers. Legs and cere yellow.

Voice and Diet   Gives harsh, loud, repeated *kee-kee-kee* calls when agitated or close to the nest. Hunts by hovering motionless in mid-air, searching for suitable quarry below, before diving suddenly onto prey. Can snatch perched or feeding birds in a dashing swoop. Will also sit on an open perch, watching for insects. Occasionally hawks insects on the wing. Feeds on a wide range of small rodents, birds, insects and worms.

Habitat and Status   A common, widespread breeding species found in a wide range of habitats, including mountainous cliffs, moorlands and bogs, open farmland, woodlands, parks, and towns and cities. Frequently seen hovering over road verges. Nests on cliff ledges, old derelict buildings, in old nests, in hollow trees and occasionally on highrise buildings. In winter, tends to leave more mountainous areas.

Merlin 27–33cm
Falco columbarius   Meirliún

A small, agile falcon with short, pointed wings. **Males** show a dark grey crown, a faint moustachial stripe, a whitish supercilium, streaked cheeks and a buff to rust-brown nape. Grey upperparts show thin streaking. Grey tail shows broad bars. Buff to rust-brown underparts show dark streaking. In flight, shows a streaked and barred underwing. **Females** and **immatures** show a brown crown, streaked cheeks, a diffuse moustachial stripe and a pale nape. Upperparts grey-brown. Creamy tail shows dark bars. Creamy underparts heavily streaked. In flight, shows a heavily streaked and barred underwing. Legs yellow. Cere yellow on adults, bluish on immatures.

Voice and Diet   Gives a shrill, repeated, Kestrel-like *kiik-kiik-kiik* call when agitated or disturbed at the nest. Prey consists mainly of birds, with small mammals and insects taken occasionally. Hunts by flying fast and low over the ground, sometimes snatching feeding or perched birds. Will occasionally hawk insects on the wing.

Habitat and Status   A scarce, resident breeding species found in all regions. In summer, found on upland moorland and bogs, on well-vegetated lake islands and in conifer plantations. Nests on the ground or in old crows' nests. In spring and autumn, a passage movement is noted. In winter, found along coastal areas and on low-lying inland bogs. Numbers increase in winter with the arrival of birds from Iceland and Scotland.

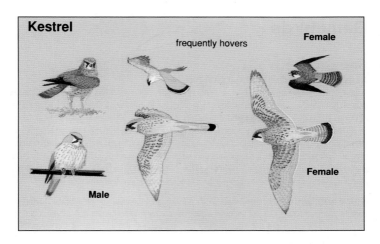

Kestrel

frequently hovers

Female

Male

Female

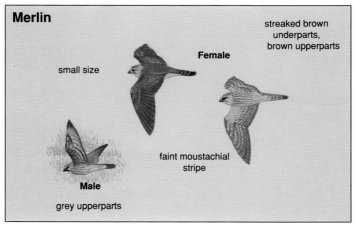

Merlin

small size

Female

streaked brown underparts, brown upperparts

faint moustachial stripe

Male

grey upperparts

Kestrel

Merlin

Gamebirds

Red Grouse 33–40cm
Lagopus lagopus   Cearc fhraoigh

A dark, plump bird showing a stout, short bill and short, rounded wings. Usually only seen when flushed. **Summer males** show a deep red-brown plumage with heavy dark barring, white-feathered legs and a bright red comb above the eye. Can appear black at a distance. **Winter males** appear darker. **Females** smaller, and show a yellower plumage with coarse barring and spotting, and a less prominent red comb. **Immatures** similar to females, but lack red combs and show a duller plumage. Flushes noisily from the ground, flying with rapid, whirring wing beats and long glides on bowed wings. Red Grouse found in Ireland belong to a specific race (*see* Introduction).

Voice and Diet   When disturbed, gives a fast, cackling *kowk-ko-ko-ko* call. During the breeding season, Red Grouse engage in displays which involve the distinctive, crowing *go-bak, go-bak, go-bak-bak-bak-bak* call. Feeds on heather shoots, flowers and seeds. Also takes a variety of berries, buds and some insects. Will feed on cereals when available.

Habitat and Status   A scarce but widespread resident breeding species. Found on upland blanket bog, low-lying bogs, open moorland and heather slopes. Numbers appear to be gradually declining due to habitat loss and upland management. Nests in cover of heather, rushes and tussocks on the ground. In severe winter conditions, Red Grouse can occasionally perch in bushes or trees to feed on berries. Birds of the darker British race have been introduced in the past by gun clubs.

Pheasant 53–89cm
Phasianus colchicus   Piasún

A large, striking species showing a very long, barred tail. **Males** show a metallic blackish-green head, bright red facial skin and small tufts on rear of crown. Some can show a white collar and eyebrow. Plumage copper-red with black crescents on underparts, and black and white fringes on upperparts. Short, rounded wings greyish-brown. In flight, shows a grey rump and a long, barred buff tail. Small bill ivory-white. **Females** show a shorter tail, a buff-brown plumage with dark barring and spotting on the breast, flanks and upperparts. **Immatures** resemble short-tailed, dull females. Flushes noisily, flying with rapid, whirring wing beats and gliding on bowed wings.

Voice and Diet   Males give distinctive, far carrying, resonant, choking *korrk-kook* calls and a repeated *kutok, kutok* note. Females, when alarmed, give whistling-type notes. Feeds on a wide range of plant material, including roots, seeds, fruit, berries, leaves and stems. Will also take insects, worms, slugs and occasionally small rodents and amphibians.

Habitat and Status   An extremely common, widespread, resident breeding species found in all counties. Frequents agricultural lands, rough pastures, woodlands, upland scrub and marshes. Nests on the ground in dense cover. Each year, large numbers are introduced into the countryside by gun clubs. First introduced into Ireland from Asia in the sixteenth century.

Red Grouse

dark, plump bird

dark reddish-brown plumage with dark barring

Male **Female**

Pheasant

Female

Male

large game bird with very long, pointed tail

Red Grouse **Pheasant**

Gamebirds

Grey Partridge 29–32cm
Perdix perdix   Patraisc

A shy, rotund species which shows short, rounded wings and a short, bright rufous tail. **Males** show an orange-red face, a grey neck and upper breast, a brown crown and nape, and pale streaking and dark spotting on brown upperparts. Pale lower breast shows a conspicuous, inverted dark chestnut horseshoe, while buff-washed flanks show chestnut barring. **Females** similar, but show a paler face, browner upperparts and a buff-grey breast. The inverted chestnut horseshoe is usually reduced to blotches on the lower breast and, on some birds, may be totally absent. Short, stout bill and legs greyish. Flies with rapid, whirring wing beats and glides on bowed wings.

Voice and Diet   When alarmed, Grey Partridge can give a slow, cackling *krikric-ric-ric-ric* call while the song consists of loud, hoarse *kirr-ic, kirr-ic* notes. Feeds on a wide variety of seeds, grain, roots, fruit and leaves. Will also take small insects such as ants. Occasionally feeds on slugs and worms.

Habitat and Status   An extremely rare, thinly distributed, resident breeding species. Formerly found in all counties. Now occurs in very small numbers in northern, eastern, south-eastern and midland counties. Frequents agricultural belts, especially wheat and corn-growing areas. Also found on pastures with hedgerow borders or overgrown verges, and on bogs, marshes and upland moorland. Nests in dense cover on the ground.

Quail 17–19cm
Coturnix coturnix   Gearg

A tiny, elusive gamebird, more often heard than seen. **Adult males** show a whitish central crown-stripe, a dark crown and a whitish supercilium. Whitish throat shows a black central stripe and lower border. Underparts sandy rufous with warmer smudges on breast and black-edged, pale streaking on the flanks. Upperparts dark with buff barring and black-edged whitish streaks which are very conspicuous in flight. Tail brownish, short and appears pointed. **Females** show unmarked pale throats, brown and cream head markings, and dark spotting on breast. Bill short. Hard to flush, Quail fly short distances on bowed, sandy wings before dropping back into cover.

Voice and Diet   Adult males give a very distinctive *kwit, kwit-wit* song which is loud, repeated and far-carrying. Quail can call both by day and by night and are also ventriloquial, making their precise locations difficult to judge. Females give a low, wheezing *quep-quep* call. Feeds on a wide range of seeds and insects.

Habitat and Status   A scarce summer visitor, with small breeding populations based at traditional sites in midland counties. Some breeding may also take place in western, northern and south-eastern regions. Seen regularly on passage on coastal headlands and islands, more frequently reported in spring than autumn. Found in crop fields and rough pastures.

Grey Partridge

mottled grey and brown plumage, chestnut face

Male

dark 'horseshoe' on underparts, fainter on female

Female

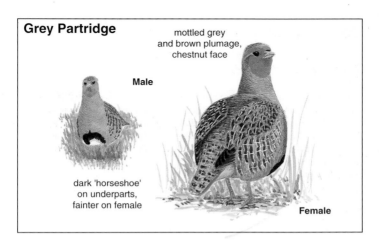

Quail

small size, streaked brown plumage

striking head pattern

Female

female duller with pale, unmarked throat

Male

Grey Partridge

Quail

Corncrake and Water Rail

Corncrake 25–27cm
Crex crex   Traonach

Corncrakes are shy and hard to see, the distinctive call often being the only indication of their presence. **Adult males** show a brown, streaked crown with blue-grey cheeks and supercilium, and a chestnut eye-stripe. Breast buffish-grey with chestnut smudges on breast sides. Flanks show chestnut, white and thin black barring, fading on undertail. Upperparts show yellow-buff and greyish edges to dark-centred feathers. Wings bright chestnut, striking in flight. Short tail yellow-buff. **Females** show less grey in plumage. Short bill and legs yellow-brown. Prefers to run through thick cover, dropping quickly back into cover if flushed. Flight weak and floppy, with legs dangling.

Voice and Diet   Males give a very distinctive, loud, rasping *kerrx-kerrx* call which is repeated. Tends to call more frequently at night, but will call during the day. Feeds on seeds, plants and invertebrates.

Habitat and Status   Formerly an extremely common summer visitor, Corncrakes have suffered a drastic population decline during this century. Between 1968 and 1972, Corncrakes were still breeding in all counties, but now are only present in small numbers along the Shannon Callows and areas in the west and north-west, with numbers still declining. Now a rare breeding bird. Found in rough pastures, meadows, flooded meadows and crop fields.

Water Rail 27–30cm
Rallus aquaticus   Rálóg uisce

A secretive bird with a long red bill. **Adults** show dark streaking on olive-brown crown, nape and upperparts. Wing feathers olive-brown with dark centres. Face, throat and breast blue-grey with a dark line through eye. Chin white. Flanks barred black and white. Undertail white. Eye reddish with a black pupil. Legs pinkish-brown. **Juvenile** birds show a paler bill, a whitish throat, brown mottling on buff face and underparts, and brown and buff flank barring. **Sub-adults** similar to adults, but show a large whitish chin patch, a brownish face, and dark barring in grey-brown throat and breast. Walks in a slow, deliberate manner with tail cocked. Flies on rounded wings with trailing legs.

Voice and Diet   Gives loud, explosive, pig-like squealing calls. Also gives a variety of grunting calls. Song is a rhythmic, hammering, repeated *kupp* call. Feeds on a variety of invertebrates, plants, berries and seeds.

Habitat and Status   A widespread, common resident species, with numbers increasing in winter due to the arrival of birds from Iceland and Europe. Found in dense reed-beds, sedges and marshes, and rivers with dense vegetation. Very difficult to see, the distinctive calls often being the only indication of a bird's presence. Nests in sedges, reeds and dense grass close to water.

Corncrake

greyish on neck

striking bright chestnut wings

Water Rail

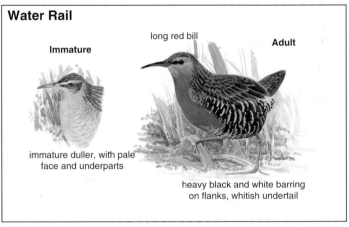

long red bill

Immature

Adult

immature duller, with pale face and underparts

heavy black and white barring on flanks, whitish undertail

Corncrake

Water Rail

Moorhen and Coot

Moorhen 30–35cm
Gallinula chloropus   Cearc uisce

A very distinctive bird with a brightly coloured frontal shield and bill, and a blackish plumage. **Adults** blackish-brown on head and upperparts with short, brownish wings. Underparts greyish-black with a broad, broken, white flank stripe. Undertail white with a black central stripe. Eye reddish-brown with a black pupil. Shows a bright red frontal shield and a short, yellow-tipped red bill. Legs and feet olive-green with small red garters on tibia. **Immatures** show brownish upper and underparts, a whitish throat and belly, a buffish flank stripe, a white undertail and a greenish-brown bill. Swims buoyantly with a jerking head and cocked tail. Flies with rounded wings and trailing legs.

Voice and Diet   Gives a throaty *kurruk* alarm call and a repeated, high-pitched *krik* call. Feeds on a variety of seeds, aquatic plants, grass, worms and insects. Seldom dives for food, preferring to pick from water surface. Can also graze on pastures, walking in a deliberate, hen-like manner.

Habitat and Status   A widespread, common resident species. Found along slow streams and rivers, canals, marshes, reed-beds, lakes, flooded fields and ditches. Also found feeding on pastures and along hedgerows. Nests in reeds, grass, bushes or trees close to water.

Coot 36–41cm
Fulica atra   Cearc cheannann

A distinctive, slaty-black bird with a heavy, rotund body and short, rounded wings. **Adults** show a glossy black head with a contrasting broad, white frontal shield and a white bill. Upperparts and wings greyish-black with white tips to secondaries showing as a thin white trailing edge to the wings in flight. Underparts greyish-black. Eye reddish with a black pupil. Legs greenish-grey with red garters on the tibia and long, lobed toes. **Immatures** show brownish upperparts, a whitish face with a dark ear-covert patch and a whitish neck, breast and belly. The small frontal shield and bill are greyish. Runs across the water when taking off. Flies on rounded wings with trailing legs.

Voice and Diet   Gives a high-pitched, sharp *pitt* call. Can also give a loud, piping, repeated *kock* call. Feeds by diving or by grazing on land close to water. Takes a variety of insects and other invertebrates and also aquatic plants, grasses and seeds.

Habitat and Status   A common, resident species with a range that is not as widespread as that of Moorhen. In winter, can gather in large flocks on lakes in the midlands, west and north. Populations may increase in winter with the arrival of birds from continental Europe. Found on areas with open water such as lakes and reservoirs, occasionally wintering in salt-water areas. Nests in reeds, grasses and other aquatic vegetation.

Moorhen

Immature

red shield and bill with yellow tip

brownish, with dark bill and white on undertail

black centre to white undertail

Adult

Coot

Immature

greyish bill

striking white shield and bill

brownish with pale underparts and dark undertail

Adult

Moorhen

Coot

Waders

Oystercatcher 40–45cm
Haematopus ostralegus   Roilleach

A noisy, stocky, black and white wader, best recognised by the long orange bill which is tipped yellowish. **Summer adults** show a black head and breast, with black upperparts showing a white wingbar, obvious in flight. Underparts white. White tail shows a black subterminal band. White rump extends as a conspicuous white wedge onto back. **Winter adults** show a white band from the throat to the sides of the neck. Adults have red eyes and an orange-red eye-ring. Stout legs are flesh-pink on adults. **Immatures** show browner upperparts, a duller bill, a white neck band, yellowish eye-rings and greyish legs.

Voice and Diet   Oystercatchers are among the noisiest wading birds found in Ireland. In flight they give loud, sharp *peik,* sometimes finished with *kapeik.* In song, or when displaying over feeding territories, these notes develop into long, loud trilling calls. Probes for worms on tidal mudflats or fields. Also feeds on molluscs which are either prised or hammered open.

Habitat and Status   A very common Irish bird, primarily found on coastal estuaries and mudflats. Can form large flocks in winter. Nests in scrapes made in shingle, sand or grass, usually along coastal stretches. Rarely nests inland. In winter, can sometimes be found on playing fields or farmland where they probe for worms. A resident species, numbers increase with wintering birds from northern Europe and Iceland.

Avocet 41–46cm
Recurvirostra avosetta   Abhóiséad

A striking, black and white wader with a long, up-curved bill. The black forehead, crown and nape contrast with the white throat and neck. A strong black scapular stripe and the thick black stripe on the wing coverts form the diagnostic black oval pattern which contrasts sharply with the otherwise white upperparts. The primaries are also black. The underparts and tail are white. The long, up-curved bill is black and the legs are bluish-grey. In flight, black wingtips and black covert and scapular stripes create a striking pattern. Feeds with distinctive side-to-side head sweeps. In deep water, head may be totally submerged.

Voice and Diet   Gives a loud, excited, fluty *klo-whitt* call when disturbed or alarmed. Also gives a shorter *klip* call. The distinctive sweeping motion when feeding allows the sensitive bill to sift water for worms, insects and crustaceans.

Habitat and Status   Formerly a regular winter visitor to the east and south coasts, Avocets are now uncommon in Ireland. Breeding occurred once in the 1930s. Normally found on estuaries and mudflats as well as on shallow lagoons. Small influxes can occur, with up to twelve birds present along eastern and south-western coastal counties in November 1992.

Oystercatcher

orange bill

Adult (summer)

striking black and white plumage

Avocet

long, thin, upcurved bill

graceful, long-legged, black and white bird

Oystercatcher

Avocet

Waders

Woodcock 32–36cm
Scolopax rusticola   Creabhar

A large, chunky bird with a long, heavy, straight bill and shortish legs. Unlike most waders, Woodcock are found in damp woodland areas and are usually seen at dusk and dawn. The large black eye is set high and back in the head. The steep forehead is greyish, with broad, dark and pale bars on the crown and nape. Dark loral stripe present. Upperparts a complicated pattern of black, buff and cream barring with a broad, creamy mantle stripe. Underparts pale with greyish-brown barring. Sides of breast show rufous tones. In flight, shows broad, plain, rounded wings. Tail dark brown with pale tips. Bill pale pinkish with a dark tip. Short pale legs. **Immatures** similar to adults.

Voice and Diet   Usually silent when flushed, Woodcock occasionally give an almost Snipe-like *schaap* call. During the breeding season, males give a display flight (known as roding) low over treetops while giving a low, repeated, guttural song consisting of *quorr-quorr-quorr-tsietz*. Feeds on damp ground or in puddles, taking earthworms, insects and larvae.

Habitat and Status   An uncommon but widespread breeding species, found in deciduous and coniferous woodlands with open clearings. Nests in scrapes under bracken, trees or bushes. Populations increase in winter when birds arrive from northern Britain and the Continent.

Buff-breasted Sandpiper 18–21cm
Tryngites subruficollis

A tame, attractive wader with a short, pointed, dark bill, a large, conspicuous, black eye and mustard-yellow legs. **Immatures** show pale buff underparts, with a paler rear belly and undertail, a plain buff-coloured face, fine streaking on the crown and nape, and dark spotting on the sides of the breast. Buff-centred upperpart feathers have sharp whitish buff edges and dark submarginal crescents, giving a neat scalloped appearance. **Adults** are similar, but show dark centres to upperpart feathers with buff fringes. Buff on the underparts also extends further down. In flight, shows a plain upperwing and rump. Underwing white, with black tips to primaries, secondaries and primary coverts.

Voice and Diet   Normally a quiet species, Buff-breasted Sandpiper can give a low *pr-r-reet* call. A sharp *tic* call is also heard on occasions. Feeds in a dainty, active fashion, picking flies, insects, beetles and larvae from the ground.

Habitat and Status   A rare but regular autumn vagrant from North America. Usually found on short grass or sandy areas close to coastal marshes or lakes. Rarely found feeding in water. An extremely tame species, Buff-breasted Sandpipers are easy to overlook should they crouch down or freeze. Tends to run ahead of observers instead of flying.

100

Woodcock

broad bars on crown and nape

very long, straight bill

cryptic brown, black and white plumage

Buff-breasted Sandpiper

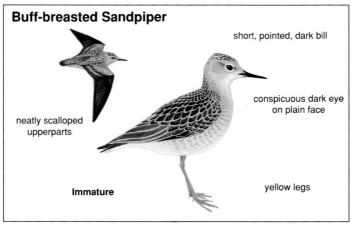

short, pointed, dark bill

conspicuous dark eye on plain face

neatly scalloped upperparts

Immature

yellow legs

Woodcock

Buff-breasted Sandpiper

Waders

Ringed Plover 18–21cm
Charadrius hiaticula   Feadóg chladaigh
Small, banded plover with a striking face pattern and bright orange legs. **Breeding adults** show a white forehead patch, a black forecrown patch, and black from base of bill onto ear-coverts. White supercilium above and behind dark eye. Thin, indistinct eye-ring. White throat and collar contrast with black breast band. Thick, short bill is orange with a black tip. Crown and upperparts greyish-brown. Underparts white. In **winter,** plumage and bill duller. **Immatures** show duller legs, a blackish bill, greyish-brown head and upperparts, and a white supercilium and forehead patch. Thin, brownish breast band usually incomplete. In flight, shows a white wingbar and white sides to the rump. Tail dark.

Voice and Diet   Gives a distinctive, fluty *too-ip* call which rises in pitch. On the breeding grounds, can give a trilling display song. Feeds in the typical stop-start fashion of plovers. Takes a variety of insects, molluscs and other invertebrates which are picked from the surface.

Habitat and Status   A very common coastal plover found throughout the year. Breeds on shingle and sandy beaches around the coast, the nest consisting of a scrape in the ground. In autumn and winter, is found in large numbers on mudflats and estuaries.

Turnstone 21–24cm
Arenaria interpres   Piardálai trá
A small, stocky wader with a stubby, dark bill and orange-yellow legs. **Summer males** show a white head with black crown streaking and a black line from forehead, through eye, down to broad black breast band. White neck collar contrasts with breast band. Mantle and scapulars blackish, contrasting with chestnut upperparts. Underparts white. **Females** similar, but show rufous tones to head. In **winter,** both show a duller plumage with a brownish-grey head. **Immatures** similar to winter adults, but show buff edges to dark brownish upperpart feathers. In flight, shows blackish tail with a contrasting white uppertail, rump and back. Wing dark with a white wingbar and inner coverts. Underwing white.

Voice and Diet   When disturbed, gives a rolling *tuk-i-tuk* call, with shorter *tuk* calls given when in feeding parties. Feeds by turning over stones or tossing seaweed aside in search of food items. Will take insects, worms, crustaceans and also carrion.

Habitat and Status   A very common passage migrant and winter visitor from breeding grounds in Greenland, Iceland and northern Europe. Found feeding in parties along rocky coasts, shorelines with stones and seaweed, harbours and piers.

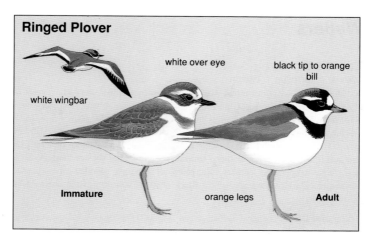

Ringed Plover

white over eye

black tip to orange bill

white wingbar

Immature

orange legs

Adult

Turnstone

Adult (summer)

orange legs, with stubby black bill

striking black and white face, chestnut on upperparts

duller in winter

Adult (winter)

Ringed Plover

Turnstone

Waders

Lapwing 29–33cm
Vanellus vanellus   Pilibín

A distinctive plover with a broad breast band. **Summer males** show a long crest with black on the crown and face. Chin and throat black, meeting breast band. Neck white. Nape dark. Upperparts deep green with copper sheens. **Females** show white flecking on chin and throat, a shorter crest and duller upperparts. Underparts white. Undertail orange-buff. Winter adults show white chin and throat, black patches on a buff face, and buff tips to some wing feathers. **Immatures** similar but show a shorter crest and buff fringes to upperpart feathers. Flight buoyant with dark, rounded upperwings, and striking black and white underwings. Black band present on a white tail. Legs dull flesh. Bill dark.

Voice and Diet   The most distinctive call is a loud, bubbling, excited *pee-wit*, which rises in pitch on the second note. On the breeding grounds, gives a repeated *perr-u-weet-weet* call which is occasionally associated with downward plunges as part of a display flight. Feeds in the stop-start manner of plovers, taking invertebrates, insects and seeds.

Habitat and Status   A very common bird, breeding on grasslands and grassy wetland areas. The nest consists of a simple scrape in the ground. In winter, the population increases with the arrival of birds from northern Britain. In winter, found along the coast on mudflats and estuaries, as well as far inland on open grassland or ploughed fields.

Dotterel 20–24cm
Charadrius morinellus   Amadán móinteach

A tame plover with a large black eye and a broad supercilium which meets in a V on the nape. **Immatures** and **autumn adults** show a streaked crown and a pale buff supercilium. Breast and belly buff-brown, separated by a narrow, creamy breast band. Upper breast streaked. Upperpart feathers show pale fringes, warmer buff on immatures. In flight, appears uniform. Underwing pale. **Summer adults** show a black crown and a white supercilium and throat. A blue-grey neck and upper breast is separated from the chestnut-brown of the lower breast and upper belly by a white breast band. Belly black, undertail white. Upperpart feathers show buff fringes. Dark, short bill. Legs yellowish.

Voice and Diet   Although usually quiet when seen in Ireland, they can occasionally give a soft *peet* call which can be repeated. Dotterels can also give a trilling alarm call. Feeds in the stop-start manner of plovers, picking up a wide variety of insects, including flies, spiders and beetles.

Habitat and Status   A rare but regular visitor from Europe, with a single Irish breeding record from 1975 when a pair nested in Co. Mayo. Can occur in the mountainous regions of the south-west on spring migration. Most records refer to autumn, when birds are found on coastal islands or headlands. Usually seen in areas of short heather growth or on fields or grassy areas along the shore. Their excellent camouflage can make Dotterels difficult to spot.

Lapwing

long crest

rounded wings

Male

shorter crest and buff edges to upperpart feathers

Immature

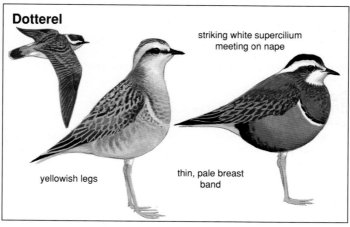

Dotterel

striking white supercilium meeting on nape

yellowish legs

thin, pale breast band

Lapwing

Dotterel

Waders

Golden Plover 27–30cm
Pluvialis apricaria   Feadóg bhuí

A large plover with a short dark bill, dark legs, gold-spangled upperparts and a diagnostic white underwing and axillaries. In **breeding plumage,** the face, throat, breast and belly are black, bordered by a white stripe from the supercilium, down sides of neck and breast and along flanks. Undertail white with gold and black barring. Crown, nape and upperparts are dark with gold spangling. Wing tips equal to tail length. **Immatures** and **winter-plumaged adults** show brownish upperparts with gold fringes to the feathers, a large conspicuous black eye in a yellow-buff face and dark streaking on the breast. Belly and undertail whitish. In flight, shows a narrow white wingbar.

Voice and Diet   Gives a rather plaintive, whistling *too-lee* call, both on the ground and in flight. On the breeding grounds, gives a mournful *per-wee-oo* song, often associated with a flight display. Feeds in the typical stop-start fashion of plovers, taking insects, beetles, earthworms and other invertebrates, as well as seeds, grasses and berries.

Habitat and Status   A breeding bird found in small numbers on mountains and bogs in the west and north-west. In autumn, numbers increase dramatically with the arrival of migrant birds from Europe and Iceland, most of which over-winter. Found on arable lands and ploughed fields, both inland and along coastal areas. Also found on mudflats and estuaries in winter.

Grey Plover 28–32cm
Pluvialis squatarola   Feadóg ghlas

A large, big-headed plover with a stout, dark bill, dark legs, and with black axillaries contrasting with a white underwing. **Summer adults** show a black face, breast, belly and flanks. The broad, white supercilium continues onto sides of neck and breast, but not along the flanks. Undertail always white. Crown and nape pale grey. Upperparts grey with broad black spotting. **Winter plumage** shows a large eye in a pale grey face, dark streaking on breast and light grey upperparts with dark spotting. **Immatures** similar to winter adults, but show yellowish tones to the upperparts. In flight, the upperwing shows white wing stripe. White rump obvious against the barred tail.

Voice and Diet   Gives a diagnostic, loud, whistling call, consisting of *tee-oo-ee,* the second note of which is lower in pitch. Feeds on marine molluscs, crustaceans and worms in the typical stop-start manner of plovers.

Habitat and Status   A common winter and passage visitor from the breeding grounds in western Siberia, arriving by late summer. Found on coastal estuaries, mudflats and beaches. Rarely seen on arable lands or ploughed fields. Never forms a tight feeding flock like Golden Plovers.

Golden Plover

gold-spangled dark upperparts

large dark eye

whitish underwing

wingtips equal to tail length

Immature

Adult (summer)

Grey Plover

pale face

black face and underparts white undertail

black axillaries

yellowish tones to upperparts

Immature

Adult (summer)

Golden Plover

Grey Plover

Waders

Ruff 22–32cm
Philomachus pugnax   Rufachán

A highly variable, small-headed, medium-sized wader with a shortish, slightly decurved bill. **Males** (Ruffs) are larger than **females** (Reeves). **Immatures** are orange-buff on the head and breast, with neat pale fringes to the dark upperpart feathers giving a strongly scalloped appearance. The belly and undertail are white. **In summer, adult males** show head and neck plumes which vary greatly in colour, while **females** show strong but variable markings on the head, breast and flanks. In flight, shows two white, oval rump patches, a white wing stripe and a white underwing. Bill dark with a pinkish base on adults. Leg colour varies, from greenish on immatures to orange or pink on adults.

Voice and Diet   Generally a quiet species, although a gruff *ku-uk* call can occasionally be given. Feeds in a Redshank-like manner, walking with deliberate strides, occasionally wading into deep water. Eats worms, insects, molluscs, crustaceans, as well as seeds. Probes into soft mud with the bill or picks from the surface.

Habitat and Status   An uncommon but regular autumn visitor from Europe, with small numbers occasionally over-wintering. Found on muddy verges of coastal, freshwater or brackish pools and lakes. Sometimes encountered on saltmarshes, although seldom seen on mudflats or estuaries.

Pectoral Sandpiper 19–23cm
Calidris melanotos

A very tame wader with a heavily streaked breast which stops abruptly, showing a strong demarcation with the pure white belly and undertail. The slightly decurved bill is dark with a pale base. Legs yellowish. The warm crown, nape and ear-coverts are streaked with a dark loral smudge, sometimes obvious before the eye. The broad supercilium is white. **Immatures** show dark-centred upperpart feathers with warm chestnut, buff and white fringes creating white braces on the mantle and scapulars. **Adults** are generally duller, especially on the upperparts. In flight, shows white sides to rump and a faint white wing stripe. Underwing white, contrasting with the streaked breast.

Voice and Diet   Pectoral Sandpipers can often be heard before they are seen, giving a distinctive, harsh, sharp *krrit* or *trrit* call which is loud and sometimes repeated. Feeds in a deliberate, steady, head-down manner, either picking from the surface or probing. Feeds on insects, larvae, worms and crustaceans.

Habitat and Status   An uncommon but regular visitor from North America, usually seen in autumn, with occasional records in summer. Found along edges of grass-fringed pools and wetlands, usually at coastal locations. Occasionally seen on open mudflats. An extremely tame bird and easy to overlook among tall grass or sedges.

Ruff

Males (summer) **Female (reeve)** **Male (ruff)**

Pectoral Sandpiper

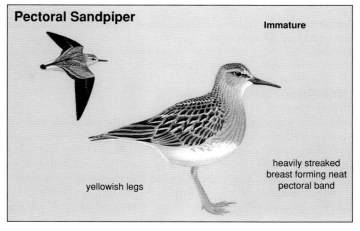

Immature

heavily streaked
breast forming neat
pectoral band

yellowish legs

Ruff **Pectoral Sandpiper**

Waders

Sanderling 19–22cm
Calidris alba Luathrán

A small, hyperactive wader with a short, straight, black bill and black legs which lack a hindclaw. In **winter,** the plumage is pale grey on the upperparts, with a distinctive black patch on the bend of the wing. Underparts pure white. Occasionally seen in **summer** plumage when the head and upperparts are chestnut-brown with broad black centres to the upperpart feathers. Also shows a streaked, chestnut-brown breast band in summer. **Immatures** similar to adult winter, but show black spangled upperparts, black streaking on crown and faint streaking on the sides of the neck which can show a buff wash. In flight, shows a prominent white wingbar and white sides to rump and uppertail.

Voice and Diet   Gives a hard, quiet *kick* call, occasionally repeated. Feeds in a hyperactive fashion, almost recalling a clockwork toy. Takes a wide variety of invertebrates, including insects, worms, molluscs and small fish.

Habitat and Status   A common winter visitor to the coastline, arriving in early autumn from breeding grounds in the Arctic. Usually found chasing the waves up and down the beach, or feeding along the tideline on debris and seaweed washed ashore. On migration, can also occur on mudflats or on coastal marshes.

Little Stint 12–14cm
Calidris minuta

A tiny wader with a fine, short, black bill and black legs. **Immatures** show bright chestnut-buff edges to the upperpart feathers with white fringes to the mantle, creating the distinctive, white mantle braces. A whitish supercilium extends onto the warm brown crown, creating a diagnostic split supercilium. Ear-coverts and breast sides warm buff and streaked. Underparts clean white. **Breeding adults** show streaking on a warm buff head and breast, a white throat, and chestnut-buff, dark-centred upperpart feathers with whitish fringes to the mantle. **Winter adults** show brown-grey upperparts and white underparts. Narrow white wing stripe, obvious in flight. White sides to rump.

Voice and Diet   Gives a short, sharp, high-pitched *stit* call which can be repeated. Feeds in an active fashion, taking insects, worms and molluscs, occasionally seeds. Often found among flocks of Dunlin in autumn.

Habitat and Status   A regular autumn visitor from breeding grounds in north-eastern Europe and Siberia. Occasionally recorded in winter and spring. Usually found on coastal estuaries, mudflats or lakes, often associating with large, mixed wader flocks.

Sanderling

prominent white wingbar

very pale with black carpal patch

Immature
black-spangled upperparts

Adult (summer)

Adult (winter)

Little Stint

tiny wader

white mantle braces on rufous upperparts

short, thin, black bill

plain grey upperparts

Adult winter (rare)

Immature

Sanderling

Little Stint

Waders

Dunlin 16–19cm
Calidris alpina   Breacóg

A small wader with black legs and a blackish bill, decurved at the tip. Dunlin vary greatly in size, plumage and bill length. In **winter** shows greyish-brown upperparts. White underparts show faint streaking on the breast. **Summer adults** show a striking black belly patch and rufous edges to mantle and scapular feathers. Crown and nape warm buff, with heavy spotting on the breast. Moulting adults show a mixture of both plumages. **Immatures** show black centres and warm buff edges on mantle and scapulars. Coverts fringed buff. Breast shows a diffuse buff wash. Belly and flanks show dark spotting. In flight, shows a white wingbar, white sides to rump and uppertail, and a greyish tail.

Voice and Diet   Gives a distinctive, sharp *treep* call in flight. On the breeding grounds, the song consists of a purring trill. A fast, active feeder, probing and picking off the surface. Feeds on molluscs, worms, insects and crustaceans.

Habitat and Status   An abundant autumn and winter wader, with a small breeding population based in the midlands, west and north-west. In autumn, birds arrive from Iceland and northern Europe, with large numbers wintering on estuaries, mudflats and coastal lakes. Nests in grass and tussocks on marshes, bogs and wetlands.

Curlew Sandpiper 18–20cm
Calidris ferruginea   Gobadán crotaigh

A slender wader with a long, slightly decurved bill and black legs. **Immatures** show neatly scalloped upperparts with pale fringes to the feathers. Crown and nape streaked with a well-defined supercilium. Underparts clean, creamy white, with a delicate peach wash on breast sides. **Breeding plumage** is unmistakable, with chestnut-red underparts, neck and head. Scapulars and mantle have black centres with pale and rufous fringes. Wing coverts appear greyish. **Moulting adults** can show blotchy red underparts and some dark-centred upperpart feathers. **Winter birds** are greyish-brown above and white below, with a strong supercilium. In flight, shows a white rump, a dark tail and a white wingbar.

Voice and Diet   Gives a rippling, gentle *chirrup* call. Feeds by probing or picking from the surface but can wade into deep water. Takes a variety of worms, molluscs, crustaceans and insects.

Habitat and Status   A regular autumn visitor from breeding grounds in Siberia. Occasionally seen in large numbers, with wintering birds sometimes reported. Found on coastal lakes, estuaries and mudflats. Curlew Sandpipers can associate with Dunlin flocks. Can show a tendency to feed in deeper water, making them more noticeable when in large, mixed flocks.

Dunlin

long, decurved bill
rufous upperparts

brown-grey upperparts

Adult (summer)

Adult (winter)

black belly patch

Curlew Sandpiper

white rump and wingbar

neatly scalloped
upperparts

long, decurved
bill,
well defined
supercilium

Adult (summer)   **Adult (winter)**   **Immature**

Dunlin

Curlew Sandpiper

113

Waders

Knot 24–27cm
Calidris canutus   Cnota

A medium-sized wader with a short, straight, black bill and greenish legs. **Winter adults** are plain grey on the upperparts with pale fringed feathers. The underparts are whitish, with heavy streaking on breast, and barring on the flanks. **Immatures** similar, but show a buff wash on the breast, yellow-green legs and buffish-grey upperpart feathers appearing scalloped due to pale buff fringes and dark submarginal lines. **Summer adults** show chestnut-red face and underparts, with spotting on the sides of the breast and a barred whitish undertail. Upperparts show black-centred feathers with rufous and buff fringes. In flight, shows a narrow white wingbar, and a pale rump and uppertail.

Voice and Diet   A generally quieter wader than other species, Knot can give a soft *knut* call. Feeds in flocks, probing or picking from the surface. Eats a variety of molluscs, crustaceans, worms and insects, but can occasionally take vegetable matter.

Habitat and Status   A reasonably common autumn and winter visitor from breeding grounds on the high Arctic regions of Greenland, Canada and Iceland. The main arrival occurs in October and by November the main wintering flocks are present. Found on coastal estuaries, mudflats and saltmarshes.

Purple Sandpiper 17–21cm
Calidris maritima   Gobadán cosbhuí

A tame, rather drab wader with a long, slightly decurved, yellow-based dark bill and yellowish legs. **Winter adults** show a dark grey head and upperparts, with a faint purple gloss on scapulars and mantle, and greyish fringes to the coverts. Throat and breast dark grey with streaking on breast onto flanks. Belly and undertail white. **Immatures** show rufous tones on the crown, a faint supercilium and dark upperpart feathers with whitish and buff fringes. **Summer adults** show a brown crown, a white supercilium, heavily streaked breast and flanks, and chestnut and white fringes to dark upperpart feathers. In flight, shows a striking white wingbar and white sides to the rump and the uppertail.

Voice and Diet   Gives a short, twittering *wheet* call when disturbed. Feeds on a variety of insects, molluscs and crustaceans which are found on rocky shorelines.

Habitat and Status   An uncommon winter visitor from breeding grounds in Greenland, Iceland and northern Europe. Purple Sandpipers are found along rocky shorelines, occasionally searching for prey items among seaweed. They can be extremely tame and this, as well as their coloration, can make them easy to overlook. Often found feeding with flocks of Turnstones.

Knot

stocky build

plain grey upperparts

straight black bill, greenish legs

Adult (summer)

Adult (winter)

Purple Sandpiper

thin white wingbar

dark wader, yellow-based dark bill

Adult (summer)

Adult (winter)

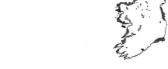

Knot

Purple Sandpiper

Waders

Whimbrel 40–45cm
Numenius phaeopus   Crotach eanaigh

A short-necked wader, smaller and with a shorter, more kinked bill than Curlew. **Adults** show a distinctive head pattern of a creamy crown-stripe, a dark lateral crown-stripe, a whitish supercilium and a dark eye-stripe. Cheeks, throat and neck whitish with heavy streaking. Breast creamy with heavy streaking which extends along flanks. Belly and undertail whitish. Upperparts brownish, with pale fringes and notches on feathers. **Immatures** show a shorter bill and a warm buff wash on breast. In flight, shows a coarsely marked upperwing with a white rump and back appearing as a wedge. Tail brown with dark barring. Bill dark, occasionally with a paler base to lower mandible. Legs bluish-grey.

Voice and Diet   Gives a distinctive, whistling, rolling *ti-ti-ti-ti* call which is flat-toned and delivered faster than Curlew. Feeds by probing for insects, molluscs, crabs and worms.

Habitat and Status   A common spring and autumn passage migrant, with small numbers present in summer. Birds occasionally winter in southern areas. Passage is recorded in early spring, as birds move north from wintering grounds in Africa to the breeding grounds of Iceland and northern Europe. Found on estuaries, mudflats, coastal wetlands and coastal pastures. Birds of the North American race, known as Hudsonian Whimbrel, are very rare vagrants, and differ by showing a brown rump and back.

Curlew 51–60cm
Numenius arquata   Crotach

A large wader with a long, decurved bill. **Adults** pale buff on head and neck with heavy streaking. Throat pale. Breast whitish, with heavy streaks extending onto flanks. Belly and undertail whitish. Mantle and scapulars show buff edges. Coverts show dark centres with pale edges. Secondaries and greater coverts dark with pale notches. **Immatures** similar, but show a shorter bill and buff tones to breast. In flight, shows a coarsely marked plain wing with paler secondaries and greater coverts. Tail and rump white, with heavy barring and spotting. Back white and shows as a contrasting white wedge. Underwing whitish with barring. Long bill shows a pinkish base to lower mandible. Legs bluish-grey.

Voice and Diet   Gives a very distinctive, rolling, far-carrying *cour-lee* call. When alarmed, gives a repeated *kyuyu* call. Feeds by probing with the extremely long bill for molluscs, crabs, worms and insects. Will also take plant material.

Habitat and Status   A widespread breeding species, with birds nesting on moorlands, bogs, damp meadows and farmlands. Breeding occurs in most regions, except some areas in the south-west and south-east. Winters on estuaries, mudflats and coastal grasslands. In winter, numbers increase with the arrival of birds from Scotland, northern England and Scandinavia.

Whimbrel

striking head pattern

slightly smaller and with a
shorter bill than Curlew

Adult

Curlew

large brown wader with
very long, decurved bill

Adult

Whimbrel   **Curlew**

Waders

Bar-tailed Godwit 33–41cm
Limosa lapponica   Guilbneach stríocearrach

A large wader with a long, slightly up-curved, pink-based, dark bill and dark legs. Similar to Black-tailed Godwit, but in flight shows plain wings, a barred tail and a white rump extending as a wedge up the back. **In winter,** the upperparts are brownish-grey and appear streaked. Underparts white with brownish streaking on the breast. Head brownish-grey, with a whitish supercilium most prominent behind the eye. **In summer** shows a brick-red head, a dark eye-stripe, a streaked crown and a broad supercilium. Underparts completely brick-red. Upperparts dark, with blackish, brown and chestnut notches on the feathers. **Immatures** similar to winter adults, but show a buff wash on the breast.

Voice and Diet   Calls frequently in flight, giving a low, barking *kirruk* call. Can also give a short, repeated *ik* call. Feeds by probing in soft mud, taking a variety of lugworms, flatworms and molluscs. Will also feed on insects.

Habitat and Status   A common winter visitor from breeding grounds in northern Europe. Birds arrive in late summer, with the peak arrival in September. Most depart in late spring, although small flocks occasionally spend the summer in Ireland. Found in all coastal counties. Feeds on sandy estuaries and mudflats. In some areas, particularly in the south-east, flocks can be found feeding on fields during high tides.

Black-tailed Godwit 36–44cm
Limosa limosa   Guilbneach earrdhubh

A large wader with a long, straight, pink-based, dark bill and long dark legs. Similar to Bar-tailed Godwit, but shows a striking white wing stripe, a black tail and a white rump in flight. **In winter,** the grey upperparts are unstreaked. White underparts show a greyish breast. Head grey with a dark eye-stripe and a short supercilium before eye. **In summer,** shows an orangy head, a streaked crown, a dark eye-stripe and a pale supercilium fading behind the eye. Throat pale orange, with dark barring on white belly. Upperparts plain grey, with some black and chestnut feathers on mantle and scapulars. **Immatures** show a warm buff wash on the throat and breast, and orangy edges to dark upperpart feathers.

Voice and Diet   In flight, flocks give a very distinctive, repeated *wikka-wikka* call. Can also give a short *tuk* call on occasions. On the breeding grounds, Black-tailed Godwits are very noisy and give a *krru-wit-tsew* song during display flights, the emphasis being on the last phrase. The song may sound like *whatta-we-do*. Feeds by probing or picking from the surface. Takes a wide range of worms, molluscs, insects and small crustaceans.

Habitat and Status   A common winter visitor from Iceland, found in all coastal counties feeding on mudflats and estuaries. Also a very rare breeding species of some midland counties.

Bar-tailed Godwit

Adult (winter)

Adult (summer)

streaked brownish-grey
upperparts

long, slightly
up-curved bill

plain wings, barred tail and
white, wedge-shaped rump

Black-tailed Godwit

long, straight bill

Adult (summer)

striking white wing stripe,
black tail and white rump

plain, unstreaked
upperparts

Adult (winter)

Bar-tailed Godwit

Black-tailed Godwit

Waders

Redshank 26–31cm
Tringa totanus   Cosdeargán

A medium-sized, greyish-brown wader with bright orange-red legs and a reddish base to a straight, medium-length, dark bill. In **winter,** the upperparts and head are plain greyish-brown. White eye-ring obvious against a dark eye-stripe. Underparts pale greyish-white, with dull breast and flank spotting. **Breeding birds** show heavy streaking on the head, breast and underparts. Upperparts brown, buff and cinnamon, with a variety of dark brown barring. **Immatures** show heavily streaked underparts, warm buff edges and spots to upperpart feathers, paler legs and a duller base to the bill. Easily recognised in flight by the all-white secondaries and inner primaries. Rump and back are white. Tail barred.

Voice and Diet   An extremely excitable and noisy wader which gives a loud, yelping *teeuu* call which is repeated continuously. In flight, gives a *teeu-u-u* call. During display flights on the breeding grounds, the song consists of *ty-uu* notes, delivered rapidly and loudly. Feeds by probing or picking from the surface, taking worms, insects, molluscs and crustaceans.

Habitat and Status   A very common winter and autumn wader. Redshanks breed in very small numbers in Ireland, with breeding populations concentrated around the midland lakes and Lough Neagh. Nests on the ground on open, wet grasslands. In autumn, numbers increase with the arrival of Icelandic birds which, together with birds from Scotland and northern England, winter in Ireland.

Spotted Redshank 29–33cm
Tringa erythropus

An elegant wader with long, red legs and a long, dark bill, showing a red base to the lower mandible. In **winter,** the upperparts are pale grey, underparts white. A strong white supercilium contrasts with a dark eye-stripe. In **summer,** the plumage is black, with white spots on the upperpart feathers. **Immatures** show dusky grey-brown upperparts with white spots and edges to the feathers. Told from immature Redshank by the white supercilium obvious before the eye, the longer, duller bill, and the underparts which appear more barred than streaked. In flight, shows a plain wing with a white oval on the back. This contrasts with darkish rump and tail. Legs extend well beyond the tail in flight.

Voice and Diet   Gives a very distinctive, sharp, loud *tch-uit* call in flight. They are often heard before they are seen. Feeds by picking or probing on a wide range of prey items, including molluscs, crustaceans, worms and insects.

Habitat and Status   An uncommon visitor from breeding grounds in northern Europe. Seen in autumn and spring on passage, with small numbers wintering in Ireland. Found on coastal estuaries in winter, occasionally feeding in deep water. On passage, also recorded on brackish coastal lakes and lagoons.

Redshank

all-white secondaries and inner primaries

white, wedge-shaped rump

bright orange-red legs

Adult (winter)

Spotted Redshank

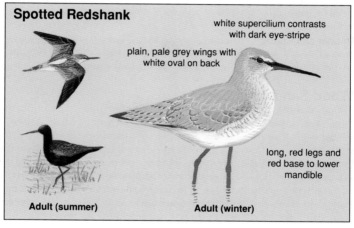

white supercilium contrasts with dark eye-stripe

plain, pale grey wings with white oval on back

long, red legs and red base to lower mandible

Adult (summer)

Adult (winter)

Redshank

Spotted Redshank

Waders

Greenshank 29–33cm
Tringa nebularia   Laidhrín glas

A large, grey and white wader with a long, slightly up-curved bill and long, pale green legs. In **winter**, **adults** show a pale greyish-white head and grey upperparts. Faint streaking obvious on nape and sides of breast. Underparts white. **Adults in summer** show a heavily streaked head and breast, with streaking onto the flanks. The upperparts also show broad black markings. **Immatures** appear greyish-brown on the upperparts, with buff fringes on the scapulars and streaking on the head and breast sides. In flight, shows a dark, plain upperwing which contrasts with the white wedge on the back, the white rump and the pale tail which appears white at a distance. Dark bill shows a pale green base.

Voice and Diet   Gives a very loud and distinctive *tue-teu-teu* call, delivered quickly and occasionally repeated. On the breeding grounds, gives a soft, repeated *teo-oo*. Feeds in a very active manner, walking with deliberate strides, sometimes chasing prey in shallow water with lunges and sweeps. Also probes in soft mud. Takes molluscs, crustaceans, insects, worms and small fish.

Habitat and Status   A common autumn and winter visitor from breeding grounds in Scotland. Breeding took place in Ireland at one site in Co. Mayo in 1972 and 1974. Breeds on open moorland. Usually found on estuaries, mudflats and saltmarshes.

Wood Sandpiper 19–22cm
Tringa glareola   Gobadán coille

Small, slim, elegant wader, similar to Green Sandpiper, but with a long, dark-tipped bill and greenish-yellow legs. Most sightings refer to **immatures** which show a clear white supercilium beyond eye, a dark brown crown with creamy streaking, a dark eye-stripe, and coarse, pale buff spotting on brown upperparts. Underparts white with delicate breast streaking and spotting. **Summer adults** similar, but show white spotting on darker brown upperparts, and heavy streaking on foreneck and breast extending as barring onto flanks. In flight, similar to Green Sandpiper, showing a plain upperwing and a white rump, but differing by showing pale underwings and longer legs.

Voice and Diet   Wood Sandpipers give a very distinctive, rapid, high-pitched, shrill *chiff-iff-iff* call, especially when flushed. Feeds by probing in soft mud or by picking delicately from the surface of shallow pools. Feeds on a variety of insects, larvae, worms, molluscs, small crustaceans and occasionally small fish.

Habitat and Status   A scarce but regular autumn passage migrant from north-eastern Europe. Most records refer to August and September. Rarer in spring. Very few records refer to wintering birds. Most sightings are along eastern and southern coastal regions, although recorded in all coastal counties. Found feeding on muddy edges of coastal lakes, pools and marshes. Occasionally found along open shoreline.

Greenshank

long, slightly
up-curved bill

very pale overall

pale green legs

Adult (winter)

Wood Sandpiper

clear white supercilium

Immature

plain upperwing
and white rump

coarse, pale spotting on
upperparts

greenish-yellow legs

Greenshank

Wood Sandpiper

Waders

Green Sandpiper 22–25cm
Tringa ochropus　Gobadán glas

A stocky, dark wader with yellowish-green legs. Straight bill shows a greenish base and a dark tip. **Summer adults** show dark greenish-brown upperparts with coarse pale spots, a streaked greenish-brown crown, a white supercilium before eye, and a white eye-ring. Neck and upper breast show heavy brown streaking. Underparts white. **Immatures** show buff spots on dark upperparts, a brownish-grey crown, a white eye-ring and a white supercilium before eye. Neck and upper breast brownish-grey. **Winter adults** show small buff upperpart spots and a heavily streaked neck and breast. In flight, shows a square white rump, a dark tail with strong white barring, a plain dark upperwing and a dark underwing.

Voice and Diet　When flushed, gives a loud, high-pitched *weet-tweet* call which can be repeated. Can also give a series of loud *too-leet* notes. Feeds by probing in soft mud or shallow water, taking a variety of beetles, flies, larvae and crustaceans.

Habitat and Status　A common passage migrant from northern Europe. Most reports refer to autumn, with birds occurring from June to October. Small numbers are recorded in March and April. Birds occasionally occur in summer and winter in most regions, but uncommon in some western and north-western areas. Frequents a variety of wetland habitats, including lake fringes, pools, rivers, ditches and on brackish coastal lagoons.

Common Sandpiper 18–21cm
Actitis hypoleucos　Gobadán

A small wader with a constantly bobbing long tail extending well beyond the wings. Shows dull green-yellow legs and a straight, dark-tipped brownish bill. **Summer adults** show brownish upperparts with thin streaking and barring, a brownish crown, dark lores, an indistinct, pale supercilium, and a white eye-ring. Underparts white, with brown streaking on sides of breast. **Immatures** show pale brown and dark edges to upperpart feathers, with pale tips and brown subterminal bars on coverts. In flight, shows a white wingbar and trailing edge to secondaries. Tail shows faint barring and white edges. Flies on stiff, bowed wings.

Voice and Diet　Gives a clear, distinctive *swee-wee-wee* call. On the breeding grounds, can give rapid, high *kitti-weeti* song notes which can be delivered both in flight or on the ground. Feeds in a careful, deliberate manner, picking from the surface or from vegetation. Takes a wide range of prey items, including insects, larvae, worms, molluscs, tadpoles and crustaceans. Can occasionally feed on seeds.

Habitat and Status　A common, widespread breeding species present in most regions each summer. Small numbers winter in the south-west. Largest breeding populations are in midland and western counties. Found on edges of rocky streams and rivers, and on shingle shores of lakes. In some regions, frequents mountain lakes and rivers, while in the south-west can breed on coastal shingle areas. On passage, found on coastal estuaries and lagoons.

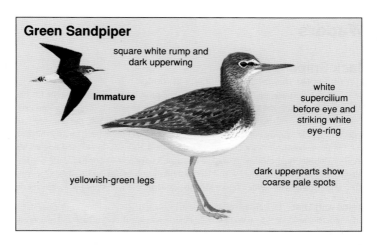

Green Sandpiper

square white rump and dark upperwing

Immature

white supercilium before eye and striking white eye-ring

yellowish-green legs

dark upperparts show coarse pale spots

Common Sandpiper

buff notches on tertials

white wingbar and trailing edge to secondaries

dull greenish-yellow legs

long tail

Immature

Adult (summer)

Green Sandpiper

Common Sandpiper

Waders

Jack Snipe 18–20cm
Lymnocryptes minimus   Naoscach bhídeach

Small, long-billed wader with rounded wings and prominent golden stripes on the back. When flushed, Jack Snipe fly in a straight line before quickly dropping into cover. Rarely calls when flushed. Best told from Snipe by the shorter bill, the rounded wings with a thin, pale trailing edge, prominent golden stripes on the back and by the darker tail. On the ground, shows a distinctive dark crown and a dark, isolated line within a creamy double supercilium. A dark eye-stripe continues to form a dark border to ear-coverts. Underparts pale, with heavy streaking on breast and flanks. Upperparts dark, contrasting with golden upperpart stripes. Bill pale with dark tip. Legs greenish.

Voice and Diet   Usually silent when flushed, Jack Snipe can give a quiet, weak *gach* call on occasions. Feeds in a crake-like manner, picking off the surface and probing less often than Snipe. Also has a habit of bobbing the body up and down when feeding. Takes insects, worms, molluscs and seeds.

Habitat and Status   An uncommon winter visitor from northern Europe, Jack Snipe can easily be overlooked due to their habit of remaining motionless, relying on their camouflage for safety. Found in grassy wetlands, freshwater marshes, bogs, saltmarshes and along the fringes of reed-beds. Rarely found feeding in open water or exposed mudflats.

Snipe 25–29cm
Gallinago gallinago   Naoscach

A long-billed wader with creamy stripes on the back and crown. When flushed, usually calls loudly and flies rapidly, zig-zagging to a good height before dropping back into cover a good distance away. Told from Jack Snipe by the longer bill, less prominent back stripes, less rounded wings, and the flight pattern and call. On the ground, shows a creamy central crown-stripe and supercilium and a dark lateral crown-stripe. Dark eye-stripe does not form border to ear-coverts. Underparts pale, with heavy streaking on the breast. Flanks barred. Upperparts dark with creamy back stripes. **Immatures** show buff fringes to wing coverts. Straight, dark tipped, pale brownish bill. Legs greenish.

Voice and Diet   An easily alarmed bird, flushing noisily and giving a loud, harsh *sccaap* call. On the breeding grounds, gives a short, repeated *chic* call. During display flights, dives with spread outer-tail feathers which create a rapid, muffled, 'drumming' sound. Feeds by probing deep with fast, 'sewing machine' head movements. Feeds on insects, worms and seeds.

Habitat and Status   A common resident breeding species, with numbers increasing in winter with the arrival of birds from the Baltic and Britain. Nests on the ground in marshes, bogs, wet fields, and river and lake shorelines. In winter, found in similar habitats, as well as coastal marshes. Can feed in deep, open water or on exposed mudflat areas.

Jack Snipe

prominent golden stripes on back

long bill

dark eye-stripe and border to ear coverts

streaked flanks

Snipe

extremely long bill

creamy stripes on back

barred flanks

Jack Snipe

Snipe

Waders

Red-necked Phalarope 17–19cm
Phalaropus lobatus   Falaróp gobchaol

An elegant wader with a fine black bill and greyish legs. **Summer females** show a blue-grey crown and neck, darker ear-coverts, a white spot above eye, a white throat, and a red foreneck extending up sides of neck to rear of ear-coverts. Upperparts dark with warm buff mantle stripes and edges to wing feathers. Breast and flanks grey. Belly and undertail whitish. Tail greyish. **Summer males** drabber. In flight, shows white wing stripes and sides to uppertail coverts and rump. **Immatures** show buff upperpart stripes, a white patch on bend of wing, a whitish face with a dark crown, and a dark ear patch curving down behind eye. **Winter adults** are pale grey above and white below, with a thin black ear patch.

Voice and Diet   Gives short, low-pitched *prek* or *whit* calls. Feeds by wading or swimming buoyantly, occasionally spinning in circles or up-ending. Takes a wide range of insects and larvae, either picking them quickly from the surface of the water or from stones and vegetation.

Habitat and Status   An extremely rare breeding species found at one site in the west. Numbers have dwindled since 1920s, with none seen between 1974 and 1978. Has also bred at other sites in southern and western regions. Found in freshwater marshes with open pools and dense vegetation. Nests in vegetation and grass tussocks. Incubation and chick-rearing performed by males only. On passage, found on coastal freshwater marshes. Winters at sea.

Grey Phalarope 19–22cm
Phalaropus fulicarius   Falaróp gobmhór

Small wader with a thick, black bill and bluish-grey legs. **Immatures** show a dark crown, a whitish face and a square, blackish ear patch which does not curve behind eye. Whitish underparts can show a peach-tinged breast. Dark upperparts show buff edges to feathers and an inconspicuous buff mantle stripe. Some grey winter feathers can show on mantle and scapulars. **Winter adults** are pale grey above and white below, with a black ear patch and a pale base to the bill. In flight, shows white wingbars and white sides to uppertail-coverts, recalling Sanderling. **Summer adults** show completely red underparts with a white face, a dark crown, lores and chin, and dark buff-fringed upperparts.

Voice and Diet   Gives a short, sharp *wit* call, higher in pitch than the similar call of Red-necked Phalarope. Feeds by swimming buoyantly, occasionally spinning, and wading. Takes a wide variety of insects, larvae, worms, molluscs and crustaceans.

Habitat and Status   A regular autumn passage bird, also occurring in early winter. Rarely seen on spring passage. Breeds in Arctic regions, wintering off western coasts of Africa. In autumn, especially following strong winds or gales, frequently reported from seawatching points in the west and south-west, with birds also reported in the south-east. Also found on coastal lakes, freshwater pools and marshes. Extremely tame.

Red-necked Phalarope

buff stripes on upperparts

Immature

Female (summer)

fine black bill

Grey Phalarope

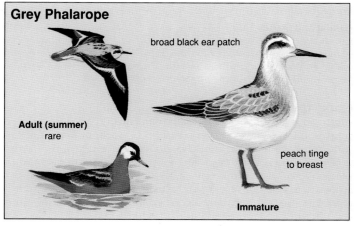

broad black ear patch

Adult (summer) rare

peach tinge to breast

Immature

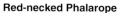

Red-necked Phalarope

Grey Phalarope

Skuas

Arctic Skua 38–49cm
Stercorarius parasiticus   Meirleach Artach

A light skua with narrow-based, pointed wings. **Pale-phase adults** show a dark cap, a yellowish face, whitish underparts and a diffuse breast band. Dark, plain brown upperwings show whitish shafts to outer primaries appearing as crescents on the underwing. Rump brown. Dark tail shows long, pointed, central feathers. **Dark-phase adults** show all-dark underparts and face. Bill and legs dark. **Immatures** show warm brown, buff-edged mantle, wings and rump. Crown and underparts buff with dark barring and streaking. Nape paler. In flight, shows white primary bases, barred underwing and undertail-coverts, and short, pointed central tail feathers. Bill shows a blue-grey base. Legs blue-grey.

Voice and Diet   Rarely heard when seen off Ireland. However, when in pursuit of a gull or tern, Arctic Skuas can sometimes utter hard, high-pitched *tuuk-tuuk* calls. Feeds by chasing and harassing gulls and terns, pursuing them until they drop or disgorge food. Will also feed on fish, small mammals, birds and eggs. Will readily eat carrion and offal.

Habitat and Status   A common spring and autumn passage migrant from breeding grounds in the Scottish Isles, northern Europe and Iceland. Seen off islands and headlands on all coastal counties. Winters in the south Atlantic. The highest numbers are recorded in autumn, peaking in August and September. Has also been recorded on large inland lakes. Several reports refer to birds seen during summer and winter months.

Long-tailed Skua 38–55cm
Stercorarius longicaudus   Meirleach earrfhada

A light, slender-winged skua similar to Arctic Skua. **Adults** show very long central tail feathers, a yellowish nape, a black cap, greyish upperparts and whitish underparts. In flight, greyish wings show little white on primaries and a black secondary bar. Dark underwings do not show pale crescents. In flight, **immatures** show grey-brown upperparts and wings, a black secondary bar and almost no white on primaries. Barred underwings show pale crescents. Nape and sides of head pale. Underparts greyish, breast darker. Rump, flanks and undertail heavily barred. Dark tail shows blunt central feathers, varying in length. Bill shows a bluish-grey base. Legs greyish.

Voice and Diet   On passage, Long-tailed Skuas are silent, the shrill calls only being heard on the breeding grounds. Unlike other skuas, seldom chases gulls and terns, feeding chiefly on fish caught at sea. Also attracted by carrion and offal.

Habitat and Status   A rare but regular passage migrant from breeding grounds in Arctic Europe, with numbers fluctuating from year to year. Exceptional movements occur occasionally, with most records from western and northern coastal counties. In spring, peak movements occur in May, while late August and September provide the largest autumn counts. Has also been recorded inland. Winters in the south Atlantic.

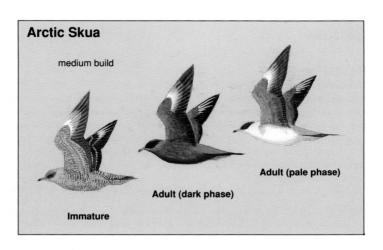

Arctic Skua

medium build

Adult (dark phase)

Adult (pale phase)

Immature

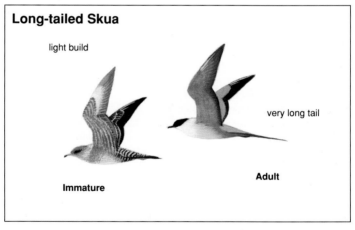

Long-tailed Skua

light build

very long tail

Immature

Adult

Arctic Skua

Long-tailed Skua

Skuas

Pomarine Skua 43–54cm
Stercorarius pomarinus   Meirleach pomairíneach

A heavy, deep-chested bird, like Arctic Skua but showing broad-based wings, and long, blunt, twisted, central tail feathers. **Pale-phase adults** show a yellowish face, a dark cap, whitish underparts and a dark breast band. Upperwing brown with whitish outer primary shafts. Underwing shows white crescents. **Dark-phase adults** show dark underparts. Heavy bill and legs dark. **Immatures** show brown, buff-edged upperparts. Head grey-brown, appearing barred. Buff underparts evenly barred. In flight, shows white primary bases, double white underwing patches, heavy barring on rump, and short, blunt, central tail feathers. Bill shows a blue-grey base. Legs greyish.

Voice and Diet   Generally silent on passage. However, the harsh, distinctive *whit-yuu* call can occasionally be given. Like Arctic Skua, Pomarines feed by chasing and harassing gulls and terns, pursuing them until they drop or disgorge food. Will also feed on fish, small mammals, birds and eggs. Also attracted to stranded fish, carrion and offal.

Habitat and Status   A regular but uncommon spring and autumn passage migrant. Breeds in Arctic Russia, wintering in the south Atlantic. Seen off islands and headlands on all coastal counties. The highest numbers have been recorded in spring, peaking in May. However, seawatching off western locations has revealed that large southern movements occur off Ireland in the autumn. Occasionally found in Irish waters in winter.

Great Skua or Bonxie 56–62cm
Stercorarius skua   Meirleach mór

A very large, broad-winged skua with striking white flashes across the primaries. Could be mistaken for a large immature gull, but in flight appears deeper-chested, with the bright wing flashes obvious with every deep, heavy wing beat. **Adults** show a dark brown crown, a yellowish-streaked brown neck, and streaked, brown upperparts. Dark brownish tail shows slightly elongated central feathers. Greyish-brown underparts show brown streaking on throat and along flanks. Wings brown with contrasting darker flight feathers and striking white primary flashes. **Immatures** appear darker than adults and show smaller wing flashes. Shows a large, dark, hooked bill. Legs dark.

Voice and Diet   The harsh, gruff calls are rarely heard away from the breeding grounds. Feeds by agilely chasing and attacking other bird species including gulls, terns and even Gannets. Usually pursues these birds relentlessly until they either drop or disgorge food. Will readily take fish, birds and eggs. Attracted by offal from trawlers.

Habitat and Status   The commonest skua species found off Ireland, they are regular autumn and spring passage migrants from breeding grounds in Iceland and the northern Scottish Isles. Seen off all coastal regions, most records refer to movements off seawatching points on the south-west and west coasts. Some records refer to birds present on large inland lakes. Occasionally found in Irish waters in winter.

Pomarine Skua

heavy build, deep-chested

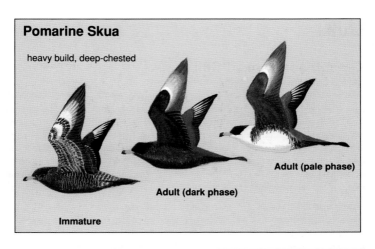

Immature

Adult (dark phase)

Adult (pale phase)

Great Skua or Bonxie

Adult

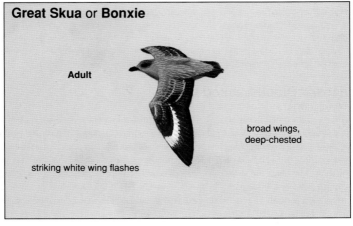

broad wings, deep-chested

striking white wing flashes

Pomarine Skua

Great Skua or **Bonxie**

Gulls

Great Black-backed Gull 69–70cm
Larus marinus   Droimneach mór

A very large gull with a heavy bill and pinkish legs. **Adults** show a white head, underparts and tail. Head unstreaked in winter. Upperparts black with white scapular and tertial crescents, large white tips to black primaries, and, in flight, a white trailing edge to wing. Bill yellow with a red gonys spot. Eye yellow. **1st year birds** show a black bill, a dark eye, a whitish head and underparts, barred brownish-grey upperparts and dark primaries. In flight, tail shows an ill-defined band. **2nd years** show whiter underparts and head, a pale-based bill and some black mantle feathers. **3rd years** as adult, with some immature feathering and dark subterminal markings on bill.

Voice and Diet   Gives a deep, barking *aouk* call and a long, trumpeting *ee-aouk-ouk-ouk*. When disturbed on the breeding grounds, gives deep *uk-uk-uk* calls. Feeds on a wide variety of fish, molluscs, worms, crustaceans, offal and carrion. Also found at rubbish tips, feeding on scraps and waste. Will take weak or small mammals and seabirds.

Habitat and Status   A common resident breeding species found in all coastal counties. Breeds in small colonies or singly on coastal cliffs or islands, building a large nest of feathers, plant material, seaweed and sticks. Also found breeding on lake islands at inland sites in northern and western regions. In winter, present along all coastal counties, on estuaries, mudflats or at rubbish tips. Small numbers also occur at inland sites in winter.

Lesser Black-backed Gull 51–56cm
Larus fuscus   Droimneach beag

A large gull, similar in size to Herring Gull. **Adults** show a white head and underparts, and yellow legs. Head streaked and legs duller in winter. Dark grey upperparts contrast with white-tipped black primaries. Underwing dusky on inner primaries and secondaries. Bill yellow with red gonys spot. Eye yellow with red eye-ring. **1st year birds** show a black bill, a dark eye, barred brownish upperparts, dark primaries and a whitish head and underparts. In flight, shows a broad tail band and a contrasting upperwing pattern. Legs pinkish. **2nd years** show a pale-based bill and some grey mantle feathers. **3rd years** as adult, with some immature feathering and dark subterminal markings on bill.

Voice and Diet   The calls are louder and deeper than Herring Gull. Gives a loud, deep *kyow* call and a long, shrill, trumpeting *kyee-kyee-kyee-aou-aou-aou*. When disturbed, gives loud *kee-ya* calls and deep *gak-gak-gak* calls. Feeds on a wide variety of fish, molluscs, worms, crustaceans, offal and carrion. Also found at rubbish tips, feeding on scraps.

Habitat and Status   A common breeding species found in most coastal counties. Primarily a summer visitor from southern Europe and North Africa. In recent years, large numbers winter at coastal and inland sites. Breeds in colonies on coastal headlands and islands, nesting on the ground on flat, sloping areas or on well-vegetated lake islands at inland sites. Found on estuaries, mudflats, farmlands and rubbish tips.

Great Black-backed Gull

very large size,
all black back and wings

Adult (winter)

pink legs

1st year

Adult (summer)

Lesser Black-backed Gull

dark grey upperparts,
black primaries

Adult (winter)

yellow legs

1st year

Adult (summer)

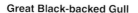

Great Black-backed Gull

Lesser Black-backed Gull

Gulls

Herring Gull 54–64cm
Larus argentatus Faoileán scadán

A familiar large gull, similar in size to Lesser Black-backed, but showing pink legs. **Adults** show a white head and underparts. Head streaked in winter. Pale grey upperparts contrast with white-tipped black primaries. Bill yellow with red gonys spot. Eye yellow with orange-yellow ring. **1st year birds** show a pale base to black bill, a dark eye, barred brownish upperparts, dark primaries, and a pale brownish head and underparts. In flight, shows a tail band and a dark outer wing contrasting with paler inner primaries. **2nd years** show some grey mantle feathers and a blotchy tail band. **3rd years** as adult, with some immature feathering and dark subterminal markings on bill.

Voice and Diet Gives a loud *kyow* call and a long, shrill, trumpeting *kyee-kyee-aou-aou-aou*. When disturbed, gives loud *kee-ya* calls and deep *gak-gak* calls. Calls are almost identical to Lesser Black-backed, but not as deep. Feeds on a wide variety of fish, molluscs, worms, crustaceans, offal and carrion. Also found at rubbish tips, feeding on scraps and waste. Takes weak, small mammals. During the breeding season, kills seabird chicks.

Habitat and Status An extremely common, widespread, resident breeding species found in all coastal counties. Breeds in colonies on coastal cliffs or islands. Builds a nest on sloping or flat ground. Also found breeding on lake islands at inland sites. In recent years has bred in towns and cities, nesting on rooftops and chimneys. In winter, present along all coastal counties, on estuaries, mudflats or at rubbish tips. Good numbers winter inland.

Mediterranean Gull 37–41cm
Larus melanocephalus

A heavy, stocky gull, similar to Black-headed Gull but showing a broader, more drooped bill. **Summer adults** show a black hood, a black subterminal band, and a yellow tip to a deep red bill. Legs red. Upperparts pale grey which, unlike Black-headed, show pure white primaries. Underparts and tail white. **Winter adults** show a black patch behind eye. **1st winter birds** show a pale base to a dark bill, a pale grey mantle and dark brown primaries. In flight, shows a striking upperwing pattern, resembling Common Gull. Tail shows a thick, dark tail band. **1st summers** show extensive black on the head. **2nd years** as adults, but show variable amounts of black on the primaries.

Voice and Diet Gives deep, harsh *kee-oh* calls which are deeper in tone and pitch than those of Black-headed Gull. Feeds in association with other gull species, taking a wide assortment of small fish, worms, molluscs and insects. Occasionally found on rubbish tips feeding on waste and scraps.

Habitat and Status Formerly a very rare migrant from south-east Europe, has now become a scarce but widespread annual visitor to coastal counties. Most records refer to a period from autumn to spring. Several sightings have referred to juvenile birds, and it is possible that this species will breed, or is breeding, in Ireland.

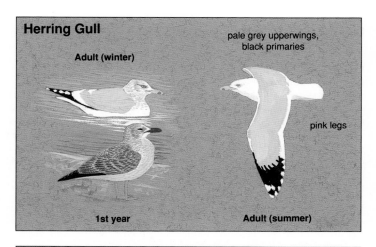

Herring Gull

Adult (winter)

pale grey upperwings, black primaries

pink legs

1st year

Adult (summer)

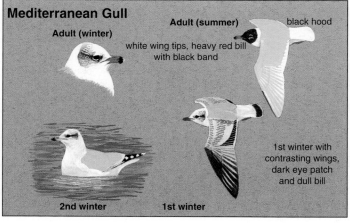

Mediterranean Gull

Adult (winter)

Adult (summer)

black hood

white wing tips, heavy red bill with black band

1st winter with contrasting wings, dark eye patch and dull bill

2nd winter

1st winter

Herring Gull

Mediterranean Gull

Gulls

Glaucous Gull 58–69cm
Larus hyperboreus   Faoileán glas

A large, powerful gull. **Winter adults** show a streaked white head, white underparts, pale grey upperparts, and short white primaries. Eye yellow. Bill yellow with red spot. Legs pink. **1st winter birds** show delicate barring on pale buff upperparts, rump and tail, creamy underparts, and short creamy-white primaries. Heavy, pale pink bill shows a black tip. Eye dark. **2nd winters** appear whiter, show a yellow eye and a dark ring on a pink bill. **3rd winters** as adult, with buff feathers on whitish wings and tail, and black markings on yellow bill. Told from Iceland Gull by larger size, heavy bill, a flat-crowned appearance, a more aggressive expression and shorter primaries.

Voice and Diet   The most commonly heard note of this generally silent species is a deep *kyow,* similar to, but shriller than, Herring Gull. When agitated will give loud *gak-gak-gak* calls like most large gulls. Feeds on a variety of carrion, offal, fish, worms and molluscs. Also feeds on waste and scraps at rubbish tips.

Habitat and Status   An uncommon but regular winter visitor from Iceland and Greenland. In some years, extremely large numbers have occurred. Found along most coastal counties, the highest concentrations being in northern, western and southern regions. Frequents fishing ports, harbours, docklands and rubbish tips. Occasionally found inland. Most reports refer to a period from January to early March. Smaller numbers recorded in autumn, early winter, spring, and occasionally in summer.

Iceland Gull 50–57cm
Larus glaucoides

A white-winged gull, smaller than Glaucous Gull. **Winter adults** show a streaked white head, white underparts, grey upperparts, and long, attenuated white primaries. Eye yellow. Bill yellow with red gonys spot. Legs pink. **1st winter birds** show delicate mottling on pale buff upperparts and tail, creamy underparts and whitish primaries. Medium-sized dark bill shows a pinkish base. Eyes dark. **2nd winters** whiter, with a yellow eye and dark ring on pink bill. **3rd winters** as adult, with buff on whitish wings and tail, and black markings on yellow bill. Told from Glaucous by smaller size, medium-sized bill, rounded crown, gentle expression and long primary projection.

Voice and Diet   Iceland Gulls are a reasonably quiet species away from the breeding grounds. Calls are similar to Herring Gull, consisting of shriller *kyow* and agitated *gak-gak-gak* calls. Like Glaucous Gull, feeds on a variety of carrion, offal, fish, worms and molluscs. Also feeds on waste and scraps at rubbish tips.

Habitat and Status   Uncommon but regular winter visitor from Greenland. Although scarcer than Glaucous Gull, large influxes can occur in some winters. Found along most coastal counties, with the highest concentrations in northern, western and southern counties. Frequents fishing ports, harbours, docklands and rubbish tips. Very rarely found inland. Most reports refer to a period from January to early April. Extremely rare in summer.

Glaucous Gull

Adult (winter)

large build,
heavy bill

short primaries

1st winter

white wing tips

Iceland Gull

Adult (winter)

medium-sized bill

long primaries

white wing tips

1st winter

Glaucous Gull

Iceland Gull

Gulls

Ring-billed Gull 41–46cm
Larus delawarensis

A stocky gull similar to, but slightly larger and deeper-chested than, Common Gull. **Adults** show a black ring on a broad, parallel yellow bill. Eye yellow with a dark pupil. Legs yellow. Upperparts paler grey than Common, with smaller mirrors on the primaries and a thinner tertial crescent. Head and underparts white. Head streaked in winter. **1st year birds** show a dark tip to a heavy, orange-pink bill. Head and breast heavily spotted. In flight, shows a pale grey mantle, dark primaries and secondaries, pale grey greater coverts, and a blotchy tail band. **2nd years** as adults, but show dark primary coverts and can show traces of the tail band and secondary bar.

Voice and Diet   Ring-billed Gulls, though rarely heard when found in Ireland, give high-pitched, shrill calls similar to those of Common Gull. Feeds on a wide range of molluscs, fish, worms and insects. Like Common Gull, will take offal, dead fish, small birds, mammals and eggs. Can also be found on rubbish tips feeding on scraps and waste.

Habitat and Status   A rare but regular vagrant from North America. First found in Ireland in 1979, Ring-billed Gulls have now become annual visitors. This is probably due to a population expansion in North America. Found with gull flocks on estuaries, mudflats, marshes, inland pastures and rubbish tips. Most records refer to a period from winter to early spring, with some birds occasionally over-summering. May breed in Ireland in the near future.

Common Gull 38–42cm
Larus canus   Faoileán bán

A medium-sized gull, with **adults** showing a slender, pointed yellow-green bill and legs, a dark eye, a white head, tail and underparts, and dark grey upperparts showing a thick, white tertial crescent. White-tipped, black primaries show two large white mirrors. **Winter adults** show a narrow dark band on the bill and a streaked head. **1st year birds** show a pinkish-grey base to a slender, dark-tipped bill, dark spots on head, a dark grey mantle, contrasting pale-edged brown tertials and coverts, and dark brown primaries. In flight, shows a well-defined, dark tail band. **2nd years** as adults, but show dark primary coverts and a broad, dark band on a dull yellowish bill.

Voice and Diet   Common Gulls give shrill, whistling *keee-ya* calls which can develop into longer, trumpeting notes. The calls are shriller and higher-pitched than those of the larger gull species. Feeds on a wide range of insects, molluscs, worms and fish. Will also take offal, dead fish, small birds and mammals and eggs. Can also be found on rubbish tips feeding on scraps and waste.

Habitat and Status   A widespread species found along most coastal counties in autumn and winter. Breeds in colonies on small lake or coastal islands, usually nesting on the ground. The main breeding populations are based in western and northern regions. In autumn and winter, numbers increase with the arrival of birds from Europe and Iceland. In winter, found on estuaries, mudflats, coastal fields and on inland lakes and pastures.

Ring-billed Gull

Adult (summer)

Adult (winter)

yellow eye,
black ring on broad
yellowish bill

1st winter

Common Gull

Adult (summer)

2nd winter

slender yellow-green bill,
dark mantle

1st winter

Ring-billed Gull

Common Gull

141

Gulls

Black-headed Gull 35–39cm
Larus ridibundus   Sléibhín

A small gull, with **summer adults** showing a chocolate-brown hood, white eye crescents, a dark red bill and legs, and white underparts. Upperparts pale grey with black-tipped primaries. In flight, wings show a white leading edge and contrasting dusky underprimaries. Tail white. **Winter adults** show a white head with a dark ear spot and brighter legs and bill. **1st winter birds** similar to adult winter, but wings show a pale brown carpal bar and a black secondary bar. Tail shows a dark band. Like adults, wings show a white leading edge and dusky underprimaries. **1st summers** can show a dark hood. **Juveniles** warm buff on head, hindneck, sides of breast and upperparts.

Voice and Diet   An extremely noisy gull giving loud, harsh *kuarr* and short, abrupt *kwup* calls. Particularly noisy when nesting. Takes a wide range of food items, including fish, worms, molluscs, insects, seeds, berries and other plant material. Also found on rubbish tips feeding on waste and scraps. Can occasionally be seen disturbing prey by paddling vigorously in wet mud, sand or shallow pools. Will also hawk flying insects in the air.

Habitat and Status   A very common widespread resident breeding species found in all counties. Largest breeding populations based in western and north-western regions. Nests in colonies on dunes, coastal islands, moorland pools, bogs and on freshwater lake islands. In winter, numbers increase with birds from Britain and northern Europe. Found in winter on inland pastures and ploughed fields, reservoirs, and on coastal estuaries and mudflats.

Little Gull 27–30cm
Larus minutus

A tiny gull with rounded wings. **Winter adults** show a white head, black eye crescents and ear spot, a greyish crown and a blackish bill. Underparts white. Upperparts pale grey. In flight, shows pale grey wings, with white-tipped primaries and secondaries forming a white trailing edge, and contrasting blackish underwings. Legs red. **Summer adults** show a black hood and a pink flush on underparts. In flight, **1st winter birds** show a blackish covert bar and leading edge, forming a striking W upperwing pattern similar to 1st year Kittiwake. Underwing whitish. Head as winter adult. Bill blackish. Legs reddish. **2nd winters** as adults, but show black on wing tips and paler underwings.

Voice and Diet   Gives low-pitched, repeated *kek* and harsher, louder *ke-aa* calls. Feeds in a very Black Tern-like manner, flying buoyantly low over the water and dipping to pick food from the surface. Will occasionally hawk flying insects on the wing. Feeds on a variety of small fish, molluscs, worms and insects. Will take plant matter on occasions.

Habitat and Status   A scarce but regular winter and passage visitor to coastal counties, with occasional inland sightings. Most records occur when birds are blown close inshore during bad weather. A regular movement is noted annually off southern and eastern coasts in spring and autumn. Found on coastal stretches, harbours and lagoons. Also frequents coastal marshes, and, occasionally, inland lakes. Breeds in central and eastern Europe.

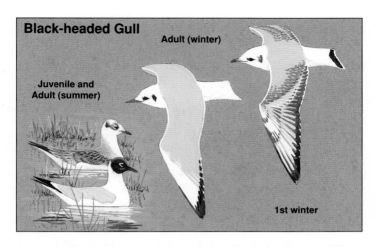

Black-headed Gull

Adult (winter)

Juvenile and Adult (summer)

1st winter

Little Gull

2nd winter

Adult (winter)

1st winter

**Adult winter
2nd winter
1st winter**

Summer adults

Black-headed Gull   **Little Gull**

143

Gulls

Kittiwake 38–42cm
Rissa tridactyla   Saidhbhéar

A slender gull with long, pointed wings. **Summer adults** show a white head, underparts, rump and tail. Upperparts dark grey. In flight, shows clear-cut black wing tips and dark grey coverts fading to a white trailing edge to secondaries and primaries. **Winter adults** show a greyish hindneck and rear crown, and a dark ear spot. Bill greenish-yellow. Legs dark. Eye dark with a red orbital ring. **1st year birds** show a greyish rear crown, a dark ear spot and a black half collar on the hindneck. In flight, the greyish-white secondaries and inner primaries contrast with the black leading edges and covert bars which form a distinctive W on the wings. Forked tail shows a black terminal band. Bill dark.

Voice and Diet   The distinctive, loud, repeated *kitti-waak* calls are usually only heard at the breeding cliffs. Feeds on a wide range of fish, crustaceans, worms and insects. Feeds by picking delicately from the surface in flight or when settled. Occasionally dives.

Habitat and Status   A common, widespread breeding species present in most coastal counties. During the breeding season, found on sheer cliffs, nesting on narrow ledges. Will occasionally build nests on sides of buildings, piers or on light standards. Spring and autumn movements are noted annually from the south-west. In winter, disperses to open oceans and seas, although small numbers are usually present in ports and harbours. Kittiwakes are more pelagic than other gull species and are rarely found inland.

Sabine's Gull 32–35cm
Larus sabini

Summer adults show a blackish-grey hood, white underparts, rump and tail, and a yellow-tipped black bill. In flight, shows a black leading edge, dark grey coverts and mantle, and white inner primaries and secondaries forming a striking white triangle. Outer primaries show white tips. **Winter adults** show a dark smudge on the head. Legs dark. **1st years** show a grey-brown mantle extending onto head and sides of breast, grey-brown coverts contrasting with a black leading edge and white 'triangle', and a black terminal band to a forked tail. Bill dark. Immature Kittiwakes can resemble Sabine's Gulls but show a mostly white head, a black W on the wings and a black collar on the neck.

Voice and Diet   Although rarely heard in Ireland, Sabine's Gull can give a harsh, tern-like call. Feeds on a wide range of molluscs, worms, small fish and insects. Feeds by picking off the surface of the water in flight. Will also feed actively on mudflats.

Habitat and Status   A rare but regular autumn passage vagrant from the high Arctic regions of Canada, Greenland and Spitzbergen. Usually seen following strong westerly winds when birds are recorded around the coast. Most records come from western and south-western regions. While most records refer to autumn, there have been several winter and spring reports. Sabine's Gulls are almost wholly pelagic, rarely being found inland.

Kittiwake

cliff-nester

1st winter

Adult (summer)

Sabine's Gull

striking
upperwing
pattern

Immature

Adult (winter)

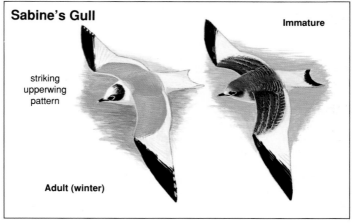

Kittiwake

Sabine's Gull

Terns

Arctic Tern 30–39cm
Sterna paradisaea   Geabhróg Artach

A dainty species with a shortish, blood-red bill. **Adults** show a rounded black crown and nape, white cheeks, whitish underparts which can show a dark greyish wash, and pale grey upperparts. When perched, shows short red legs and a wing length which is shorter than the long tail streamers. Flies with shallow, quick wing beats and shows a plain grey upperwing with no primary wedges. The underwing is pure white and shows a narrow, black trailing edge to the primaries. Rump and long tail white. **Juveniles** show an all dark bill, pale red legs, a white forehead and lores, a pale grey mantle and wings, and a faint carpal bar. Shows white primaries and secondaries in flight.

Voice and Diet   Gives a *kee-aar* call similar to Common Tern, although shorter and delivered in a less harsh manner. Can also give a whistling *kee-kee* call. Juveniles give harsh *kik-kik* calls. Feeds on a wide range of small fish and invertebrates which are caught by skilful dives following mid-air hovers.

Habitat and Status   A widespread summer visitor, with breeding taking place in most coastal counties. Tends to be more maritime in behaviour than Common Tern, although small numbers breed on inland lakes, often in mixed tern colonies. Found along coastal areas and large inland lakes. Nests on small islands and undisturbed shorelines, with the nest an open scrape on the ground. Wintering on the Antarctic pack ice, Arctic Terns are reputed to see more daylight than any other bird species.

Common Tern 30–36cm
Sterna hirundo   Geabhróg

An elegant species with a long, black-tipped red bill. **Adults** show a black crown and nape, white cheeks and underparts, and a pale grey mantle and wings. When perched, shows red legs and long wings which are equal to the tail length. Flies lazily on long wings, showing pale grey upperwings with a distinctive dark wedge on the mid-primary and dark outer primaries tips. Underwing silvery-grey with a broad, dark trailing edge on outer primaries. Rump and long tail white. **Juveniles** show a pale base to a dark bill, red legs, a white forehead and lores, and a brownish mantle with pale edges to feathers contrasting with a dark carpal bar. Shows dark grey secondaries and primaries in flight.

Voice and Diet   Gives loud, grating *kee-aaar* and *kiip* calls. Juveniles give hard, repeated *kik* calls. Feeds on a variety of small fish which are skilfully caught by diving from a height following a mid-air hover.

Habitat and Status   A widespread summer visitor, with breeding populations present in most coastal and some inland counties. Winters off West Africa. Breeding takes place in colonies, usually on small coastal and lake islands. Nest an open scrape on the ground. Found along coastlines, inland rivers and lakes, and off headlands on passage.

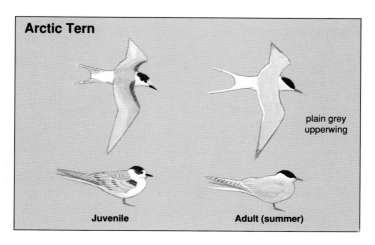

Arctic Tern

plain grey
upperwing

Juvenile   **Adult (summer)**

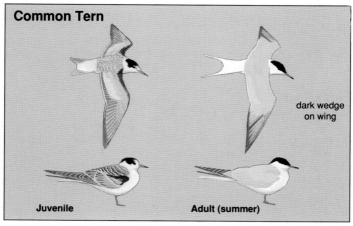

Common Tern

dark wedge
on wing

Juvenile   **Adult (summer)**

Arctic Tern   **Common Tern**

Terns

Roseate Tern 32–41cm
Sterna dougallii　Geabhróg rósach

A delicate species with a dull red base to a blackish bill. **Adults** show a black crown and nape, white cheeks, white underparts which show a pink wash in summer, and whitish-grey upperparts. When perched, shows orange-red legs and long tail streamers extending well beyond the wings. Flies lazily and shows a very pale upperwing with grey outer primary wedges in late summer. White underwing lacks a dark trailing edge to the primaries. **Juveniles** show a black cap with a white loral spot, a black bill and black legs. Mantle shows dark brown scalloping which gives a dark, saddle-like effect in flight. Wings pale with faint greyish primary tips and a faint carpal bar. Underwing whitish.

Voice and Diet　Gives a distinctive, high-pitched *tchu-ick* call, not unlike that of Spotted Redshank. Also gives loud, harsh *raaak* calls. Feeds on a variety of fish which are caught by diving from mid-air hovers.

Habitat and Status　A rare breeding species which, following a serious decline in recent decades, is now beginning to breed successfully in coastal counties in the east, south-east and north. Maritime in habitat, Roseate Terns breed in colonies on small islands or beaches, nesting in hollows or under vegetation. Winters off West Africa.

Black Tern 23–26cm
Chlidonias niger　Geabhróg dhubh

A small, compact species with short wings and a shallow fork to the tail. **Summer adults** are very distinctive with a black head and underparts, white undertail-coverts, grey upperwings, rump and tail, grey underwings, a black bill and dark legs. **Moulting adults** can show black mottling on underparts. **Immatures** show a diagnostic black shoulder patch, white underparts and a black ear-covert and crown patch. Upperwing grey with a strong, conspicuous, black carpal bar. Mantle grey, slightly darker than grey rump and tail. Flight is bouncy with shallow, stiff wing beats. Feeds by picking from the surface while in flight. Does not plunge-dive like other tern species.

Voice and Diet　Not as vocal as other tern species, Black Tern can sometimes give a high-pitched, squeaky *kitt* call. Feeds on a wide variety of insects which are delicately picked from the surface of lakes and marshes.

Habitat and Status　A regular autumn passage migrant from continental Europe. Also recorded irregularly in spring. Successful breeding occurred on one occasion at Lough Erne, Co. Fermanagh, in 1967. Breeding was attempted at the same locality again in 1975 but the nest and eggs were abandoned. Found feeding over freshwater lakes, marshes and reservoirs. Usually found in coastal counties, but has also been reported at inland sites. Black Terns are also occasionally seen during seawatches.

148

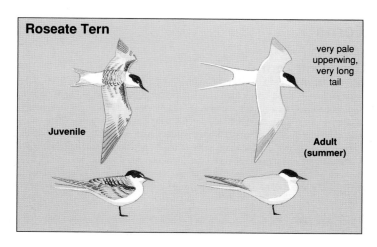

Roseate Tern

Juvenile

very pale
upperwing,
very long
tail

**Adult
(summer)**

Black Tern

Adult (winter)

Immature

dark overall,
grey rump

Adult (summer)

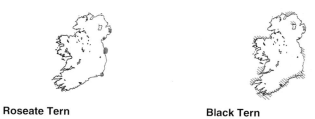

Roseate Tern

Black Tern

Terns

Sandwich Tern 38–44cm
Sterna sandvicensis   Geabhróg scothdhubh

A large, long-winged tern with a slender, yellow-tipped black bill and black legs. **Summer adults** show a black cap with a shaggy crest, white underparts and pale grey upperparts. In flight, shows slender pointed wings with dark wedges to primaries. Rump and short forked tail white. **Winter adults** show a white forehead, with the black cap and shaggy crest confined to the rear of the crown. Some birds can show a white forehead by the end of the breeding season. **Juveniles** show a slender black bill, a black cap with white speckling on the forehead, and a scalloped mantle and carpal bar. The tertials and tail also show dark markings. Flight is strong and direct, with shallow wing beats.

Voice and Diet   Gives a distinctive, loud, grating *kirr-rik* call. Feeds on a variety of fish which, like other tern species, are caught by skilful dives following mid-air hovers. Will also take worms and molluscs.

Habitat and Status   A common summer visitor found breeding in noisy colonies on quiet, undisturbed islands or shingle beaches in most coastal regions. Small colonies are also present at some inland sites. Nests in a scrape on open ground or on grass. One of the earliest summer visitors to Ireland, Sandwich Terns can be seen along most coastal regions from early March onwards. Found on open coastal waters, bays and harbours. Most depart by September, wintering off the coast of West Africa.

Little Tern 24–27cm
Sterna albifrons   Geabhróg bheag

A tiny long-winged tern with a black-tipped yellow bill and orange-yellow legs. **Adults** show a white forehead patch which contrasts strongly with a black loral stripe, crown and nape. Upperparts bluish-grey with long wings. Throat, neck and underparts white. In flight, the long wings show a dark leading edge to the primaries. Rump and short forked tail white. **Immatures** show a dark, brownish bill, yellow-brown legs, a buff to white forehead and lores, a black streaked crown, and a blackish eye patch. Greyish upperparts show brown barring on the mantle and scapulars and, in flight, the wings show a complete dark leading edge. Flight appears bouncy with fast wing beats.

Voice and Diet   Little Terns are generally very noisy around the breeding grounds, giving loud, shrill *krii-ek* calls. Also gives a repeated, sharp *kitt* call and chattering *kirrik-kirrik-kirrik* calls. Feeds on a range of crustaceans and small fish by diving from mid-air hovers.

Habitat and Status   A summer visitor to most coastal counties except those in northern and north-eastern regions. Rarely found inland. Breeds in small colonies on shingle and sandy beaches, the nest consisting of a scrape in the ground. The eggs and chicks are perfectly camouflaged and difficult to see. Unfortunately, because of this, and their habit of nesting on beaches, Little Terns are prone to human disturbance.

Sandwich Tern

large size

Juvenile

Adult
(summer)

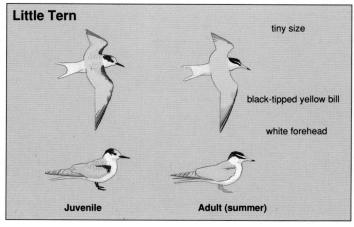

Little Tern

tiny size

black-tipped yellow bill

white forehead

Juvenile

Adult (summer)

Sandwich Tern

Little Tern

Auks

Guillemot 40–44cm
Uria aalge   Foracha

A slim auk with a dark, pointed bill and dark legs. **Summer adults** show a dark chocolate-brown head, throat, neck and upperparts, with a thin white line formed by white tips to the secondaries. Underparts white with dark flank streaking. The **Bridled forms** show a white eye-ring and a white eye-stripe from behind eye. **Winter adults** show a white throat, neck and cheeks, with a thin black stripe obvious behind the eye. Crown, nape and hindneck chocolate-brown, forming a collar on sides of breast. In flight, shows white sides to rump, a short, rounded tail, a white trailing edge to secondaries, whitish underwing coverts and dark axillaries. **1st winter birds** show less flank streaking.

Voice and Diet   Extremely noisy at the breeding colonies, with birds making harsh, rolling *oarrr* calls. Feeds by diving, swimming underwater by flapping the wings. Takes a variety of fish, marine worms, molluscs and crustaceans.

Habitat and Status   A common breeding species, with large colonies present in summer on cliffs and islands on southern and western coastal sites. Small colonies also present in eastern and northern regions. Breeds on sheer cliffs, perching precariously on narrow ledges. Juveniles leave the cliffs before they can fly and are fed at sea by the parents. Guillemots winter off the Irish coast and are found in harbours, bays and offshore waters.

Razorbill 39–43cm
Alca torda   Crosán

A stocky auk with black legs and a dark, stubby bill showing a white band and a thin white line from the eye along the upper mandible. **Summer adults** show a black head, throat, neck and upperparts, with a thin white line formed by white tips to the secondaries. Pointed tail obvious when swimming. White underparts unstreaked. **Winter adults** show a white throat and neck, with white extending behind contrastingly black ear-coverts. Crown, nape and hindneck black, forming a short collar on sides of breast. In flight, shows white sides to rump, a longish pointed tail, a white trailing edge to secondaries, and clean whitish underwing coverts. **1st winter birds** similar to winter adults.

Voice and Diet   At the breeding grounds, give low, weak, growling, whistling and grunting calls. Rarely heard away from the breeding colonies. Feeds by diving, swimming underwater by flapping the wings. Feeds on a wide variety of prey items, taking fish, marine worms, molluscs and crustaceans.

Habitat and Status   Common breeding species, present in summer among mixed auk colonies on cliffs and islands on southern and western coastal sites. Small colonies are also present in eastern and northern regions. Nests in crevices, under boulders or on sheltered ledges. Juveniles leave the cliffs before they can fly and are fed at sea by the parents. Winters off the Irish coast and found in harbours, bays and on offshore waters.

Guillemot

Bridled form

Adult (summer)

pointed bill, streaking on flanks

Winter

Razorbill

Adult (summer)

Winter

thick bill, clean flanks

Guillemot

Razorbill

153

Auks

Black Guillemot 33–36cm
Cepphus grylle   Foracha dhubh

A striking auk with bright red legs and a dark bill showing a bright red gape. **Summer adults** show an all sooty-black plumage with striking white wing covert patches. In flight, these patches are the most conspicuous feature. **Winter adults** show a very white head with a dark grey area around the eye, a greyish crown and nape, and white underparts with blackish streaking along the flanks. The blackish mantle shows broad white edges to feathers, giving a barred and mottled appearance. The tail and wings remain blackish in winter, the large white wing covert patches being less conspicuous. **Immatures** are similar to winter adults, but show dark barring on wing patches and duller legs.

Voice and Diet   On the breeding areas, can give loud, whistling *spiiiiieh* calls, which can finish in trilling notes. Feeds by diving for marine prey items including fish, worms, molluscs and crustaceans.

Habitat and Status   A widespread resident species, present in all Irish coastal counties. Found on rocky cliffs and islands, nesting under boulders, in caves, holes and even using crevices in walls and piers. Breeding occurs in most regions where there is a suitable rocky coastline. In winter, found in sheltered bays and harbours, usually remaining close to shore.

Puffin 29–32cm
Fratercula arctica   Puifín

An unmistakable, dumpy, black and white auk with a colourful bill. **Summer adults** show a triangular blue-grey, yellow and reddish-orange bill with a yellow-edged gape. Whitish face shows a greyish wash on the cheeks, and dark shading above eye extending as a thin rear eye-stripe. Crown, nape and neck black. Upperparts and tail black, contrasting with white underparts. Legs bright orange. Eye dark with a red eye-ring. In **winter,** shows a smaller, duller bill, a dusky, greyish face, and yellowish legs. **Immatures** show a stubbier bill, a dark greyish face and dusky rear flanks. Flies with rapid wing beats, showing a black upperwing and rump, and dark underwings. Stands in an upright posture.

Voice and Diet   A normally silent species. However, in the breeding burrows, Puffins can be heard to give low, moaning, growling *arr-ow-arr* calls. Feeds on a wide variety of marine life, taking fish, worms, molluscs and crustaceans. At breeding sites, can often be seen returning from feeding forays with up to ten sand-eels draped cross-wise in the bill.

Habitat and Status   A summer visitor to some Irish coastal counties, with the highest populations based at colonies in north-western, western and south-western regions. Smaller, more widely scattered colonies are present along north-eastern, eastern and south-eastern coasts. Found on grassy slopes on quiet, undisturbed islands and cliffs, nesting in old rabbit and shearwater burrows. In winter, most birds disperse to the Atlantic and are seldom seen offshore.

Black Guillemot

striking white wing patches

Winter

Adult (summer)

red legs

Puffin

Adult (summer)

bright bill and legs

Adult (winter)   duller bill and face

Black Guillemot   **Puffin**

Doves

Rock Dove 31–36cm
Columba livia   Colm aille

The ancestor of the domestic and feral pigeon, wild Rock Doves are shy and unapproachable. **Adults** show a blue-grey head and neck with a green and purple neck patch. Breast, belly and undertail pale grey. Upperparts pale grey, with two broad black wingbars across tertials and secondaries, and median coverts. Primaries dark grey. Tail blue-grey with a darker terminal band. In flight, shows a small white rump contrasting with grey tail and upperparts, swept-back wings which show striking black bars on the secondaries and median coverts, and silvery-white underwings. Can glide on V-shaped wings. Eye reddish-orange. Bill grey with white cere. Legs pinkish. **Immatures** duller with brownish tones.

Voice and Diet   Gives a soft *coo-roo-coo* song occasionally associated with a strutting, fan-tailed display. Engages in display flights which consist of slow wing beats, wing claps and long glides on V-shaped wings. Feeds on a wide variety of grains, cereals and seeds. Will also take other plant material and occasionally molluscs.

Habitat and Status   A resident species, pure wild Rock Doves are now only found along the south-western, north-western and northern coasts. Found in small numbers on rocky sea cliffs, headlands and islands, feeding in coastal fields. Nests in caves and crevices in rocks.

Stock Dove 32–36cm
Columba oenas   Colm gorm

A stocky, compact species which lacks white in the plumage and shows a dark eye and a pale tip to a bright reddish bill. **Adults** show a blue-grey head with an emerald-green neck patch and a purple-tinged breast. Belly, undertail, mantle and rump blue-grey. Wings show two small blackish bars on the inner coverts and tertials. The secondaries, primaries and primary coverts are dark. Short, blue-grey tail shows a very broad, dark terminal band. In flight, appears compact, short-winged, and shows a distinctive dark border to edge and rear of wings. Underwings greyish. **Immatures** show a browner plumage, a darkish bill and lack the emerald-green neck patches.

Voice and Diet   Gives a deep, sharp *coo-ah* call which can be repeated. Engages in display flights which involve flying straight with slow, deep wing beats with wing claps and glides on shallow, V-shaped wings. Feeds on a wide variety of seeds, cereals and other plant material. Can also take small invertebrates.

Habitat and Status   A common, widespread resident species found in most counties, with the highest concentrations in eastern and south-eastern regions. Found on farmlands, woodlands, parks and along coastal cliffs and dune systems. Nests in holes in trees, old ruined buildings, cliff crevices and even rabbit burrows.

Rock Dove

white cere

double wingbar,
pale rump

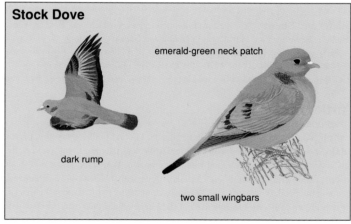

Stock Dove

emerald-green neck patch

dark rump

two small wingbars

Rock Dove

Stock Dove

Doves

Collared Dove 29–32cm
Streptopelia decaocto   Fearán baicdhubh

A slim, pale, sandy-brown dove with a longish tail. **Adults** show a pinkish-brown head, with a conspicuous black and white neck collar. Breast pinkish-brown with belly and undertail pale sandy-brown. Upperparts greyish-brown, with a pale greyish band on the wing and darker primaries. Rump and tail sandy-brown with white outer tips to tail. From below, shows a diagnostic undertail pattern of a very broad white outer band contrasting with dark inner undertail. In flight, shows rounded wings with pale grey middle, dark primaries and pale underwings. Eye dark reddish. Bill slim and dark. Legs pinkish-brown. **Immatures** lack the half-collar, appear duller and show pale edges to upperpart feathers.

Voice and Diet   Gives a deep, cooing song consisting of *coo-cooo-oo*, the emphasis being on the second syllable. In flight or when alarmed, gives a harsh, nasal *cwurr* call. Feeds on a wide variety of grain and seeds, also visiting bird tables to take any available scraps.

Habitat and Status   A widespread, common species which was first recorded in Ireland in 1959, breeding in that year in Dublin and Galway. Now found in all counties. Formerly an eastern European species, the range of Collared Dove began to expand westwards in the 1930s. By the 1970s, the species had reached Iceland. Found in towns, parks, gardens and farmlands, often seen in the vicinity of mills. Will also visit bird tables.

Turtle Dove 25–29cm
Streptopelia turtur   Fearán

A small, slender dove with a longish, graduated tail and boldly marked upperparts. **Adults** show a blue-grey head with black and white neck patches. Breast pinkish. Belly and undertail whitish. Mantle and rump grey-brown. Scapulars, lesser and median coverts, inner greater coverts and tertials rufous with black centres. Secondaries, greater and primary coverts pale greyish, contrasting with dark primaries. Tail greyish-brown with a white terminal band and a dark subterminal band. Undertail dark with a narrow white tip. In flight, shows pointed wings with greyish underwings. Eye and legs reddish-brown. Bill dark with reddish cere. **Immatures** duller and lack neck patches.

Voice and Diet   Gives a very distinctive, soft, purring *torr-r-r* song, delivered from a prominent perch. Feeds on a wide variety of seeds and grain.

Habitat and Status   A scarce passage migrant from continental Europe, found in spring and autumn. Some may over-summer and breeding has taken place on occasions. Most frequently found on passage on coastal headlands and islands, but can occur in open country with hedgerows and small woodlands. Nests in bushes and small trees.

Collared Dove

black and white neck collar

slim, pale, long tail

Turtle Dove

black and white on tail

small, slender, boldly-marked rufous upperparts

Collared Dove

Turtle Dove

Woodpigeon and Barn Owl

Woodpigeon 39–44cm
Columba palumbus   Colm coille

A small-headed, plump bird with a longish tail. **Adults** show a grey-blue head, a green and purple gloss on the side of the neck, and conspicuous white neck patches. Breast purplish-brown with rest of underparts creamy greyish-white. Upperparts grey-brown, with a striking white line on bend of wing. Primary coverts and primaries dark. Rump and uppertail blue-grey with a dark terminal band to tail. Flies with swept-back wings, deep chest, head held high, showing white across middle of wing and greyish underwings. Eye yellowish. Bill orange-yellow with white cere. **Immatures** browner, lacking neck patches and showing dark eyes and duller bills. Flushes noisily with wing clatters.

Voice and Diet   Gives a muffled, rhythmic cooing song consisting of *cooo-coo, coo, coo-cu* delivered from a prominent perch. Engages in display flight which involves flying steeply upwards, wing clapping and gliding downwards. This display can be repeated several times. Feeds on a wide variety of seeds, cereals, leaves and other plant material. Can also take some invertebrates.

Habitat and Status   A very common resident species present in all counties. Can be found in many habitats, including towns, cities, parks, gardens, farmlands, woodlands and open country. Will feed in flocks. Nests in trees, hedges or on the ground.

Barn Owl 32–36cm
Tyto alba   Scréachóg reilige

A distinctive species usually encountered as a ghostly white shape flying in the night. Can occasionally hunt at dusk when the delicate plumage can be seen. Shows black eyes set in a white, heart-shaped face. Crown, mantle, wings, rump and tail are orange-buff with varying amounts of grey speckling. Underparts white but can show a buff tinge. **Females** can show more speckling on the upperparts and fine dark spotting on the underparts. **Juveniles** similar to adults but often show tufts of down on the head, mantle and underparts. When perches, appears upright with a large head and longish legs. Flies with grace and ease, moving with slow, deep wing beats. Hovers with dangling legs when hunting.

Voice and Diet   Gives a very eerie, drawn-out screech, often delivered in flight. At the nest, both adults and young give loud snoring and hissing calls. Feeds by flying on rounded, silent wings, hovering and pouncing on prey. Will take small mammals like rats, mice and shrews. Will also feed on small birds and sometimes insects.

Habitat and Status   A scarce but widely distributed resident breeding species. While present in most Irish counties, they are absent or in very low numbers in some parts of the west and north-west. Numbers seem to be declining. Found near old buildings, ruins, farms, church towers and even in towns and cities. Will also nest in hollows in trees. In winter, can be found in woodlands. Hunts over fields and open ground.

Woodpigeon

large size,
small headed, plump,
longish tail

vivid white
wing patches

striking white neck patch

Barn Owl

very pale in flight

heart-shaped
face with dark
eyes

Woodpigeon

Barn Owl

Owls

Long-eared Owl 34–37cm
Asio otus   Ceann cait

A slim, upright, nocturnal species with striking long tufts on the head. A greyish-brown crown contrasts with an orangy face which shows pale eyebrows and striking black vertical lines from the tufts to the bill. Eyes bright orange. Pale buffish-white underparts show dark streaking to belly and onto flanks. Upperparts greyish-brown with fine barring and streaking. In flight, shows an orangy upperwing with mottling on the coverts, barring on the secondaries and primaries, and a distinctive orangy primary patch. Underwing white with fine barring on the tip and a dark carpal patch. Tail shows indistinct barring. In flight, shows rounded wings. Flies with deep wing beats interspersed with glides.

Voice and Diet   In spring, gives a very distinctive, low, muffled, repeated *oo* call. Can also give a variety of wheezes, barks and screams. One call resembles the *cwurr* call of Collared Dove. Young birds can give a far-carrying, squeaking call. During display flights engages in wing-clapping. Feeds on a wide range of small mammals, birds and insects.

Habitat and Status   A widespread but uncommon resident breeding species. Found in woodlands, favouring areas of pine or spruce. Nests in old crow or Magpie nests, old squirrel dreys and occasionally on the ground. On passage, found on coastal headlands and islands, roosting in small trees, hedgerows and occasionally on the ground. Many birds seen on passage are probably migrants from the Continent.

Short-eared Owl 36–40cm
Asio flammeus   Ulchabhán réisc

A stocky owl usually seen hunting, roosting on the ground or perched on a post during daylight hours. A pale, sandy-buff crown shows two indistinct tufts, while a pale face shows bright yellow eyes set in black eye-rings. Dark streaking on pale buffish-white underparts usually confined to the breast, with faint flank streaking. Upperparts pale sandy-buff with dark, heavy blotching. In flight, shows a pale buff upperwing with heavy mottling on coverts, strong barring on primaries and secondaries, a white trailing edge, a dark carpal patch, and a striking pale primary patch. Underwing white with a solid dark tip and carpal patch. Tail strongly barred. Flies with slow, deep wing beats. Glides on raised wings.

Voice and Diet   Gives a shrill, barking *kwock* call. Can also give a low-pitched *bo-bo-bo* call near breeding areas. Will engage in flight displays involving wing-claps. Feeds on small mammals, small birds and occasionally insects.

Habitat and Status   A scarce, thinly distributed passage and winter visitor to Ireland from Iceland, northern Europe, Scotland and northern England. Breeding has occurred in the west and south-west, with summering birds being recorded in other regions on occasions. Found on the ground or perched on posts close to rough vegetation, usually in coastal marshes or dunes. Also found in stubble fields, bogs and moorlands. Nests on the ground in heather, grass or gorse.

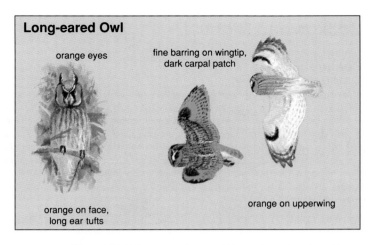

Long-eared Owl

orange eyes

fine barring on wingtip,
dark carpal patch

orange on face,
long ear tufts

orange on upperwing

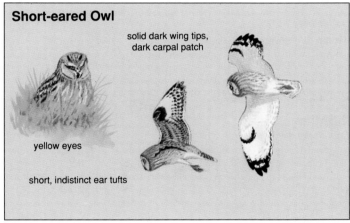

Short-eared Owl

solid dark wing tips,
dark carpal patch

yellow eyes

short, indistinct ear tufts

Long-eared Owl

Short-eared Owl

Cuckoo and Nightjar

Cuckoo 32–35cm
Cuculus canorus   Cuach

A long-tailed, parasitic species appearing hawk-like in flight. **Adults** show a bluish-grey head, throat and upper breast, while the white underparts show narrow, dark grey barring. Upperparts also bluish-grey, with slightly darker wings which can be held drooped. The long, graduated, dark grey tail shows white spotting. Pointed, dark bill shows a yellowish base. Eyes yellow with a dark pupil. Legs yellow. **Females** can show brownish tones to the upperparts and a buff wash on the breast. **Juveniles** show brownish upperparts with black barring, buffish-white underparts with dark barring, and distinctive white nape patches. Flies with rapid, shallow wing beats on pointed wings.

Voice and Diet   Males give the very distinctive, far-carrying *cuc-coo* call which is usually delivered from a prominent perch or on the wing. Females, though rarely heard, give long, bubbling, chuckling calls and repeated *wah-wah* calls. Feeds on a variety of insects and larvae. The female, when laying an egg in a nest of a foster parent, will usually remove an egg from that nest and eat it.

Habitat and Status   A common summer visitor to all regions, usually arriving by mid-April. Adults depart by July, immatures in August and September. Found on farmlands, moorlands, woodland edges, sand-dunes and coastal islands and headlands. The young Cuckoo, on hatching, will systematically remove all other eggs and chicks from the nest, thus receiving the full attention of the unfortunate foster parents.

Nightjar 25–28cm
Caprimulgus europaeus   Tuirne lín

A distinctive, delicately camouflaged, crepuscular bird which flies with easy, buoyant wing beats interspersed with floating glides on raised wings. In flight, shows long wings and tail, a broad, flattened head and a very short wide-gaped bill. **Adult males** show a greyish-brown plumage with a complicated pattern of black, brown, buff and cream barring, mottling, spotting and streaking. In flight, males show white spots to the three outer primaries and white tips to the outer-tail feathers. **Adult females** and **immatures** are similar, but lack the white wing spots and tail tips. During daylight hours, Nightjars sit still among ground vegetation or on low, horizontal branches.

Voice and Diet   The song of Nightjar is an unmistakable, rapid, rhythmical churring which rises and falls in pitch. The song can continue for long periods of time. In flight, gives a sharp *quu-ic* call. On the breeding grounds can also engage in loud wing-clapping displays. Feeds on a variety of insects which are caught on the wing.

Habitat and Status   Formerly a widespread summer visitor, Nightjar is now a very rare breeding species and passage migrant. Frequents felled woodland and conifer plantations with open moorland areas. On passage, found on coastal headlands and islands.

Cuckoo

hawk-like flight

long tail,
barred underparts

Adult

Juvenile

Nightjar

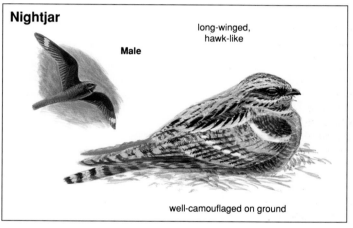

long-winged,
hawk-like

Male

well-camouflaged on ground

Cuckoo

Nightjar

Swallow and House Martin

Swallow 16–22cm
Hirundo rustica   Fáinleog

A familiar summer visitor, easily recognised by the long tail streamers. **Adults** show a glossy bluish head, a dark red forehead and throat patch, and a dark bluish breast band. Lower breast, belly, flanks and undertail-coverts creamy white. Upperparts and rump dark glossy blue. Wings browner. The diagnostic tail shows elongated streamers. White subterminal patches on the central feathers form a distinctive white band on the undertail, and narrow white markings on the uppertail. Tail streamers longest on males. **Immatures** show shorter tail streamers, buffish throat and forehead patches, and a greyish-brown breast band. Flies with effortless swoops and glides. Short legs and bill dark.

Voice and Diet   Gives a high, tinkling *vitt* call, sometimes repeated. Song combines various twittering, warbling and trilling notes. Feeds on a wide variety of insects which are skilfully caught on the wing. Drinks on the wing by swooping low over streams and rivers and dipping the bill into the water.

Habitat and Status   A very common summer visitor to all counties. Arrives from the wintering grounds in southern Africa by March or April. The nest is made of mud pellets and built under rafters, on ledges and under eaves of old sheds, barns, farm out-houses and porches. Can be very faithful to nest sites, returning year after year to the same location. Found on farmlands, in suburbs, and over lakes and rivers. Will roost in reed-beds.

House Martin 12–14cm
Delichon urbica   Gabhlán binne

A compact bird with a forked tail and a large, conspicuous white rump. **Adults** show a metallic dark blue head and upperparts. Throat, breast, belly, flanks and undertail pure white. Wings appear browner. Large white rump contrasts strongly with the dark upperparts and the dark, metallic blue forked tail which lacks the elongated tail streamers of Swallow. **Immatures** show a brownish wash on the sides of the breast, a dull brownish crown, brownish wings, and white tips to the tertials. In flight, shows a more triangular wing shape than Swallow. Flies with fluttering wing beats, interspersed with frequent glides and swoops. Bill short and dark. Legs and feet feathered white.

Voice and Diet   Gives a clear, hard *tchirrrip* call along with a sharp *tseep* when alarmed. Song consists of weak, chirruping, twittering notes, similar to but less varied than that of Swallow. Feeds on a wide variety of insects which are caught on the wing.

Habitat and Status   A very common summer visitor from wintering grounds in Africa. Arrives in March or April, leaves by mid-October, with a few records of birds seen during winter months. Found in towns, villages, farms and around cliffs. Nests in colonies. Builds a nest made of mud which is cupped under eaves of houses, bridges or on cliffs.

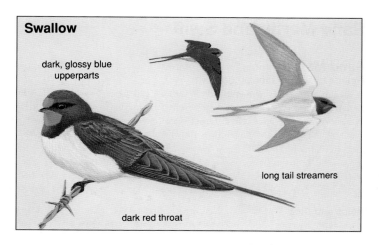

Swallow

dark, glossy blue
upperparts

long tail streamers

dark red throat

House Martin

conspicuous white
rump

short, forked tail

Swallow

House Martin

Sand Martin and Swift

Sand Martin 11–13cm
Riparia riparia   Gabhlán gainimh
A small brown and white martin with a short tail and a brown breast band. **Adults** show a dull brown crown, nape and ear-coverts. Chin and throat are white, contrasting with a broad brown breast band. Lower breast, belly, flanks and undertail-coverts white. Mantle, wings and rump brown. Brown tail is short and shows a very shallow fork. **Immatures** show pale edges to wing and upperpart feathers, creating a scaly appearance. In flight, shows brownish underwings. Flies with fluttering wing beats, gliding less frequently than Swallow. Highly gregarious, often seen in large flocks, occasionally associating with Swallows and House Martins. Short bill and eyes dark.

Voice and Diet   Gives a short, sharp, dry *tchrrip* call which can be repeated. Song is a weak, harsh twittering. Feeds on a wide variety of flying insects which are caught on the wing.

Habitat and Status   A common summer visitor to all counties from wintering grounds in southern Africa. Sand Martins are subject to fluctuations in numbers, with the species suffering severe population crashes from time to time. Found in areas close to water. Nests in colonies, building tunnels in sand or earth banks. Will roost in reed-beds.

Swift 16–18cm
Apus apus   Gabhlán gaoithe
An agile, all-dark bird with long, scythe-like wings and a short, forked tail. **Adults** show a small, inconspicuous pale throat patch which can contrast with the sooty-brown head, upperparts and underparts. The sooty-brown tail is short and shows a deep fork which is not always obvious as the tail can be closed to a point. **Immatures** show a slightly larger throat patch and appear browner. Small bill, eye and legs dark. Flies on stiff wings with rapid wing beats and skilful glides. Highly adapted to an aerial life, eating, sleeping and mating on the wing, only perching during the breeding season. Highly gregarious, occasionally forming large, noisy flocks.

Voice and Diet   Gives a long, loud, shrill, piercing screech, often delivered during rapid aerial chases around rooftops. Takes a wide variety of flying insects which are caught on the wing. Feeds by flying with open mouth, swooping on prey items which can then be stored in the throat. This can give the throat a bulging appearance.

Habitat and Status   A very common passage and summer visitor, arriving in late April, leaving by August or early September. Found over towns, villages, cliffs and open country. Often found feeding over rivers, lakes and marshes. Nests in colonies in holes in eaves, under roof tiles, church towers and cliffs.

Sand Martin

short tail

brown breast band

white throat

Swift

long scythe-like wings

dark plumage, paler throat

Sand Martin

Swift

Hoopoe and Kingfisher

Hoopoe 26–28cm
Upupa epops   Húpú

An exotic species with a bold plumage and a long, curved bill. Crown shows a long, pinkish-brown, black-tipped crest. This can be fanned, but is usually depressed, giving the head a hammer-like appearance. Apart from a thin, dark eye-stripe, the face, and the nape, throat, mantle and scapulars are pinkish-brown, contrasting with the bold black and white pattern of the wings. Breast pinkish-brown, fading to white on the belly, flanks and undertail. Tail black with a white central band. Flight appears lazy and undulating, the wings closing briefly following each series of wingbeats. In flight, the striking wing pattern and the boldly patterned rump are obvious. Feeds on the ground in a methodical fashion.

Voice and Diet   The distinctive, low *poo-poo-poo* song, from which the species derives its name, is rarely heard in Ireland. On occasions, gives a quiet, chattering alarm call. Feeds in a methodical manner, searching for a wide range of worms, larvae and insects which are either picked off the ground or probed for in soft earth or sand.

Habitat and Status   A scarce but annual vagrant from southern Europe. Hoopoes have been recorded in every month, but most reports refer to early spring, with a smaller passage noted in autumn. Can be found in a wide range of habitats, including farmland, rough coastal pastures, sand-dunes, parklands and gardens. On passage, occurs on coastal islands and headlands, with most reports originating from the south-east, south and south-west.

Kingfisher 15–17cm
Alcedo atthis   Cruidín

A small, brightly coloured, short-winged bird with a long, dagger-like bill. **Adults** show a bright blue-green crown and moustachial stripe with pale barring and spotting. Nape dark blue-green. Dark loral stripe contrasts with bright orange-chestnut loral spot and ear-coverts. Throat and neck patch white. Underparts bright orange-chestnut. Mantle to rump pale turquoise. Short green-blue wings show pale spotting on the scapulars and coverts. Short tail bright blue. Bill dark with an orange-red base, more extensive on females. **Immatures** greener with paler underparts. Legs orange-red. Eye dark. Flies rapidly with whirring wing beats, the bright turquoise mantle and rump being very conspicuous.

Voice and Diet   Gives a shrill, harsh *chee* or *chrii* call which often attracts attention. The song is seldom heard and consists of a short trill. Feeds on a wide variety of small fish and aquatic insects. Dives into the water from overhanging branch or open perch, opening wings on impact.

Habitat and Status   A common resident bird found in all counties. Found along rivers, streams, on lakes, canals and marshes. In winter, can occur on coastal estuaries and bays, occasionally found feeding on channels on tidal marshes. Nests in excavated tunnels on banks of rivers, streams and canals.

Hoopoe

long bill
and crest

striking black
and white wings
and tail

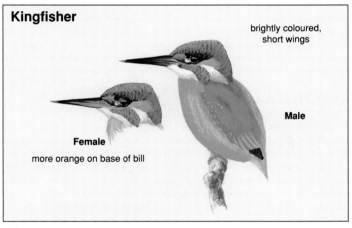

Kingfisher

brightly coloured,
short wings

Male

Female

more orange on base of bill

Hoopoe

Kingfisher

171

Larks and Pipits

Skylark 17–19cm
Alauda arvensis   Fuiseog

A large lark, more often heard than seen. **Adults** show a long streaked crest which can be raised or flattened on the head. Face appears plain, with a creamy supercilium, a thin eye-stripe behind the eye and thin streaking on brownish cheeks. Heavy streaking on the buffish breast extends as a malar stripe onto the paler throat. Underparts creamy. Upperparts brown with heavy blackish streaking. Flight undulating, showing a white trailing edge to the wings and white edges to the long tail. Pale bill thick and pointed. Legs pinkish and show a very long hindclaw. **Immatures** appear scaly and show a very short crest.

Voice and Diet   The song is delivered from high in the air, the bird hovering in a stationary position. Also sings during fluttery display flights. Can sing from posts or trees. The song consists of a continuous, strong, loud, clear warbling. When flushed or in flight, gives a rippling *chirrup* call. Feeds on a variety of seeds, worms, insects and larvae.

Habitat and Status   A common, widespread, resident breeding species found in all counties. Found in a variety of habitats, including moorlands, farmlands, rough pastures, sand-dunes and saltmarshes. Also found on stubble fields in autumn. Very inconspicuous on the ground, flushing at the last moment. Nests on the ground in grass or crops. When returning to the nest, lands some distance away before running, in cover, to the nest site.

Rock Pipit 15–17cm
Anthus petrosus   Riabhóg cladaigh

A rather drab pipit, slightly larger and taller than Meadow Pipit. Upperparts dull olive-grey with dark streaking and showing inconspicuous, creamy-buff wingbars. Shows a faint, pale supercilium and a thin, dark eye-stripe which highlights a narrow, pale eye-ring. Ear-coverts show a dark lower border. Dull creamy underparts show a dark malar stripe and heavy brown streaking on the breast and flanks. This heavy streaking may even extend onto the paler belly. In flight appears long-winged. Unlike other pipits, the darkish tail shows creamy or buffish outer feathers. Long, dagger-like bill is pale with a dark tip. Legs appear blackish but, when seen well, show a dull pinkish hue.

Voice and Diet   Gives a loud, full, harsh *pseep* call. Song is similar to that of Meadow Pipit but is a louder, more musical series of accelerated notes given during a rising display flight. The song finishes with a loud, strong trill given while descending during a parachuting glide. Feeds on a wide variety of small insects and worms. May feed on seeds.

Habitat and Status   A common resident breeding species found in all coastal counties. Rarely found inland. Frequents areas of rocky coastline and islands, occasionally occurring on mudflats and estuaries in winter. Nests in holes or crevices in rocks or cliffs. While numbers peak at some locations in autumn, this is not due to a strong passage movement but rather reflects a population increase due to recently fledged, immature birds.

Skylark

conspicuous crest

thick, pale bill

a large lark

Rock Pipit

drab plumage

faint supercilium

dark legs

Skylark

Rock Pipit

Pipits

Meadow Pipit 14–15cm
Anthus pratensis   Riabhóg mhóna

A small, active pipit, similar to Tree Pipit. In **spring,** shows brownish upperparts with dark streaking on the back and crown. A pale supercilium fades behind the eye while a faint eye-stripe behind the eye gives the face a plain appearance. Underparts show a dark malar stripe and heavy streaking which, unlike Tree Pipit, extends as heavy flank streaking. Whitish underparts show a faint buffish wash on the breast. In **autumn**, the upperparts show greenish tones with a strong yellowish-buff wash on the breast and flanks. Rump unstreaked. Tail brownish with white outer feathers. Legs pinkish-orange with long hindclaw. Bill pale, thin and pointed with a dark tip.

Voice and Diet   Gives a very distinctive, thin *tsip* call which can be repeated and delivered in a strong manner. On the breeding grounds, rises in a display flight, giving a series of accelerated, thin, tinkling, piping notes before descending in a parachuting glide, giving a rapid, musical trill. Feeds on a wide range of small insects, larvae and worms. Will also take seeds in the autumn. Feeds in a busy, active manner.

Habitat and Status   A very common, widespread breeding species found in all counties. Frequents areas of open country, being present on rough pastures, farmland, sand-dunes, moorlands and bogs. Also found on offshore islands. Nests in a shallow depression on the ground, usually in heavy cover of grass tussocks or heather. In winter, the higher ground is abandoned and many move to more southern counties.

Tree Pipit 14–15cm
Anthus trivialis   Riabhóg choille

A small pipit, similar to, but slightly larger and more slender than, Meadow Pipit. In **spring**, shows greenish upperparts with streaking on the back and crown. Supercilium strong behind the eye, contrasting with a prominent eye-stripe which may extend across the lores. Underparts show a dark malar stripe and strong, defined streaking which, unlike Meadow Pipit, becomes thin and faint on the flanks. Underparts show a strong orangy-buff wash on the breast which contrasts with a whiter belly. In **autumn**, the breast can show a creamy wash. Rump unstreaked. Tail shows white outer feathers. Legs pinkish with a short hindclaw. Thick, pale bill shows a dark tip.

Voice and Diet   Gives a very distinctive, buzzing *tzeep* call which can be repeated and delivered strongly. Can also give a very soft *sip* call. The song is a very loud, accelerated series of Chaffinch-like notes, given during a rising display flight, usually launched from a tree or bush. The song finishes with repeated *seea* notes during a descending, parachuting glide. Feeds in a slow, methodical manner, taking a wide range of small insects.

Habitat and Status   A scarce but annual spring and autumn passage migrant from Britain and Europe. Most records refer to the south-east and south-west. Also recorded on several occasions at inland sites. Tends to perch on trees more than Meadow Pipit but, when seen in Ireland, is usually found feeding with other pipits on open, rough pastures and farmland on coastal islands and headlands.

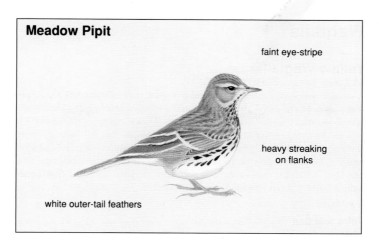

Meadow Pipit

faint eye-stripe

heavy streaking
on flanks

white outer-tail feathers

Tree Pipit

darker lores than
Meadow Pipit

light streaking on flanks

white outer-tail feathers

Meadow Pipit

Tree Pipit

Wagtails

Yellow Wagtail 16–17cm
Motacilla flava   Glasóg bhui

A slender, long-tailed species with a thin, pointed, dark bill and dark legs. **Spring males** show bright yellow underparts, throat and supercilium which contrast with a yellow-green crown, ear-coverts and upperparts. Dark wings show two narrow white bars and thin white edges to the tertials. Rump greenish. Tail dark with white outer feathers. **Females** show brownish-green upperparts with a pale, yellow-washed supercilium, throat and breast. **Immatures** similar to females with a pale supercilium and chin, and can show a dark malar stripe and breast band. **Blue-headed**, **Ashy-headed** and **Grey-headed** races occasionally occur and show distinctive head patterns.

Voice and Diet   Gives a very distinctive, thin, musical *tsweep* call which is given both on the ground when feeding or in flight. Can also give a short, warbling song which consists of simple, thin *tsip-tsip* notes. The song can be given in flight or from a perch. Feeds on a wide range of small insects and larvae. Can often be found associating with cattle, flitting suddenly into the air to catch insects disturbed by the feeding animals.

Habitat and Status   A scarce but regular spring and autumn passage migrant occurring annually. Also a rare breeding species. On passage, found at coastal locations, feeding in rough pastures, marshes and short turf. In summer, frequents lowland rough pastures, farmlands, marshes and wet meadows. Nests on the ground in cover of grass tussocks or crops. Other races are scarce to rare vagrants.

Grey Wagtail 18–20cm
Motacilla cinerea   Glasóg liath

A bright bird with a long, constantly wagging tail. **Summer males** show a grey head and mantle, a white supercilium, a black throat and white submoustachial stripes. Wings darker, with white-edged tertials. Tail black with white edges. Rump bright yellowish-green. Breast, undertail and centre of belly bright yellow. Flanks white. **Females** differ by showing a white throat, buffish supercilium, greenish ear-coverts and paler breast. **Winter males** similar to females, but show a buff-yellow breast. **Immatures** similar to winter adults, but upperparts greyish-brown. Legs pinkish. Bill thin and dark. Appears slim and long-tailed in flight, with a white wingbar and a dark underwing-covert bar.

Voice and Diet   Gives sharp, abrupt, loud *stzit* or *stzitzi* call. Song consists of a twittering, trilling warble. Feeds on a wide variety of insects which are caught among stones. Will also take molluscs and sandhoppers.

Habitat and Status   A common, widespread, resident species, with small passage movements noted in the autumn. Found in all counties, usually along fast-moving rivers and streams. Can also occur in cities, feeding along dockland areas and around park ponds. Nests in holes or on ledges under bridges, walls or old buildings close to or over water.

Yellow Wagtail

Blue-headed

Ashy-headed

Grey-headed

Female

Male

dark legs

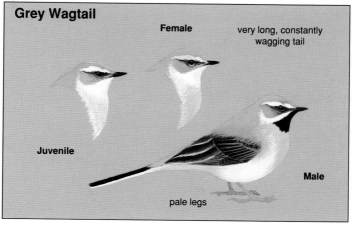

Grey Wagtail

Female

very long, constantly wagging tail

Juvenile

Male

pale legs

Yellow Wagtail

Grey Wagtail

Wagtails

Pied Wagtail 17–19cm
Motacilla alba yarrellii   Glasóg shráide

A black and white bird with a long, constantly wagging tail. **Summer males** show a white face and forehead, with a black crown and nape meeting a black bib. Back, wings and rump black. Wings show white bars and white-edged tertials. Tail black with white outer edges. Underparts white with dark grey flanks. **Summer females** show a blackish-grey back. **Winter adults** show a white throat, a black, crescent-shaped breast band and a blackish-grey back. **Juveniles** show a brownish-grey crown and back, a black rump, a buff-tinged face and throat, a messy breast band and greyish flanks. **1st winter** birds similar to winter adults, but show greyish upperparts. Legs and thin, pointed bill black.

Voice and Diet   Gives a loud, shrill *tchissick* call with an abrupt *tchik* call given in alarm. Song consists of twitters and warbles. Feeds in an active, fast manner, taking a wide variety of insects and seeds.

Habitat and Status   A very common, widespread, resident species found in all counties. In autumn, birds from Scotland and northern England may occur on passage. Found in a wide range of habitats, including towns, gardens, farms and shorelines. In winter, can occasionally be found roosting in large colonies in city centres. Nests in holes in walls, banks, out-houses, rocks or under stones or plants.

(White Wagtail) 17–19cm
Motacilla alba alba   Glasóg bhán

A race of Pied Wagtail. A black, grey and white bird with a long, constantly wagging tail. **Summer males** show a white face and forehead, with a black crown and nape which do not meet the black bib. Back ash-grey, contrasting with crown and blackish wings which show white bars and white-edged tertials. Greyish rump contrasts with black, white-edged tail. Underparts white with clean flanks. On **summer females**, grey of back extends onto nape. **Winter adults** differ by showing a white throat and a black, crescent-shaped breast band. **Immatures** show a grey crown, back and rump, paler wings with fainter bars, a thin, messy breast band and clean flanks. Can show pale yellow tones to face and throat. Legs and bill black.

Voice and Diet   White Wagtails give the same calls as those of Pied Wagtail, with a loud, shrill *tchissick* call given in flight and an abrupt *tchik* call given in alarm. Rarely heard in song in Ireland. Feeds in the same active, fast manner as Pied Wagtail, taking a wide variety of insects and seeds.

Habitat and Status   This race of Pied Wagtail is an uncommon spring and autumn passage migrant from Iceland and continental Europe. Found in open country at coastal headlands, islands, shorelines, lagoons and coastal wetlands and lakes. Occasionally associates with Pied Wagtail flocks. In spring, most records refer to northern and north-western coasts, with the south and south-east recording the highest numbers in autumn.

Pied Wagtail

Adult Male

Adult Female

dark grey flanks

Adult (winter)

1st winter

(White Wagtail)

Adult Male

Adult Female

pale flanks

Adult (winter)

1st winter

Pied Wagtail

(White Wagtail)

Robin and Dunnock

Robin 13–14cm
Erithacus rubecula   Spideog

A familiar, cheeky, rotund bird with a bright orange-red breast. **Adults** unmistakable, with an olive-brown crown, nape and upperparts. The lores, ear-coverts and breast are bright orange-red, with a grey border from behind eye to the sides of the breast. Belly and undertail white. **Juvenile** birds show a brownish head and wings, with the mantle, face and breast strongly barred. **Immatures** are similar to adults, but have pale tips to greater coverts showing as a narrow wingbar. Eye appears large and rounded. Bill dark, thin and pointed. Legs thin and blackish. Hops along the ground, frequently pausing in an upright stance with flicks of the tail and wings. A highly territorial species, usually solitary.

Voice and Diet   Gives a sharp, harsh *tic* or *tic-tic* call which can be repeated. Also gives softer *tsiip* and *tsee* calls. Song is a variety of short, high, liquid warbling phrases. Feeds on a wide selection of small insects, worms and also seeds. Will frequently visit bird tables.

Habitat and Status   A very common and widespread resident species found in all counties. In spring and autumn, some vagrants from continental Europe may occur in Ireland. Found in gardens, parks, hedgerows and woodlands. Nests in holes in walls, trees, in ivy or on ledges. Occasionally found nesting in most unusual places such as tin cans or watering cans.

Dunnock 14–15cm
Prunella modularis   Dunnóg

A small, rather drab, grey and brown bird with a dark, slender, pointed bill. **Adults** show a grey head with brownish crown and ear-coverts. Mantle rufous-brown with blackish streaks. The rufous-brown wings show dark centres to the feathers, adding to the streaked appearance of the upperparts. Rump and tail greyish-brown. The breast, belly, flanks and undertail are grey, with brown streaking present on the flanks. Eye deep reddish-brown. **Immatures** show a browner head with a white throat, dark streaking on buffish breast and flanks, and less rufous upperparts. Usually seen singly, feeding near cover. Moves with a shuffling gait, twitching the wings on occasions.

Voice and Diet   Gives a high, piping *tseep* call. The song is a hurried, high, pleasant, broken jingle. Sings from a prominent perch. Feeds on a variety of small insects and seeds. Will visit bird tables, but usually prefers to feed on the ground below them, taking scraps that might have fallen.

Habitat and Status   A very common, widespread, resident species. Found in areas with good cover and undergrowth. Present in towns and cities, being found in parks and gardens. In country areas, found along hedgerows and woodland fringes. Nests in dense cover in bushes and small trees.

Robin

unstreaked upperparts

conspicuous orange-
red face and breast

Dunnock

dull grey and brown
plumage

brown streaking
on flanks

Robin

Dunnock

Redstarts

Black Redstart 14–15cm
Phoenicurus ochruros   Earrdheargán dubh

A dark bird which shows a conspicuous, bright orange-red tail and rump in flight. **Winter adult males** have a blackish-grey crown, nape and mantle, with blackish wings showing white patches. Cheeks and throat blackish, extending onto breast. Belly and undertail pale greyish. In **summer**, the upperparts, the throat and the breast are black. **Females** are greyish-brown on upperparts and on underparts from the chin to the belly. Undertail paler. **Immatures** similar to adult females. In all plumages, the rump and tail are orange-red with dark central tail feathers. The tail can sometimes be flicked. Bill thin, dark and pointed. Legs blackish. Dark eye shows a very thin eye-ring.

Voice and Diet   The scratchy, hissing song of Black Redstart is rarely heard in Ireland. Usually silent on passage, wintering birds can occasionally give a short, soft *tsit* call. Feeds on a wide range of insects. Will also take berries.

Habitat and Status   An uncommon but regular spring and autumn passage migrant from central Europe. Each year, small numbers over-winter. Unlike Redstart, prefers open areas. Found on fields, rocky beaches, around power stations and old ruined buildings. Wintering birds are usually found at coastal locations. Tends to perch prominently on open rocks, walls or even on the top of buildings.

Redstart 14–15cm
Phoenicurus phoenicurus   Earrdheargán

A slim bird which shows a striking orange-red tail and rump in flight. **Summer males** show a black throat and ear-coverts, a white forehead and supercilium, orange-red underparts and a blue-grey crown, nape and mantle. Undertail pale. Wings brownish. **Autumn** and **1st winter males** show pale mottling on underparts and throat, with **immatures** being browner above with an obscure supercilium. **Adult females** are warm brown above and creamy-buff below, usually with a white chin. Can show a peach wash on breast and flanks. **Immature females** similar. All plumages show an orange-red rump and tail with dark central tail feathers. Eye dark with pale eye-ring. Thin, pointed bill dark. Legs dark.

Voice and Diet   Gives a Willow Warbler-like *hooweet* call, occasionally preceded by *tchuc* calls. The song consists of hurried warbling notes and twitters, and ends weakly. The song can recall a mixture between Chaffinch and Robin. Feeds on a wide variety of insects. Will also take berries.

Habitat and Status   A very rare breeding species, and an uncommon but regular spring and autumn migrant. In summer, occurs in mature deciduous woodland, with most breeding records referring to eastern counties. Breeding has also been recorded in the north, north-west and south-west. Nests in holes in trees or old walls. On migration, can be found in gardens and areas with good cover on coastal headlands and islands.

Black Redstart

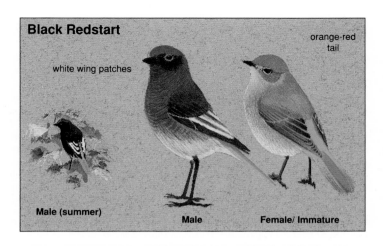

orange-red tail

white wing patches

Male (summer)

Male

Female/ Immature

Redstart

pale chin

black throat

orange-red rump and tail

Male

Female/Immature

Black Redstart

Redstart

Chats

Whinchat 12–14cm
Saxicola rubetra   Caislín aitinn

Summer males show a blackish crown and ear-coverts, a white supercilium and dark-streaked brownish upperparts and rump. Wings dark with white innerwing coverts and primary coverts. Underparts buff, with a white border to cheeks and a whitish belly and undertail. **Females** show a brown crown and cheeks, a creamy supercilium, and paler buff breast and flanks which can show spotting. Upperparts fawn, with white tips to dark-centred feathers. Wings show a small white covert patch and a pale tertial panel. **Autumn males** and **immatures** similar to females. In all plumages, the short tail shows white or buffish-white patches on the base. Pointed bill, eye and legs dark.

Voice and Diet   Gives short, sharp *stic-stic* or *tu-stic-stic* calls, which can be repeated. Can also give a low churring-type call. The song is a brief, twittering, variable warble. Feeds on a wide variety of insects, larvae, worms and spiders.

Habitat and Status   A regular spring and autumn passage migrant along eastern and southern coastal counties. Also a summer visitor, breeding in many counties, usually at sites away from the coast. Frequents areas of rough pasture, mountain valleys, young conifer plantations and bogland edges. On passage, found on rough pastures and open areas along the coast. Nests in grass tussocks or bracken, occasionally at the base of a bush or small tree.

Stonechat 12–14cm
Saxicola torquata   Caislín cloch

Summer males show a black head and throat, a reddish-orange breast and striking white neck patches. Belly and undertail whitish. Mantle blackish with brown streaking. Wings dark with white inner covert patches. Rump whitish with dark streaking. Tail dark. In **winter**, shows buffish tips to upperpart feathers, mottling on throat and a duller breast. **Adult females** show a brown head and throat, a faint supercilium, pale sides to neck, and streaked, brown upperparts with white wing patches. Breast reddish-buff. **Immatures** similar. Eye, bill and legs dark. **Siberian races** show an unstreaked white or pale rump, females and immatures showing a pale plumage and a white throat.

Voice and Diet   Gives sharp, repeated *tsack-tsack* or *weet-tsack-tsack* calls which sound like stones clicked together. Song consists of a variety of repeated, high-pitched phrases which are delivered from a prominent perch or during a song flight. Song may recall that of Dunnock. Feeds on a wide variety of insects, larvae, worms and seeds.

Habitat and Status   A common resident species found in most counties. Frequents rough pasture, young forestry plantations and mountain valleys, usually in areas with gorse, heather or bracken. In winter, moves to low-lying areas and coastal locations. A small number also migrate to Europe in autumn. Nests in gorse or in thick cover. The rare Siberian Stonechat is an extremely rare autumn vagrant, found on coastal headlands and islands.

Whinchat

striking white supercilium

Female

Male

Autumn

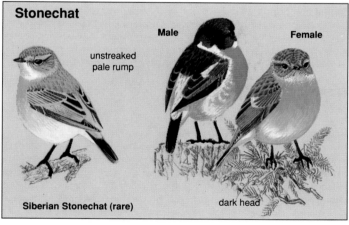

Stonechat

Male

unstreaked pale rump

Female

Siberian Stonechat (rare)

dark head

Whinchat

Stonechat

Wheatear and Waxwing

Wheatear 14–16cm
Oenanthe oenanthe   Clochrán

An upright species with a white rump and a black inverted T on a short white tail. **Summer males** show a greyish crown and mantle, a white supercilium, and a black eye mask with white lower cheeks. Wings blackish. Breast buffish. Belly and undertail white. **Autumn males** show brownish-grey upperparts and buff-edged wing feathers. **Adult females** show a brownish mask, a creamy supercilium, brownish-grey upperparts, brownish wings and a buffish breast. **Autumn females** show browner upperparts and buff-edged wing feathers. **Immatures** have brownish upperparts, a creamy or whitish supercilium, buff-edged wing feathers and sandy-buff underparts. Eye, pointed bill and legs dark.

Voice and Diet   Gives harsh *chack* or *weet-chack* calls. Song consists of harsh *chack*-type phrases combined with whistles, warbles and wheezing notes. Song can be delivered from a perch or during a display flight. Feeds on a wide range of insects.

Habitat and Status   A common summer visitor and passage migrant. Wheatears are often the first migrants to return to Ireland in spring. Found on mountains, moorlands and at coastal locations. Frequents areas of low grass, rough pastures and dunes, feeding on open ground. Perches prominently. Nests in holes in walls, scree, rocks or even old rabbit burrows. On passage, found along coastal shingle banks, beaches, islands and headlands.

Waxwing 17–19cm
Bombycilla garrulus   Síodeiteach

A tame, plump, colourful species. **Adults** show a pinkish-brown head with a long crest, a black eye mask, a black bib, sharply defined on males, and a white line from the bill. The cheeks are pinkish-brown but show warm chestnut tones. Upperparts greyish-brown. Wings show white and yellow V-tips to the black primaries, white and bright red waxy tips to the secondaries and white-tipped primary coverts. Rump grey. Tail shows a black subterminal band and a bright yellow tip. Underparts pinkish-brown with deep rufous-brown undertail-coverts. Short, dark bill slightly hooked. **Immatures** show paler, duller wings. In flight, appears very Starling-like, showing a short tail and triangular wings.

Voice and Diet   Gives a very distinctive, weak, trilling *sirrrrr* call, which may recall the distant ringing of a modern telephone. Feeds acrobatically and voraciously on a variety of berries and buds in winter. Will often sit for long periods during feeding. Will also eat fruit. In spring, can sometimes be seen fly-catching.

Habitat and Status   An uncommon to rare winter visitor from Scandinavia, found in very small numbers annually. In some years, Waxwings irrupt in search of food, and can occur throughout the country. Found anywhere with a plentiful supply of berries. Usually reported in town and city gardens where their exotic plumage and tameness often attract attention. Most records refer to northern and eastern coastal counties.

Wheatear

striking tail pattern

Male

Female

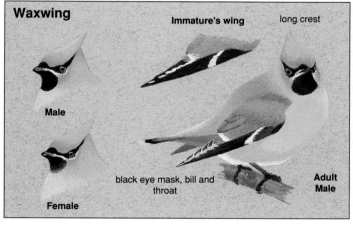

Waxwing

Immature's wing

long crest

Male

black eye mask, bill and throat

Adult Male

Female

Wheatear

Waxwing

Thrushes

Blackbird 24–28cm
Turdus merula   Céirseach

The striking **male** shows an all-black plumage which contrasts with a bright orange-yellow bill and yellow eye-ring. The **female** is dull brown with a pale throat and slightly paler underparts which can often show indistinct spotting. The bill of the female is dark with a dull yellowish base. **Immature females** are slightly paler than adults. **Immature males** are dark blackish-brown with paler underparts, and differ from adult males by lacking an orange bill and yellow eye-ring. The wings are short and do not show pale edges, this being a very useful feature to identify semi-albinistic birds which can appear very similar to Ring Ouzel. Runs along ground, frequently pausing with tail and head in the air.

Voice and Diet   Blackbirds are highly excitable birds and give loud, strong *chuck, chuck* alarm calls which usually end in an excited screech. In flight, can give a *tsee* call, thinner than that of Redwing. Song is loud and fluty, with a variety of melodic notes, usually delivered from a prominent perch. Feeds on worms, slugs, snails, insects, as well as berries and fallen fruit such as apples.

Habitat and Status   A very familiar, common bird of gardens, towns, farmlands and woodlands. Usually solitary or in pairs. Blackbirds are highly territorial and will engage in noisy disputes with neighbours. Nests in bushes and hedgerows as well as in trees, old walls and out-houses.

Ring Ouzel 23–26cm
Turdus torquatus   Lon creige

A shy, long-winged and more streamlined bird than the Blackbird, with a conspicuous white crescent-shaped patch on the breast. **Males** are black, with silvery edges to the wing feathers, long primaries and a pure white breast patch. The shorter, thicker bill is lemon-yellow in colour. Males also lack the yellow eye-ring of male Blackbird. **Females** are dark blackish-brown and show a duller breast patch and bill. **Immatures** are dark brown and lack the white breast patch, although this can appear as a pale brownish patch on some young males. Best separated from immature Blackbirds by silvery-white edges to the wing feathers, clearly visible even in flight, and by the long primaries.

Voice and Diet   Can give a loud, harsh, hollow, chattering *chak-chak* call. The song is a series of lonely piping notes, often finished with a chatter. Usually sings from a prominent perch. Feeds on worms, slugs, insects, seeds and berries.

Habitat and Status   An uncommon bird of mountainous regions, often found on areas of scree and replacing Blackbird at higher altitudes. Nests in grass on steep, rocky outcrops. A summer visitor from southern Europe and North Africa, usually arriving in early spring and departing throughout the autumn. On migration, occurs in fields and along hedgerows on coastal islands and headlands. In general, a shy, retiring bird.

Blackbird

black plumage, orange-yellow bill and eye-ring

brown with pale throat

Male

Female

Ring Ouzel

Male

lemon-yellow bill

white breast crescent

long wings

Female

Blackbird

Ring Ouzel

189

Thrushes

Fieldfare 24–28cm
Turdus pilaris   Sacán

A large, striking thrush with contrasting upperparts and heavily spotted underparts. Head and nape grey with a thin pale supercilium. Shows a blackish eye-stripe, a dark border to the ear-coverts, and blackish centres to the crown feathers. Mantle chestnut-brown, with brown wings showing dark centres to the tertials and primaries. Rump grey, contrasting strongly with the black tail. Throat white with dark malar stripe and spotting. Breast yellow-buff with very heavy inverted arrowhead spotting, fading onto whitish flanks and belly. Bill pale yellow with a dark tip. Eye and legs blackish. In flight shows a whitish underwing. Usually seen in large, mixed thrush flocks.

Voice and Diet   In flight gives a soft *tsee*, similar to but not as drawn-out as Redwing. Also gives a harsh, chattering *chik-chak-chak* call. Feeds on insects, worms, slugs and berries as well as windfall fruit.

Habitat and Status   A common winter visitor from Scandinavia and northern Europe, arriving in late autumn or early winter and departing in early spring. Found on open fields and open woodlands, moving in large flocks which often include Redwings. During hard weather will visit town gardens to feed on berry bushes. On migration, found along hedgerows and in fields on coastal islands and headlands.

Redwing 20–23cm
Turdus iliacus   Deargán sneachta

A striking, dark brown thrush with a white supercilium, heavy underpart streaking, and a bright red flash on the flanks. Crown and nape dark brown with broad white supercilium and submoustachial stripe. Ear-coverts brown. Mantle, tail and wings uniform dark brown, with **immatures** showing pale tips to greater coverts and tertials. Underparts creamy white, with heavy breast streaking extending onto throat as a malar stripe, and fading onto flanks. The most striking feature is the bright red patch on the flanks. In flight shows a reddish underwing. Eye dark. Legs pale. Bill dark with a yellow base. Usually seen in large, mixed thrush flocks.

Voice and Diet   The call is a soft, long *tseep,* often repeated and which can be heard at night as flocks pass overhead on migration. Can also give a sharp *chich-up* call. Feeds on berries, insects, worms and slugs.

Habitat and Status   A common winter visitor to all counties, arriving in late autumn and departing by early spring. Found in large flocks on open fields or open woodlands. Perches frequently in large flocks along hedgerows and trees. In autumn, lone birds can often be found on coastal islands and headlands. Can also be found alone or in small parties in town gardens feeding on berries. Breeds in northern Europe and Iceland.

Fieldfare

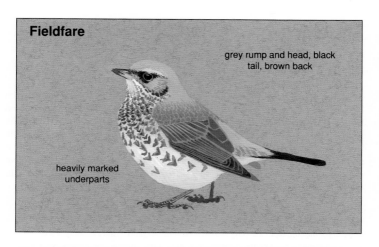

grey rump and head, black tail, brown back

heavily marked underparts

Redwing

striking white supercilium

bright red flank patch

heavily streaked underparts

Fieldfare

Redwing

Thrushes

Song Thrush 22–24cm
Turdus philomelos   Smólach

A small, shy thrush with warm brown upperparts and heavily spotted underparts. The black eye is not conspicuous in the warm yellow-buff face. Ear-coverts spotted and bordered by spots. The spotting on the throat forms a malar stripe. Breast and flanks yellow-buff with arrowhead spotting, heaviest on the breast. Crown, nape and mantle warm brown, with wings and tail the same tone. Therefore, the upperparts appear uniform and lack the contrasts of Mistle Thrush. **Young birds** similar to adults, but show pale spotting on the mantle. In flight shows an orange-red underwing. Bill brownish, with the base of the lower mandible yellow-brown. Legs pale. Rarely seen in flocks.

Voice and Diet   Can give a soft *tsip* call, often heard in flight. When alarmed, gives a sharp *chi-chip-chip* call. The song is loud and wandering, consisting of sharp, melodic notes with each phrase repeated twice. Feeds on worms, slugs, insects and berries. Also feeds on snails by smashing the shells on a favourite stone. Broken snail shells close to such an anvil stone are often a good indication of the presence of a Song Thrush.

Habitat and Status   A common bird found in gardens, parks and woodlands. In recent years, breeding numbers appear to have decreased slightly. In winter, the population increases with the arrival of birds from Scotland and northern England. A shy thrush, preferring areas of dense cover. Nests in trees or hedges and occasionally in old out-houses.

Mistle Thrush 26–29cm
Turdus viscivorus   Liatráisc

A large, pot-bellied thrush with heavy spotting on the underparts, and long wings and tail. Large black eye conspicuous in a rather pale face. Shows a dark ear-covert border and dark spots on a pale throat. Breast and flanks pale buff with heavy, broad, wedge-shaped spotting. Crown, nape and mantle greyish-brown with contrasting wings due to white tips on median and greater coverts and dark centres to the tertials and primaries. Long tail greyish-brown but with diagnostic white tips to the outer-tail feathers. In flight, shows a whitish underwing. **Juveniles** similar, but show pale edges to upperpart feathers. Legs pale. Bill horn-coloured.

Voice and Diet   When alarmed gives a diagnostic rattling *prrr-rr-rr-rr* call which is repeated continuously. This sounds very like the rattles that were once carried by football supporters. The song is quite Blackbird-like, but with the melodic phrases uttered in a faster and sharper tone. Usually sings from a prominent perch. Feeds on insects, worms, fruit and berries. Is also known to take nestlings occasionally.

Habitat and Status   A common resident bird of parks, woodlands, graveyards, towns and mountains. Less shy than Song Thrush, being found on more open ground away from cover. Nests in trees. In late summer and winter, they are highly gregarious, often forming quite large flocks. In hard weather can visit gardens.

Song Thrush

warm brown
upperparts

yellow-buff face

heavily spotted underparts

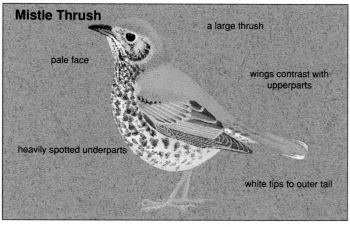

Mistle Thrush

a large thrush

pale face

wings contrast with
upperparts

heavily spotted underparts

white tips to outer tail

Song Thrush

Mistle Thrush

Dipper and Wren

Dipper 17–19cm
Cinclus cinclus   Gabha dubh

A plump, short-tailed species with a striking plumage. Seen along fast-flowing rivers, perching on rocks and bobbing continuously before plunging into the water. **Adults** show a dark brown head, a blackish mantle, wings, rump and tail, and a striking white throat and breast. This white gorget is bordered below by a dull chestnut band which fades into the blackish belly and flanks. Short bill dark. Legs greyish. When perched, flashes a white eyelid when blinking. **Juveniles** show a dark greyish head and upperparts, and a dirty, off-white gorget. Flight fast and direct, usually low over the water. Dippers belong to a specific race (*see* Introduction).

Voice and Diet   Gives a loud, sharp *zit-zit* call, usually in flight. Can also give a hard *klink* note. The song is a mixture of rippling, warbling and grating notes. Feeds by walking along the bottom of a stream or swimming on or below the surface of the water, searching for a variety of aquatic insects. Also takes molluscs, small fish, worms and tadpoles.

Habitat and Status   A scarce but widely distributed resident breeding species present in all counties. Found along fast-flowing streams and rivers, usually in upland regions. Dippers also occur on suitable stretches of water in low-lying areas. Builds a domed nest on walls, ledges, under bridges or among tree roots, always nesting above or close to water. In winter, many birds leave upland regions. Birds of the Continental race have occurred in Ireland in late autumn and winter.

Wren 9–10cm
Troglodytes troglodytes   Dreoilín

A tiny, busy species which shows very short, rounded wings and a stubby cocked tail. **Adults** show a rufous-brown head and a striking pale buff supercilium. Upperparts and short wings rufous-brown with dark barring. Short, cocked, rufous-brown tail also shows thin, dark bars. Underparts pale buff with dark brown barring on the flanks and white spots on the undertail. Thin, pointed dark bill is slightly curved. **Juveniles** similar, but show mottling on the crown and throat, a fainter supercilium, and lack spots on the undertail. A very active bird, constantly on the move, usually in deep cover. Flight is fast and straight, flying with rapid, whirring wing beats.

Voice and Diet   Gives harsh, loud, repeated *tic* calls when alarmed or disturbed. Can also give grating, churring calls. The song consists of harsh, rattling, shrill, warbling notes, followed by a rapid trill. The song is remarkably loud and far-carrying for such a small bird. Feeds on a wide variety of small insects and spiders. Will also take some seeds and can be attracted to bird tables.

Habitat and Status   An extremely common, widespread, resident breeding species present in large numbers in every county. Found in a wide range of habitats, including gardens, parks, hedgerows, farmland, woodlands, reeds, upland scrub and moorlands. Builds a domed nest in ivy, hedgerows, old buildings and broken walls. Small movements noted at some coastal islands are believed to be local birds dispersing in search of food.

Dipper

plump, short-tailed bird

striking white throat
and breast

Wren

barring on rufous
upperparts and flanks

thin pointed bill

small size, short tail

Dipper

Wren

Treecreeper and Warblers

Treecreeper 12–14cm
Certhia familiaris   Snag

A small, brown and white bird which moves up trees in a mouse-like, spiralling fashion. **Adults** show a thin, down-curved bill, a whitish supercilium, and streaked brownish crown and cheeks. Throat, breast, belly and undertail white with pale buff flanks. Mantle and wings show a complicated pattern of brown with pale buff and dark streaking and pale wingbars. Rump rufous-brown. Tail brown with stiff, pointed feathers which are pressed against the tree trunk for support. **Immatures** show brown flecks on breast and flanks, duller white underparts and colder brown upperparts. Climbs up trees in a jerky manner before dropping down to the base of another to begin again. Usually solitary.

Voice and Diet   Gives a thin, high-pitched *tzeu* call and a softer *tset*. Song almost Goldcrest-like, consisting of *tzee-tzee-tzee-tsizzi-tzee,* starting slowly but accelerating towards the finish. Feeds on a wide variety of insects which are caught with the thin bill.

Habitat and Status   A common resident species found in all counties, although not common in some parts of south-western, western and north-western counties. Found in deciduous and coniferous woodlands, parks and gardens. Tends to feed on trees with gnarled bark. Nests behind bark, in ivy or in crevices in trees.

Reed Warbler 12–13cm
Acrocephalus scirpaceus   Ceolaire giolcaí

A plain, warm brown warbler with short wings and a rounded tail. **Adults** show a warm brown head, a faint supercilium and brownish cheeks. Upperparts and wings warm brown, with short, plain primaries appearing bunched. Rump shows rufous tones. Rounded tail warm brown. Throat and underparts white with warm buff on sides of breast and flanks. This can make the throat appear conspicuously white. Undertail clean white. **Immatures** almost identical, but show a stronger rufous tone on the rump. Long, slender bill pinkish-yellow with a darker upper edge. Legs brownish-grey with yellowish feet. Eye dark and obvious in a plain face. Moves up reeds in a jerky manner. Flight low and undulating.

Voice and Diet   Gives a short, harsh, low *tchurr*. Song is distinctive, slower than that of Sedge Warbler, delivered in a lower pitch, and containing the repeated phrases of *jac-jac-jac, cerr-cerr-cerr,* interspersed with more liquid notes. Feeds on a variety of aquatic insects, slugs, worms and molluscs. Will feed on berries in the autumn.

Habitat and Status   Formerly a rare autumn vagrant to Ireland, in recent years Reed Warblers have become an established breeding species, with the main populations based in eastern and southern counties. In some areas, good numbers are present each summer and it seems likely that this colonisation will continue. Found in reed-beds, sedges and vegetation close to water. Nests in reeds and occasionally in hedges or bushes. On passage, can be found along hedgerows or in gardens on coastal headlands and islands.

Treecreeper

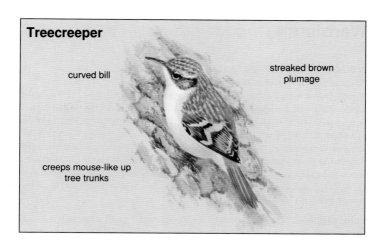

curved bill

streaked brown plumage

creeps mouse-like up tree trunks

Reed Warbler

plain, warm-brown warbler

long, pointed bill

Treecreeper

Reed Warbler

Warblers

Sedge Warbler 12–13cm
Acrocephalus schoenobaenus   Ceolaire cíbe

A pale brown warbler with streaked upperparts and a creamy-white supercilium. Adults show pale brown upperparts with dark streaking, heaviest on the crown. A broad, creamy-white supercilium is bordered by a dark lateral crown-stripe and a dark eye-stripe. Cheeks brownish. Clean underparts creamy, with a yellow-buff wash on sides of breast and flanks. Wings long with pale edges to dark-centred feathers. Unstreaked rump warm buff, contrasting with upperparts in flight. Tail feathers pale brown and rounded. **Immatures** similar, but show buffier plumage, a pale buff central crown-stripe and spotting on breast. Pointed bill dark with a paler base. Gape bright orange-red. Legs brownish.

Voice and Diet   Gives short, loud *tuc* and *chirr* calls. Song is a loud, fast sequence of harsh, grating, chattering notes mixed with musical and trilling notes. Can sing from dense cover or perched prominently on top of reeds or sedges. Will also engage in short, singing, display flights. Feeds on a variety of insects, worms and spiders. Will also take berries.

Habitat and Status   A common summer visitor present in suitable areas in all counties. Also breeds on some coastal islands with dense cover. Found in a wide range of habitats, including reed-beds, marshes, hedgerows and bushes close to ditches or wetlands, and dense vegetation near water. Nests in reeds, sedges or bushes above shallow water. On passage, can be found along hedgerows or in gardens on coastal headlands and islands.

Grasshopper Warbler 12–13cm
Locustella naevia   Ceolaire casarnaí

A shy, heavily streaked, olive-brown warbler. **Adults** and **immatures** similar, showing olive-brown upperparts with heavy streaking on the crown, mantle and rump, a faint supercilium and brownish cheeks. Wings show dark centres to feathers and short, curved primaries. Rounded tail can be held cocked. Underparts buffish-white with a whitish throat and yellow-buff sides to breast and flanks. Breast and flanks can show thin streaking. Undertail-coverts can also show dark streaking. Legs pale pink or orange. Pointed bill shows a dark upper and a pinkish lower mandible. A skulking species that moves carefully through dense vegetation.

Voice and Diet   The distinctive song is a far-carrying, single, reeling note which may recall the winding of an angler's reel. The song can also have a ventriloquial effect when the bird turns its head. The song can be given for lengthy periods, either day or night. Also gives a short, sharp *twhick* call. Feeds on a variety of insects and spiders.

Habitat and Status   A common breeding species found in suitable habitats in all counties. Frequents areas of marshland with scattered trees and bushes, moorlands with bushes and gorse, neglected hedgerows, and rough pastureland with long grass. Also found in young conifer plantations. A skulking species. Nests on or just above the ground in grass tussocks or undergrowth. On passage, found on coastal headlands and islands.

198

Sedge Warbler

striking white
supercilium

dark lores

thin, pale central
crown-stripe

Adult

Immature

Grasshopper Warbler

heavily streaked upperparts
and crown

very skulking

rounded tail

Sedge Warbler

Grasshopper Warbler

Warblers

Blackcap 13–15cm
Sylvia atricapilla   Caipín dubh

A very striking warbler with a distinctive black or chestnut crown, a longish tail and a thin, long bill. **Adult males** show a glossy black cap extending down to eye level, greyish cheeks, nape and mantle, and brownish-grey wings. Rump and tail greyish. Throat, neck and breast pale grey, with flanks and belly showing a greyish wash. Undertail whitish. **Adult females** are more greyish-brown on the upper and underparts and show a bright chestnut cap. **Immature males** show brownish tones on cap, while **immature females** appear more yellow-brown on crown. Black eye shows a thin, whitish orbital ring. Bill black. Moves in a slow, deliberate manner. Can be skulking on occasions.

Voice and Diet   When alarmed, gives a hard, often repeated *tacc* call and also harsh, churring calls. Song is shorter than the similar Garden Warbler, containing a rich variety of melodic, soft, clear warbling notes. Song occasionally starts with squeaky or scratchy notes. Sings from deep in cover. Feeds on a wide range of insects in summer, taking berries in autumn and winter. Will also visit gardens to feed on windfall apples.

Habitat and Status   An uncommon local breeding species found in most counties. A regular passage migrant seen on coastal headlands and islands in spring and autumn. Small numbers also winter in Ireland and these are believed to be late autumn arrivals from northern and eastern Europe. Frequents mixed woodland with rich undergrowth. Also found along hedgerows and gardens. Nests in hedges and brambles.

Garden Warbler 13–15cm
Sylvia borin   Ceolaire garraí

A stocky, rounded, featureless warbler with a thick, greyish bill and grey legs. **Adults** show an olive-brown head with a faint, pale supercilium, a thin eye-ring, and a greyish area on the side of neck. A large, round eye is very conspicuous in a plain face, giving a gentle expression. Mantle, rump and wings plain olive-brown, with slightly darker centres to tertials. Short, olive-brown tail is unmarked. Throat creamy-white, with breast and flanks showing a buffish-grey wash. Belly and undertail whitish. **Immatures** show warmer olive-brown upperparts and buffish flanks. Can be skulking. Moves in a slow, deliberate manner, occasionally with drooped wings.

Voice and Diet   Gives a short, hard *tchack* call and a quick, repeated *churr* call when disturbed or alarmed. Song is a prolonged, soft, even, melodic warbling similar to that of Blackcap. Usually sings from deep cover. Feeds on a wide variety of insects and takes berries in autumn.

Habitat and Status   An uncommon breeding species, with the main populations based in midland and some northern counties. Also breeds in very small numbers in other regions. A regular passage migrant, more numerous in autumn than spring. Found in woodland with dense undergrowth. Nests in low brambles and bushes. On passage, found along hedgerows and in gardens on coastal headlands and islands.

Blackcap

black cap

chestnut cap

Female

Male

Garden Warbler

grey on side of neck

plain face

Blackcap

Garden Warbler

Warblers

Whitethroat 13–15cm
Sylvia communis   Gilphíb

A large, slim, long-tailed warbler with pinkish legs. **Adult males** show a grey crown, ear-coverts and nape, a brownish mantle and brownish wings with bright, conspicuous, rufous edges to secondaries and tertials. Rump brown. Long tail grey-brown with narrow, striking, white outer-tail feathers. White throat contrasts with greyish-white underparts which can show a pinkish-buff wash on breast and flanks. **Adult females** and **immatures** similar, but show brownish heads, with immatures also showing buff-white edges to tail. Eyes pale and show a broken, narrow, white orbital ring. Bill greyish. Can perch prominently but can also be very skulking.

Voice and Diet   Gives a loud, harsh *tcak* call when disturbed or alarmed. Can also give a hoarse *tchar* call and quiet *whet, whet, whit-whit-whit* calls. Song consists of short, rapid, scratchy, warbling notes given from a prominent perch or during a dancing, aerial display flight. Feeds on a wide variety of insects. Will also feed on berries in autumn.

Habitat and Status   A widespread summer visitor and passage migrant. Whitethroat numbers took a drastic decline in the late 1960s. Since then, populations have increased but have not reached their former numbers. Found in open areas with hedges and scrub. Often found on woodland edges but never in woods or forests. On migration, found along hedgerows and in gardens on coastal headlands and islands. Nests low in dense cover.

Lesser Whitethroat 13–14cm
Sylvia curruca   Gilphíb bheag

A smart, compact, short-tailed warbler with steel-grey legs. **Adults** show a grey forehead, crown and nape, and darker lores and ear-coverts which can appear as a dark mask. Upperparts dark greyish-brown, the wing feathers lacking rufous edges. Rump grey. Short tail greyish-brown with white outer-tail feathers. Throat white, with underparts greyish-white, occasionally showing a pinkish-buff wash on breast and flanks. In autumn, adults can appear paler grey on the upperparts. Dark eye shows no orbital ring. **Immatures** show greyish-brown heads, creamy white throats and buffish tones on breast and flanks. Tail also shows off-white outer-tail feathers. Short, dark greyish bill.

Voice and Diet   Gives a loud, abrupt, harsh *tcack* call when disturbed or alarmed. Can also give a *charr* call. Rarely heard singing in Ireland. Song consists of soft warbling notes followed by a fast, far-carrying, single-note rattle. Feeds on a wide variety of insects, taking berries in autumn.

Habitat and Status   An extremely rare breeding species, but a regular spring and autumn passage migrant from Europe. Breeding has taken place on several occasions in the south-east. Frequents areas of dense vegetation with brambles, bushes and small trees. On passage, found along hedgerows and in gardens on coastal headlands and islands. Nests in dense hedges and bushes.

Whitethroat

striking white throat

rufous on wings

Male

Female

Lesser Whitethroat

Female

white throat

Male (summer)

dark cheeks, greyish-brown upperparts

Whitethroat

Lesser Whitethroat

Warblers

Chiffchaff 10–12cm
Phylloscopus collybita   Tiuf-teaf

A small, active warbler, very similar to Willow Warbler but showing dark legs and a thin, dark, pointed bill with very little orange on the base. Short wings give Chiffchaff a rotund appearance. When feeding, constantly flicks the tail. **Spring adults** show dull, olive-green upperparts, a short, yellowish supercilium, and a dark eye-stripe with pale crescents obvious above and below the eye. Plain wings show blackish alula. Underparts olive-yellow and can show buffish tones. In **autumn** shows olive-green upperparts and buffish underparts. Chiffchaffs of the **Siberian race**, *tristis*, show beige upperparts, whitish underparts, a pale supercilium and can show a short, pale wingbar.

Voice and Diet   The song is diagnostic, consisting of repeated *chiff-chaff* notes. The song can sometimes vary and the same phrase can be repeated. The song usually commences with wheezing-type noises. Also gives a sharp, short *hweet* call, similar to the call of Willow Warbler. Feeds on small insects and spiders which are picked quickly from foliage.

Habitat and Status   A very common passage and summer visitor, present in all counties. Small numbers occur each winter. Found in open woodland with undergrowth and a mixture of trees and mature hedgerows, brambles and scrub. Nests in deep cover above the ground. On passage, found along hedgerows, gardens and reeds at coastal locations. The Siberian race, *tristis*, is a rare late autumn vagrant to coastal headlands and islands.

Willow Warbler 10–12cm
Phylloscopus trochilus   Ceolaire sailí

A small, busy warbler, very similar to Chiffchaff but showing pale legs and a pale orangy base to a thin, dark, pointed bill. Long wings give Willow Warbler an attenuated, slim appearance. **Spring adults** show pale green upperparts, a well-defined, yellowish supercilium, a strong eye-stripe and blotchy ear-coverts. Pale panel obvious on the closed wing. Green tail shows a shallow fork. Underparts show a bright yellow wash on the throat and breast and a clean whitish belly and undertail. In **autumn** shows green upperparts and a lemon-yellow supercilium and underparts. Unlike Chiffchaff, does not flick the tail when feeding. In flight, appears long-winged and flycatcher-like.

Voice and Diet   The song is distinctive, consisting of thin, pleasant, liquid notes which are delivered softly at first, but which grow louder before the notes descend and fade away. The song is usually finished by a fast *tswee* note. Also gives a loud *hoo-eet* call. Feeds on a wide range of small insects and spiders which are quickly picked off foliage. Will also engage in fly-catching, chasing insects in flight. Occasionally eats berries in the autumn.

Habitat and Status   An extremely common passage and summer visitor found in all counties. Arrives in early spring. Unlike Chiffchaff, never found in winter. Frequents a wide range of habitats, including woodlands, hedgerows, copses and any areas with bushes and scrub. Builds a domed nest in good cover on or near the ground. On passage, found in gardens and hedgerows on islands, headlands and coastal stretches.

Chiffchaff

short wings

pale wingbar

dark legs

Tristis Chiffchaff (rare)

Willow Warbler

long wings

pale legs

Chiffchaff

Willow Warbler

Warblers

Wood Warbler 12–13cm
Phylloscopus sibilatrix   Ceolaire coille

A very striking, brightly coloured warbler, larger and more slender and attenuated in appearance than Willow Warbler. Upperparts very bright green, with very long wings showing conspicuous green edges to dark-centred feathers. Green crown and dark eye-stripe both contrast with the striking bright yellow supercilium, ear-coverts and throat. Rump and tail bright green. Underparts are frosty, silky white and contrast strongly with the bright yellow throat. The yellow of the throat fades into the white of the upper breast but can appear very clear-cut. Legs pale. Bill shows a pale, orangy base. When feeding, does not flick the tail but can droop the long wings.

Voice and Diet   The song is distinctive, consisting of repeated *tseep-tseep* notes which are then followed by a fast, shivering trill. On occasions the song only comprises of the trill. The song can be given during gliding display flights. Also gives a plaintive *tseu* call. Feeds on a wide variety of small insects and spiders. Will occasionally eat berries in the autumn.

Habitat and Status   A rare breeding species found in very small numbers in eastern, northern, western and south-western counties. Has also been reported summering in midland counties. Most summer records refer to birds in song with breeding not always proved. Found in areas of oak woodland and mature deciduous forests, building a domed nest in cover on the ground. Occasionally found on passage, feeding in gardens and trees on coastal headlands and islands.

Yellow-browed Warbler 10–11cm
Phylloscopus inornatus

A small, bright, busy warbler. Most records refer to **1st year birds** which show a bright olive-green crown, nape and upperparts, and greyish-white underparts which can show a faint yellowish wash along the flanks. Pale greenish ear-coverts show faint blotches. A bright creamy-yellow supercilium appears upcurved behind the eye and contrasts with a dark eye-stripe. Darker wings show two creamy-yellow wingbars on the greater and median coverts, and pale yellowish edges to dark tertials. Rump and short tail olive-green. Legs pale. Thin, pale bill shows a dark tip.

Voice and Diet   Yellow-browed Warblers tend to call frequently, giving a strong, sharp, loud *chue-eep* call, with the second phrase higher pitched. Feeds in a busy, active manner, taking a wide variety of small insects and spiders. Can also catch insects on the wing.

Habitat and Status   A rare but regular late autumn vagrant from northern Siberia. Usually found along hedgerows or in well-vegetated gardens on coastal headlands and islands. Most records refer to south-western regions, although recorded along all coastal regions.

Wood Warbler

yellow throat and face

long wings

pale legs

bright edges to wing
feathers

Yellow-browed Warbler

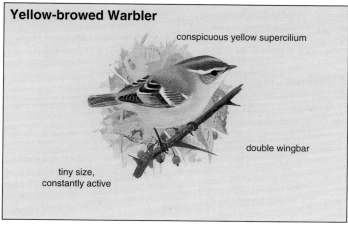

conspicuous yellow supercilium

double wingbar

tiny size,
constantly active

Wood Warbler

Yellow-browed Warbler

Warblers

Icterine Warbler 13–14cm
Hippolais icterina   Ceolaire ictireach

A sturdy, slim, long-winged warbler similar to Melodious Warbler. Shows a long, sloping forehead and a plain-faced appearance. Lacks any dark stripe between the eye and bill. Shows a very faint supercilium. In **autumn** shows a pale, greyish-green head and upperparts. Unlike Melodious, pale edges to the tertials create a panel on the closed wing, while the primary projection is about equal to the length of the tertials. Tail square-ended. Underparts creamy, with a pale yellow wash on the chin and throat. Long, wide, orange bill shows a dark culmen. Legs bluish-grey. **Spring adults** show brighter upperparts and yellowish underparts. Feeds in an active, lively manner.

Voice and Diet   Although usually silent on migration, Icterine Warblers can occasionally give a brief, hard *teck* call, not unlike that of a Sylvia warbler. Feeds on a wide variety of insects and larvae. Will also feed on ripe fruit and berries.

Habitat and Status   A rare passage migrant from northern and eastern Europe. Recorded on an almost annual basis, with most records referring to autumn. Smaller numbers have been recorded in spring, while one bird was present in Co. Dublin in November 1982. Most reports originate in southern counties where birds are seen in gardens and hedgerows on coastal headlands and islands.

Melodious Warbler 12–13cm
Hippolais polyglotta

A rounded, short-winged warbler similar to Icterine Warbler. Like Icterine, appears plain-faced, lacking any dark stripe between the eye and bill, and showing a faint supercilium. However, head shape appears more rounded. **In autumn**, head and upperparts olive-green. Wings appear plain, lacking the pale wing panel of Icterine. Primary projection short, being about half the length of the tertials with the primaries appearing bunched. Tail square-ended. Underparts yellowish, brightest on the throat and upper breast. Long, wide, orange bill shows a dark culmen. Legs brownish. **Spring adults** show brighter upperparts and yellower underparts. Feeds in a slow, methodical manner.

Voice and Diet   Like Icterine, Melodious Warblers are usually silent on migration, but can occasionally give a brief, House Sparrow-like chattering call. Feeds on a wide variety of insects and larvae. Like Icterine, can occasionally feed on ripe fruit and berries.

Habitat and Status   A rare passage migrant from southern and south-western Europe. Recorded almost annually, Melodious Warblers tend to be more scarce than Icterine Warblers. Most records refer to autumn, with smaller numbers in spring. Also tends to occur earlier in autumn than Icterine. Most reports originate in southern counties where birds are seen in gardens and hedgerows on coastal headlands and islands. Tends to be more skulking than Icterine. Could be overlooked in dense cover.

Icterine Warbler

pale wing panel,
long primary projection

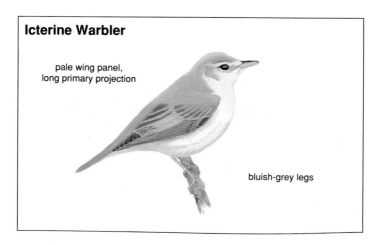

bluish-grey legs

Melodious Warbler

no pale wing panel,
short primary projection

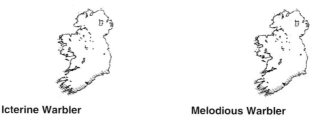

Icterine Warbler   Melodious Warbler

Crests

Goldcrest 8–9cm
Regulus regulus   Cíorbhuí

This tiny, active bird is Ireland's smallest species. **Males** show a black-edged, orange-yellow crown, and a dull greenish nape and upperparts. Wings show two white bars, white edges to the tertials and a dark wing panel. A large pale area around the dark eye gives the face a plain, open expression. The rump and short, forked tail are dull greenish. Underparts dull whitish, occasionally showing a greenish wash across the breast or along flanks. **Females** similar, but show a pure yellow, black-edged crown. **Juveniles** appear brownish on the head, lacking the yellow crown, and showing darkish crown edges. Small, thin, pointed bill dark. Legs dark.

Voice and Diet   Gives soft, high-pitched repeated *zii* calls. The song is also very soft and high-pitched, consisting of repeated *ziida-ziida* notes, and ending in a short twitter. Feeds in a busy, active manner, taking a wide variety of spiders and small insects.

Habitat and Status   A common breeding species found in all counties. In autumn and spring, occurs as a passage migrant on coastal headlands and islands. In winter, numbers may increase with the arrival of birds from Britain and northern Europe. Found in a variety of habitats, including deciduous and coniferous woodland, and in gardens with good vegetation. Nests under thick cover in conifers, or occasionally in ivy.

Firecrest 8–9cm
Regulus ignicapillus   Lasairchíor

A tiny, busy species, similar to Goldcrest but showing a striking head pattern and a very bright plumage. Like Goldcrest, **males** show a black-edged, orange-yellow crown but differ by showing a broad white supercilium and a dark eye-stripe. The ear-coverts are greenish and highlight a small, pale crescent below the dark eye. The upperparts appear bright green with distinctive bronzy patches on the shoulders. The wings show two narrow white wingbars. Rump and short forked tail. Underparts whitish, appearing cleaner than on Goldcrest. **Females** similar, but show a yellowish crown. Small, thin, pointed bill dark. Legs dark.

Voice and Diet   Gives a repeated *zit* call, which, although similar to Goldcrest, is lower-pitched and delivered in a quieter, less persistent manner. Feeds actively, taking a wide range of small insects and spiders.

Habitat and Status   A scarce but regular passage migrant, occurring almost annually. Most records refer to birds seen in autumn, with small numbers occurring in spring. There are also several winter records. On passage, found in gardens and trees on coastal headlands and islands, with most records referring to regions along the southern coastline.

Goldcrest

plain face

males show
orange on crown

yellow crown-stripe

Male

Female

tiny size,
very active

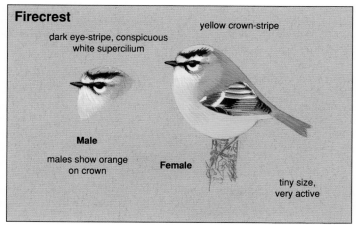

Firecrest

dark eye-stripe, conspicuous
white supercilium

yellow crown-stripe

Male

males show orange
on crown

Female

tiny size,
very active

Goldcrest   **Firecrest**

Flycatchers

Spotted Flycatcher 13–15cm
Muscicapa striata   Cuilire liath

An upright, rather drab bird, usually seen chasing insects in mid-air, hovering and twisting before returning to an open perch. Plain grey-brown upperparts show dark streaking confined to the steep forehead. Wings show pale edges to the tertials, greater coverts and long primaries. A habit of dropping and repeatedly flicking the wings exposes the grey-brown tail. The tail, which can be wagged slowly, does not show white edges or basal patches. Greyish-white underparts show brown streaking on the breast and diffuse streaking on the pale throat. Sexes alike. Long, pointed, thick black bill can sometimes be heard to snap when fly-catching. Legs dark.

Voice and Diet   Call is a soft, scratchy *tsee* or *tsee-tuc.* The song is short, containing thin, scratchy *tsip-tsic* notes repeated at intervals. Song is delivered from a perch. As the name suggests, feeds on all forms of insects, usually caught on the wing.

Habitat and Status   A bird of open wooded areas including parks and gardens. Prefers areas with open ground where fly-caching flights can be made easily. A widespread summer visitor, Spotted Flycatcher is usually one of the last migrants to arrive. Nests in holes of trees, in walls, buildings or creeping plants such as ivy.

Pied Flycatcher 12–13cm
Ficedula hypoleuca   Cuilire alabhreac

Behaves in a manner very similar to Spotted Flycatcher, but appears smaller and more rotund. **Summer plumage males** show a black head with a small white forehead patch, bold white patches on black wings, and white edges to a black tail. Underparts white. **Females** show grey-brown upperparts, white wing patches, blackish tails with white edges and whitish underparts. **Autumn males** similar to females, but retain the white forehead patch. **Immatures** similar to females, but show a thin pale wingbar on the median coverts, and usually lack a whitish primary base patch. Holds the wings drooped and flicks the wings and tail often. Shows a thin, pointed black bill and dark legs.

Voice and Diet   Call is a sharp *whiit* or, on occasions, a shorter *tik.* These calls can often be combined to give a *whit-tik.* The song can often be confused with Redstart and consists of strong, repeated *zee-iit* notes, often mingled with more scratchy, liquid notes. Feeds on insects, usually caught on the wing.

Habitat and Status   An extremely rare Irish breeding bird of deciduous woodlands. Nests are built in holes of trees and walls. Will also use nest boxes. A regular passage migrant with most records referring to autumn. On passage, found in gardens and along hedgerows on coastal headlands and islands.

Spotted Flycatcher

streaked crown and underparts

upright stance

Pied Flycatcher

white patches on wings, whitish underparts

striking black and white plumage

Female/Immature

Male

Spotted Flycatcher

Pied Flycatcher

Tits

Blue Tit 11–12cm
Parus caeruleus   Meantán gorm

An active, cheeky, colourful bird with a short, stubby, black bill and dark legs. **Adults** show a pale blue crown, with a white lower border and cheeks contrasting with a black bib and eye-stripe. Dark blue collar and nape highlight a white nape spot. Underparts bright yellow, with a dark mark down the centre of the belly. Upperparts green, with one white wingbar on bright blue wings. Rump green. Short, forked tail blue. **Juveniles** show a greenish-brown crown and hindneck, yellowish cheeks, crown border and nape patch, a diffuse black bib, more olive-green upperparts, and greenish-blue wings and tail. An extremely acrobatic species when feeding.

Voice and Diet   Gives a wide range of calls, including a rapid *tzee-tzee-tzee-tzit* and harsh churring notes. The song begins with two or three *tzee* notes which are followed by a fast, liquid trill. Feeds on a wide variety of insects, spiders, fruit, seeds, berries and grain. A common visitor to garden feeders.

Habitat and Status   An extremely common and widespread resident breeding species found in all counties. Frequents deciduous woodlands, parks, gardens, hedgerows and ditches. Nests in holes in trees or walls and will frequently use nest boxes if available. In winter, extremely common in suburban gardens. Also found in areas of reeds in winter. Occasionally associates with other tit species to form large roving parties.

Great Tit 13–15cm
Parus major   Meantán mór

A large, striking, handsome tit with a dark, pointed bill and dark greyish legs. **Adult males** show a shining blackish-blue head and throat with white cheeks and a pale yellowish nape spot. Bright yellow underparts show a black central band from the throat onto the whitish undertail-coverts. Band thickest on centre of belly. Upperparts olive-green, with bluish-grey wings showing a white wingbar and obvious white edges to the tertials. Forked, bluish-grey tail shows distinctive white outer edges. **Adult females** similar, but show a narrower band on the underparts. **Juveniles** appear duller overall, with yellowish cheeks and brownish tones to upperparts.

Voice and Diet   Gives a very large range of calls which have a metallic quality, usually louder than those of other tits. Calls include a Chaffinch-like *tzink,* a fast, repeated, short *tui,* thin, high-pitched *tzee-tzee-tzee* and harsh churring notes. Song repeated, loud *teecho-teecho* notes, similar to Coal Tit. Feeds on a variety of insects, worms, fruit, seeds and berries. A common winter visitor to nut-feeders. Occasionally kills young birds.

Habitat and Status   An extremely common and widespread resident breeding species found in all counties. Frequents orchards, deciduous woodlands, parks, gardens and hedgerows. Nests in holes in trees and, less frequently, in walls. Will frequently use nest boxes. In winter, extremely common in suburban gardens, feeding at nut- and seed-feeders. Occasionally associates with other tit species to form large roving parties.

Blue Tit

striking facial pattern
and blue crown

bright yellow underparts

Great Tit

white cheeks

males show broad black band
down centre of yellow underparts,
narrower on females

females duller

Female

Male

Blue Tit

Great Tit

Tits

Coal Tit 10–12cm
Parus ater   Meantán dubh

A small, active bird, appearing quite large-headed and short-tailed. **Adults** show a black head and chin contrasting with striking yellowish-white cheeks and nape patch. Underparts yellowish-white with buff tones on flanks. Upperparts greyish olive-buff with slightly darker wings showing two whitish wingbars. Rump olive-buff. Forked tail dark buff-grey. Small, stubby bill blackish. Legs dark. **Juveniles** show browner upperparts, sooty-black head and chin, and yellower cheeks, nape patch and underparts. Ireland has a specific race of Coal Tit (*see* Introduction). Those of the **British race** show whiter cheeks and underparts, and more olive-grey upperparts.

Voice and Diet   Gives a variety of calls, including a high-pitched, piping *tsuu* and a thin *tzee-tzee-tzee* call which is not unlike that of Goldcrest. The song is a repeated *teecho-teecho-teecho* which is similar to but sweeter and more piping than that of Great Tit. Feeds on insects, spiders and seeds. In winter, a common visitor to suburban gardens, feeding on seed and nut-feeders. Will also eat fat and, on occasions, meat.

Habitat and Status   An extremely common and widespread resident breeding species found in all counties. Frequents coniferous and deciduous woodlands, parks and gardens. Nests in holes close to the ground, using old tree stumps, walls and rocks. Will also nest in banks or in actual holes in the ground. In winter, a common visitor to garden feeding stations. The British race occurs widely. Continental race very rare.

Long-tailed Tit 13–15cm
Aegithalos caudatus   Meantán earrfhada

A tiny, active bird with a small black bill, a rounded, fluffed-up body, and an extremely long tail. **Adults** show a white head with a black stripe from above eye onto sides of neck and meeting black mantle. Throat and breast whitish, with belly, flanks and undertail showing a pinkish wash. Pinkish scapulars contrast with mantle. Wings dark, showing striking white edges. Rump dark. The long, graduated tail is black with white outer edges. **Immatures** show dark cheeks, a shorter tail, browner upperparts with whitish scapulars, and whitish underparts showing very little pink. Flight appears weak and undulating, with long tail conspicuous. A busy, gregarious, active bird, constantly on the move.

Voice and Diet   Gives a variety of calls including a distinctive, low *tsupp,* a trilling *tsrrup* and a repeated *tsee-tsee-tsee* call. Song is seldom heard and consists of a mixture of call notes. Feeds in an acrobatic manner, taking small insects and spiders.

Habitat and Status   A common resident species present in all counties. Found in woodlands and woodland edges, hedgerows, parklands and gardens. In winter, can often associate with other tit species, forming large, roving flocks on occasions. Prolonged hard winter weather can sometimes reduce populations. Nests in thorny bushes or high in trees, building an oval, mossy nest.

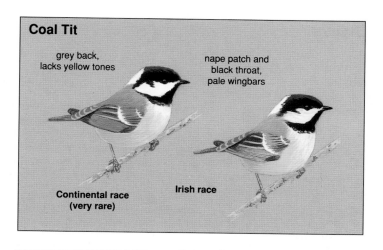

Coal Tit

grey back,
lacks yellow tones

nape patch and
black throat,
pale wingbars

**Continental race
(very rare)**

Irish race

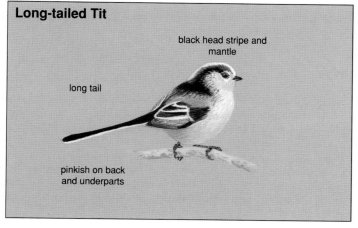

Long-tailed Tit

black head stripe and
mantle

long tail

pinkish on back
and underparts

Coal Tit

Long-tailed Tit

Crows

Raven 60–68cm
Corvus corax   Fiach dubh

The largest member of the crow family, Ravens are strong, powerful birds with a deep, heavy, dark bill and shaggy throat feathers. The plumage is completely glossy black with a purple or green sheen. In flight, the long wings have obvious primary fingers. The thick bill, along with the shaggy throat, give a large-headed profile in flight, while the diagnostic long, wedge-shaped tail is easy to see. Overall, the flight is strong and powerful, with the birds often performing acrobatic tumbles in the air. When soaring, can look like large raptors. Usually seen alone, in pairs or in small family parties. Rarely associates with other crow species.

Voice and Diet   Gives a very distinctive deep, loud, honking *prruc-pruc* call which can carry great distances. Also gives a variety of softer, quieter, croaking calls. Feeds on carrion of all kinds, but will kill weak or injured small mammals and birds. Also feeds on eggs, slugs, worms, insects and occasionally on grain.

Habitat and Status   A common resident bird of mountain glens and coastal cliffs. Nests are built on cliff outcrops or in trees, with some pairs nesting as early as January or February. A carrion eater, Ravens often suffer as a result of taking poisoned bait.

Rook 43–47cm
Corvus frugilegus   Rúcach

A common, scraggy-looking crow with a long, pointed grey bill and a whitish face patch. Forehead steep and, despite the rounded crown, often appears flat-headed. Plumage completely black with a purple sheen. Along with the grey bill and whitish face patch which extends from base of bill to chin and throat, one of the most diagnostic features is the shaggy feathers which cover the upper legs. This creates a baggy-trousers effect and is particularly useful when separating **immature** birds, which lack the pale bill and face patch, from Carrion Crows. In flight, has narrow wings, primary fingers and a long, slightly rounded tail. Moves in large flocks, often with Jackdaws.

Voice and Diet   A very noisy species, especially when roosting at dusk. Gives a sharp, grumpy *kaarg* call which is repeated continuously, often with a whole flock calling at once. Feeds on many items, including root crops, berries, insects, worms and slugs.

Habitat and Status   An extremely common resident bird found on farmland, parks, towns and cities. Feeds in large, often mixed flocks on open land. In recent years, Rooks have tended to feed on roadsides and have learned some road sense, often casually hopping out of the way of traffic. However, many are killed on the roads, although these may be young, inexperienced birds. Nests in the very tops of trees in large colonies called rookeries.

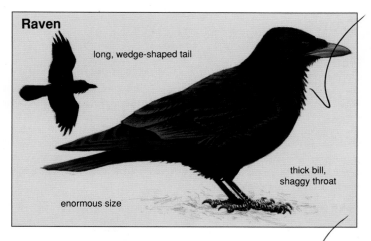

Raven

long, wedge-shaped tail

thick bill, shaggy throat

enormous size

Rook

pale grey bill, whitish face patch, all black plumage

Adult

Immature

darker bill, no face patch

shaggy leg feathers

Raven

Rook

Crows

Hooded Crow 45–50cm
Corvus corone   Feannóg

An unmistakable grey and black crow with a dark, thick-set, blunt bill. Black head, breast, wings and tail contrast strongly with the grey mantle and underparts. Lacks the baggy-trousers appearance of Rook. In flight, shows black rounded wings with primary fingers and a short, black, square tail. **Immatures** are duller grey, often with mantle markings, and with brownish wings and tails. Usually solitary, but can occur in small parties, often with Rooks and Jackdaws. **Carrion Crows**, the all-black race, occur on occasions from Britain and Europe and can be separated from immature Rooks by the blunt, thicker bill and tidier leg feathers.

Voice and Diet   Gives a loud, harsh *kaaw,* flatter in tone than Rook. Will also give a honking nasal-type *kraa* call. Takes a wide variety of food, including carrion, small birds and mammals, eggs, insects and grain. Along the coast can occasionally be seen to drop molluscs onto hard surfaces in an attempt to crack open the shells.

Habitat and Status   A common resident bird found in a wide variety of habitats, including woodland, farmland, towns, parks, coastal areas and mountains. Nests in trees, on cliffs or in old buildings. The Carrion Crow can occur at any time of the year, although most records refer to autumn and winter. When found in Ireland, Carrion Crows are usually seen in coastal locations.

Jackdaw 32–35cm
Corvus monedula   Cág

A cheeky, small, compact crow with a glossy black plumage. Nape pale ash-grey, which creates a black-capped appearance. Upper and underparts glossy black. Bill dark and pointed, considerably shorter than in other crow species. Legs dark. Eye is a whitish-grey with a dark pupil, this being a diagnostic feature. **Immatures** lack the pale grey nape and show darker eyes. In flight, has pointed wings and a short tail. Flight appears easy and buoyant, with fast wing beats interspersed with glides. On the ground, hops cheekily and is highly inquisitive. A gregarious species, Jackdaws are usually found in large flocks, often associating with Rooks.

Voice and Diet   A commonly heard bird which gives a characteristic *jak-jak* call, often repeated. Will also frequently give a *kee-yaw,* which is flatter and shorter than the similar calls of Chough. Feeds on a wide variety of food, including slugs, insects and their larvae, as well as berries and fruit. Also known to steal eggs and nestlings.

Habitat and Status   An abundant resident bird found in woodlands, parks, towns, cities, farmland and quarries. Nests in holes in trees, cliffs or occasionally on chimney pots. Often seen on open land in large flocks.

Hooded Crow

grey and black plumage

Carrion Crow
all black plumage,
lacks shaggy leg feathers

Hooded Crow

Jackdaw

pale grey nape

neat, triangular
bill, pale eye

blackish plumage

Hooded Crow

Jackdaw

Crows

Chough 36–42cm
Pyrrhocorax pyrrhocorax   Cág cosdearg

An absolute acrobat of the air, this Jackdaw-sized glossy black crow is easily identified by the long, thin, curved red bill, red legs and the distinctive *chauuh* call. **Immatures** show a pale orange bill and paler legs. The long, pointed bill is used for probing and can sometimes appear stained as a result. A shy bird, usually seen in small parties. In flight, the wings appear rounded with long primary fingers. The tail is slightly rounded. Choughs seem to enjoy themselves in flight, with easy, buoyant wing beats interspersed with swoops on closed wings. On the ground, walks or hops in a sideways manner. Sometimes associates with other crows, particularly Jackdaws.

Voice and Diet   Gives a distinctive, loud, high-pitched *chauuh* call which, although similar to that of Jackdaw, is delivered in a more explosive manner. Feeds by probing in fields or sand-dunes for worms, slugs, insects and larvae. Will also take grain.

Habitat and Status   An uncommon bird of rugged headlands and islands. Found along southern, western and northern coastal areas. Choughs are very rare in most eastern regions. Feeds in sand-dune areas or on short-cropped grass known as machair. Nests in coastal cliff holes or caves.

Magpie 42–51cm
Pica pica   Snag breac

A boldly-patterned, cheeky bird with a long, wedge-shaped tail. Initially appears black and white but, when seen well, reveals an elaborate variety of colours. Head, mantle and breast black with a bluish-purple gloss. The wings are black with blue and green sheens, but show white scapulars and white, black-edged primaries. Undertail and rump black. Long tail appears black, but shows green, purple and bronze sheens. Flies with long trailing tail and white scapulars and primaries contrasting strongly with otherwise black upperparts. Belly and flanks white. **Immatures** show a duller plumage and shorter tail. Stout, pointed dark bill. Legs and eyes dark.

Voice and Diet   A very vocal bird giving a loud, chattering *chacka-chacka-chack* call which is repeated harshly both in flight and when alarmed. Feeds on insects, slugs and seeds, but also steals eggs and nestlings, making this species unpopular with many people.

Habitat and Status   A very common resident species found in towns, cities, parks and open farmland. Often seen alone or in pairs, although sometimes forms small parties. Walks in a deliberate manner while searching for food. Builds a large, domed nest in trees or bushes. Can often remain faithful to the same nesting site.

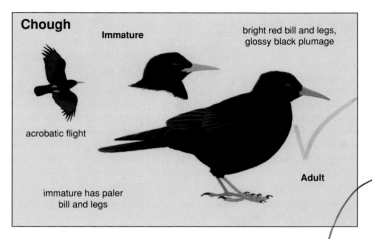

Chough

Immature

bright red bill and legs,
glossy black plumage

acrobatic flight

immature has paler
bill and legs

Adult

Magpie

striking plumage

long tail

Chough

Magpie

Jay and Starling

Jay 33–37cm
Garrulus glandarius   Scréachóg

A stocky, skulking species with a stout, dark bill, and showing a white rump and a black tail. **Adults** show a black-streaked, whitish crown, a broad black moustachial stripe, a white throat and purplish-brown cheeks, nape and mantle. Black wings show a bright blue and black barred wing patch, a conspicuous white panel formed by white bases to the secondaries, and deep chestnut inner edges to the tertials. Underparts pinkish-brown, fading to white on the centre of the belly. Undertail-coverts white. Flight appears laboured, with the white rump contrasting strongly with the black tail. Jays in Ireland belong to a specific race (*see* Introduction).

Voice and Diet   The very distinctive call can be the first indication of the presence of a Jay. Gives very harsh, loud *skkaaaa* and loud, barking *kaa* calls. Can also give a subdued mewing-type note. Feeds on fruit, berries, nuts and acorns. Known to bury food in the autumn, utilising hidden stores during hard winter periods. Also feeds on insects, worms, slugs, eggs, nestlings and small mammals.

Habitat and Status   A widely distributed resident breeding species. While present in all counties, Jays are relatively uncommon in some regions. Frequents deciduous and coniferous woodlands, open mature parklands and, occasionally in winter, orchards and suburban gardens. Nests in trees or large, mature bushes. British Jays appear paler.

Starling 20–23cm
Sturnus vulgaris   Druid

A busy species showing a long, pointed bill, a short tail and triangular wings in flight. **Summer males** show a purple and green gloss to a blackish head and underparts, buff edges to mantle and wing feathers, and a grey base to a yellow bill. **Females** similar, but show some pale underpart spots, a pink base to the bill and a thin white eye circle. **Winter males** show buff spotting on the upperparts, white spotting on the head and underparts, and a brown bill. **Winter females** show larger underpart spotting. Legs pinkish. **Juveniles** greyish-brown with a white throat, dark lores, a dark bill and dark legs. **Immatures in moult** show a mixture of juvenile and adult winter plumages.

Voice and Diet   A noisy species with a variety of calls. Very talented mimics. Usual calls comprise harsh, grating *tzheerr* and thin, whistling *tzoo-ee* notes. Song a rambling selection of warbling, whistling and clicking. Some mimicry may be included. Feeds on the ground in noisy flocks, probing with open bills in search of insects, worms and slugs. Also feeds on grain, fruit, berries, scraps and insects.

Habitat and Status   A common, widespread breeding species present in all counties in a wide range of habitats — cities, farmland, woodland, islands, shorelines. Nests in holes in trees or buildings, usually in loose colonies. In early autumn, immature birds may disperse in large flocks to headlands and islands. In late autumn, birds arrive from the Continent and in hard winters, from northern and central Europe. Can form huge winter roosting flocks.

Jay

streaked crown,
black moustaches,
bright blue wing patches

white rump

Starling

dark brown upperparts, dark lores and bill

adult all dark in summer

Adult (winter)

Immature

Jay

Starling

Sparrows

House Sparrow 14–16cm
Passer domesticus   Gaelbhan binne

House Sparrows are one of the most common, successful species found in Ireland. **Males** show a grey forehead and crown, a brownish-grey nape, a black throat and chin patch, and pale cheeks. Underparts greyish-white. Chestnut upperparts show broad dark streaks and contrast with a grey rump and uppertail-coverts. **Females** appear duller, with streaked, paler upperparts, and show a brownish crown and a pale supercilium. Underparts greyish-white. Shows a thick, short bill. A highly gregarious species, feeding and roosting in large, noisy flocks. Easily attracted to gardens to feed on any available scraps. Can occasionally be seen taking communal dust baths.

Voice and Diet   Gives a loud, repeated *chirrp* or *chirp* call. When alarmed, gives the same note delivered with more urgency. Flight call is a short *zwit*. Although primarily a seed-eater, almost any available food is taken. Recently, House Sparrows have learned to feed from nut-feeders left out for tits and finches.

Habitat and Status   A very common resident town and city species, usually found close to human habitation. In Ireland they are present in all counties. Nests in holes and cavities, often under roof tiles. On occasions, nests in trees and bushes, constructing a dome-shaped nest with a side entrance.

Tree Sparrow 13–15cm
Passer montanus   Gaelbhan crainn

Tree Sparrows are slightly smaller and more colourful than the very similar House Sparrow. **Males** and **females** are identical. Shows a striking head pattern with a deep chestnut crown and a distinctive black spot on white cheeks. The black throat and chin patch are neater than House Sparrow. Shows a white neck collar and streaked chestnut upperparts. Tail and rump warm brown. Underparts greyish-white. Thick bill short and dark. **Immatures** show a brownish-grey tinge to the centre of the crown, buffish-grey underparts and a yellowish base to the bill. Occasionally joins House Sparrow flocks in the winter.

Voice and Diet   Gives a distinctive, sharp, repeated *tek* call. When perched, can also give a loud *tritt* call which can be difficult to hear if within a mixed flock of sparrows. Feeds on a wide variety of seeds and cereals. Although primarily a seed-eater, Tree Sparrows will occasionally eat insects.

Habitat and Status   A widespread but scarce resident species, found in all regions. Found on open farmland and less frequently in towns and villages. Tree Sparrows breed in widely scattered colonies. Nests in holes in trees and old buildings.

House Sparrow

Male

grey forehead and crown

streaked, pale upperparts and pale supercilium

extensive black bib

Female

Tree Sparrow

deep chestnut crown

striking black spot on white cheeks

small, neat black bib

House Sparrow

Tree Sparrow

Finches

Chaffinch 14–16cm
Fringilla coelebs   Rí rua
Summer males show a blue-grey crown and nape, a reddish-pink breast and cheeks, and a chestnut-coloured mantle. Dark wings show a broad white shoulder patch, white-tipped greater coverts and white bases to the primaries. Primaries and tertials also show olive-green edges. Forked tail shows white outer feathers. Rump olive-green. **In winter** the plumage is paler. **Females** show similar wing markings, but the upperparts and head are greyish-brown. The centre of the crown and the nape are paler, creating dark lines from side of neck onto sides of crown. Underparts pale greyish-brown. **Immatures** similar to females. Thick bill blue-grey. Can form large flocks in winter.

Voice and Diet   Calls frequently, giving a loud *pinnk* call or, in flight, a *chhip* call. In spring and summer, males can be heard to give a *whiit* call. Song consists of scratchy chipping-type notes finished rapidly with a *ptsse-eeo* note. Feeds on seeds, berries, fruit and occasionally insects.

Habitat and Status   An abundant finch, found in every county. Frequents gardens, parklands, hedgerows and woodland. In winter, found in farmyards and on open fields when resident birds are joined by birds from northern Europe. Nests in bushes and low trees.

Brambling 14–15cm
Fringilla montifringilla   Breacán
A colourful finch with a black and orange plumage and a white rump. **Winter males** show a mottled brown head and mantle, and grey from behind eye onto nape and sides of neck. A bright orange shoulder patch and two buff wingbars are obvious on blackish wings. Upper breast orange, fading to a white lower breast, belly and undertail. Shows diffuse spotting on flanks. Deeply notched blackish tail contrasts with the white rump. **Females** similar, but show a paler head and shoulder patch, and an orange wash on the breast. **Summer males** show a black head and mantle, and orange on the throat, breast and scapulars. Thick bill black on summer males, paler on females. Legs pale.

Voice and Diet   Calls include a Chaffinch-like *chick* in flight and a *tsueek* when on the ground. Feeds on seeds and berries but also favours beechmast.

Habitat and Status   An uncommon winter visitor from northern Europe. Found in mixed finch flocks on farmlands, open fields and beech woodland. In late autumn, occurs on coastal headlands and islands. Numbers can fluctuate from winter to winter, with flocks of several hundred birds occasionally recorded.

Chaffinch

white wingbars, dull grey and brown head pattern

blue-grey crown and nape, pinkish underparts

Female

Male

Brambling

pale wingbars and rump

brown upperparts, pale orange underparts

striking black and orange plumage

Male

Female

Chaffinch

Brambling

Finches

Greenfinch 14–16cm
Carduelis chloris Glasán darach

A chunky finch with bright yellow wing and tail flashes, a thick, pale bill and pale legs. **Summer males** show an olive-green head and upperparts, and bright yellow-green underparts. Greyish wings show a bright yellow flash on the primaries. Rump yellow-green. Dark, forked tail shows yellow flashes at base. **Winter males** show brown tones to upperparts and head. **Adult females** show a faintly streaked, greyish-brown head and upperparts with yellow-tinged, whitish underparts and dull yellow wing and tail flashes. **Immatures**, while showing streaked brownish heads and upperparts, pale, streaked underparts and a brownish rump, do show yellow wing and tail flashes.

Voice and Diet In flight, gives a distinctive, soft, deep, trilling *chit* which is usually repeated. In spring, males can give a long, drawn-out, nasal *tsueee* note. The twittering song consists of a variety of call notes and is delivered from a prominent perch or during a slow, wing-flapping, bat-like flight display. Feeds on a variety of berries, seeds, fruit and occasionally insects. A regular winter visitor to nut-feeders in gardens.

Habitat and Status An extremely common, widespread, resident species found in all counties. In winter, birds from Britain and the Continent can occur. Found in a wide range of habitats, nesting in hedgerows, bushes and trees in gardens, parks, woodland edges and farmland. In winter, can be found in quite large flocks on farmlands and yards, arable fields and coastal saltmarshes. Also a common winter visitor to nut and seed feeders.

Siskin 11–13cm
Carduelis spinus Siscín

An agile finch which shows two thick yellow wingbars, a pointed, pale bill and dark legs. **Adult males** show a black crown and chin, olive-green ear-coverts, and a yellowish supercilium, throat and breast. Upperparts olive-green with faint streaking. Yellow-edged, black wings show two broad yellow wingbars. Yellow-green rump unstreaked. Short, dark, forked tail shows yellow base. Underparts white with dark streaking along flanks. **Adult females** show heavily streaked greyish-green upperparts and head. Wings similar to males. Underparts whitish with heavy streaking. Immatures similar to females, but appear browner on the upperparts and show a greyish rump.

Voice and Diet Gives distinctive, loud, shrill *tseu* or more extended *tseu-eet* calls. Song consists of a combination of call notes and more warbling, twittering notes. The song can be delivered either from a prominent perch or during a Greenfinch-like, slow, flapping display flight. Feeds on a wide range of tree seeds and will readily visit nut and seed feeders.

Habitat and Status A common, widespread, resident species found in all counties. In summer, frequents conifer plantations and occasionally mixed woodlands. Nests high in conifers. In winter, is found in areas with alder, birch and larch trees. Has become a regular visitor to gardens in towns and cities, feeding on nut- and seed-feeders. Highly gregarious, often found in quite large flocks. Will readily associate with other species.

Greenfinch

bright yellow tail
and wing flashes

thick,
pale bill

Male

Female

Siskin

black crown and chin

two yellow
wingbars and
unstreaked
yellow-green
rump

Male

Female

streaked head and upperparts

Greenfinch

Siskin

Finches

Linnet 13–14cm
Carduelis cannabina   Gleoiseach

A small brownish finch with a heavy, greyish bill and white flashes on the wings and tail. **Summer males** show a bright red forehead and breast, a grey head, a pale throat and whitish underparts. Warm brown upperparts show faint streaks and an inconspicuous wingbar. Dark primaries show extensive white flashes on outer feathers. Short, forked tail shows striking white sides. **Winter males** show a streaked grey head, with pale areas above and below eye and on cheeks. Whitish underparts show faint streaking on buff breast and flanks. **Females** similar to winter males, but show a browner head with heavy streaking on upperparts and underparts. **Immatures** show a pale-buff face and less streaking.

Voice and Diet   In flight gives a twittering, musical *tret-tret-terret* call and a drawn-out *tsweet*. Song consists of a variety of twittering, trilling, fluty notes which are delivered from a prominent perch. Feeds on a wide range of plant seeds and some insects.

Habitat and Status   A widespread and common breeding species present in all counties. Frequents a variety of habitats, including farmlands, rough pastures, waste ground, sand-dunes, saltmarshes, scrubland and young plantations. Nests in dense cover on the ground or in brambles and bushes. Many Irish birds winter in southern continental Europe.

Twite 13–14cm
Carduelis flavirostris   Gleoiseach sléibhe

A heavily streaked finch, similar to Linnet but with a pale yellow bill in winter and less extensive white wing and tail flashes. **Summer males** show a warm buff face, throat and breast, and streaked-brownish ear-coverts, nape and crown. Underparts whitish with streaking from breast onto flanks. Heavily streaked, brownish upperparts show a conspicuous pale wingbar and white flashes on outer primaries. Rump pinkish. Forked tail shows white sides. Bill dark. **Winter males** show a pale yellow bill, a buffish-pink rump and streaked, buff flanks. **Females** similar to males, but show a streaked buffish rump. Best told from Linnet by buff face and throat, small, paler bill and heavier streaking.

Voice and Diet   In flight, gives a harsh, nasal, metallic *tchweek* call which can often be the first indication of the presence of a Twite among a large, mixed finch flock. Can also give twittering calls which are similar to but harder than Linnets, and a softer *tseee* call. Song consists of a range of twittering, trilling, musical notes delivered from a prominent perch. Feeds on a variety of plant seeds and some insects.

Habitat and Status   An uncommon resident species, with breeding populations based in northern, north-western, western and south-western counties. Nests on the ground in heather, old stone walls or gorse, frequenting areas of open, upland moorlands and pastures. In winter, more commonly found along coastal stubble and crop fields, saltmarshes and estuaries. Feeds on the ground and can be quite approachable.

Linnet

Male
(summer)

Male (winter)

Female

white flashes on wings

Twite

streaked buffish rump

pale yellow bill,
pinkish rump

Female

Male

Linnet

Twite

233

Finches

Redpoll 11–13cm
Carduelis flammea   Deargéadan coiteann

A heavily streaked, brownish finch with a black-tipped yellow bill and which is smaller and more arboreal in behaviour than Linnet. **Males** show a bright red forehead, a black chin and pinkish-red tones on head, breast and upper flanks. Underparts whitish with dark flank streaking. Crown and upperparts tawny-brown with heavy streaking. Wings show two obvious whitish-buff wingbars but lack white primary flashes of Linnet. Rump pinkish. Forked, brownish tail does not show white sides. Duller in winter. **Females** show heavier underpart streaking and lack strong pinkish-red tones. **Immatures** similar to females, showing a red forehead but no pinkish-red tones to head and breast.

Voice and Diet   In flight, gives a twittering, rhythmic, repeated *chei-chei-chei* call. Can also occasionally give a drawn-out *tsweeck*. Song consists of a variety of trilling notes interspersed with call notes. Song can be delivered from a prominent perch but can also be given during a circling, slow, flapping flight display. Feeds on a wide range of tree seeds, particularly those of birch and alder. Will also take some insects.

Habitat and Status   A widespread breeding species, present in all counties. During the breeding season, found in a variety of woodlands which usually include some birch or alder. Also found in upland conifer plantations. Nests in high bushes, young conifers and woodland edges. In autumn and winter, tends to leave more mountainous and western areas. Can associate with Siskins and occasionally visits bird tables in town gardens. Largest winter populations are in north-eastern and midland counties.

Scarlet Rosefinch 14–15cm
Carpodacus erythrinus

Stout, thick-billed finch, usually found in Ireland in the drab female or immature plumage. **Summer males** show a bright pink-red head and breast, often extending down onto the whitish belly and flanks. Upperparts streaked greyish-brown. Rump pinkish-red. Notched tail greyish-brown. **Immatures** and **females** are extremely plain and nondescript, with greyish-brown upperparts and head. The paler underparts show faint streaking and an inconspicuous malar stripe. Brownish wings show two diagnostic pale wingbars on the median and greater coverts. Large black beady eye stands out in a plain face. The thick, short bill is dark horn-coloured. Legs brownish.

Voice and Diet   Occasionally heard to call in Ireland, giving a quiet *teu-ic* call. Has also been heard to sing when seen in spring. The song consists of loud, far-carrying *teu-teu* notes. Feeds primarily on seeds.

Habitat and Status   A rare but regular vagrant to Ireland from eastern Europe. Although small numbers have been recorded in spring, they are usually found in autumn on coastal islands and headlands. Feeds in fields, but perches openly on hedgerows, bushes or in gardens. Often associates with other feeding finch flocks.

Redpoll

Male

red forehead patch, black chin

males have pink flush on breast

Female

Scarlet Rosefinch

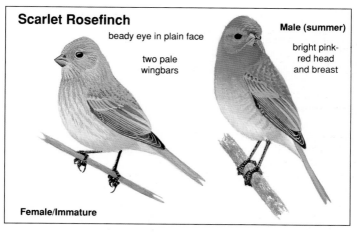

beady eye in plain face

Male (summer)

two pale wingbars

bright pink-red head and breast

Female/Immature

Redpoll

Scarlet Rosefinch

Finches

Crossbill 16–17cm
Loxia curvirostra   Crosghob

Stocky, large-headed finch with long wings and a short, deeply-forked tail. The large bill is crossed at the tip, an adaptation for taking seeds from the cones of coniferous trees. When feeding, pulls the cones from the trees, holding them in the feet while extracting the seeds. **Males** have an orange-red head, upperparts and underparts, the rump being slightly brighter. **Females** are dull greyish-green with a bright yellow-green rump. The wings of both sexes are brownish. **Immatures** are pale greyish-green and heavily streaked. Eye and legs blackish. Highly gregarious, often moving in large, noisy flocks. Flight strong and undulating. Often seen perched on the very tops of trees.

Voice and Diet   A noisy species, continuously calling to each other both in flight and when feeding. Call consists of a short, sharp *chip*. In song, gives a series of trills along with high pitched *tir-ee* notes. Feeds mainly on conifer seeds, although will take berries and occasionally insects.

Habitat and Status   Usually found in coniferous forests, frequently visiting pools to drink. An uncommon breeding bird in Ireland, nesting high in conifer trees as early as February. Populations can fluctuate drastically, with large influxes occurring in certain years. In autumn, can be found on coastal headlands and islands.

Bullfinch 14–16cm
Pyrrhula pyrrhula   Corcrán coille

Plump, thick-necked finch with a short, dark, thickset bill. **Males** show a black crown and upper nape, continuing down below the eye and onto the chin. The cheeks, throat, breast and upper belly are bright pink-red, with the lower belly and undertail white. The mantle is blue-grey and extends up the nape. The black wings show a broad white wingbar. Black tail appears square-ended. Most obvious feature in flight is the broad white rump. Duller **females** show pinkish-buff cheeks, breast and upper belly, with a greyish-brown mantle. Black crown duller. **Immatures** do not show a black cap. Black eye blends into black cap. Thick, short bill blackish-grey. Legs blackish.

Voice and Diet   Gives a soft *dieu* call. The song is a quiet variety of creaking notes. Feeds on seeds, berries and occasionally insects. Also has a liking for fresh buds of apple trees and is considered a pest in orchards.

Habitat and Status   A common resident species found in open parkland, woods, orchards and well-developed gardens. Builds nests in bushes or brambles. Unlike other finches, Bullfinches are more often seen in pairs than in flocks.

236

Crossbill

grey-green plumage

crossed mandibles

orange-red plumage

Female

Male

Bullfinch

heavy dark bill

white rump

broad white wingbar

Female

Male

Crossbill

Bullfinch

237

Finches and Buntings

Goldfinch 14–15cm
Carduelis carduelis   Lasair choille

A charming finch with colourful head and wing markings, and a white rump. Sexes alike. **Adults** show a bright red forehead and chin, black before eye, and white cheeks and throat. Crown and sides of neck black. Mantle buff-brown, extending onto lower throat, sides of breast and along flanks. Underparts white. Wings black with a bright yellow patch, yellow bases to primaries and white tips to primaries, secondaries and tertials. Rump white. The black, notched tail shows white tips. **Immatures** show a greyish-brown head and mantle, and duller wing markings. Thick bill whitish-grey and pointed. Legs pale. Rarely associates with other finch flocks. Flight undulating.

Voice and Diet   The twittering, chattering *ptswit-wit-wit* flight call is unmistakable. Can also give a loud *ee-uu* call. The song is a trill consisting of a variety of twittering notes. Feeds on a variety of seeds and is often found feeding on the tops of thistles or teazels. Also takes small insects.

Habitat and Status   A common finch found on open ground such as parks, gardens and woodland edges. Can be seen on waste ground where thistles are likely to grow. A resident species, Goldfinches nest in bushes and trees.

Yellowhammer 16–17cm
Emberiza citrinella   Buíóg

A striking bunting, **summer males** showing a bright yellow head and underparts with olive-brown head streaking, a chestnut ear-covert border and moustachial stripe, a diffuse chestnut breast band, and dark streaking on chestnut-washed flanks. Chestnut upperparts show dark streaking. Chestnut rump unstreaked. Tail shows white outer edges. **Winter males** show heavier head and underpart streaking, and darker head markings. **Females** show a pale yellow head with olive-brown ear-covert border, moustachial and malar stripes. Underparts yellowish with brown breast and flank streaking. Upperparts as male. **Immatures** duller than females with finer streaking. Bill greyish. Legs pinkish.

Voice and Diet   Gives a sharp, loud, metallic *tzwik* call. The song is a distinctive combination of repeated, high-pitched, tinkling notes finishing in a drawn-out, wheezy *chuee* note. This song is traditionally transcribed as *little-bit-of-bread-and-no-cheese,* the emphasis being on the *cheese.* Feeds on a wide range of seeds, corn, grain, berries and fruit. In summer, feeds on insects, spiders and worms.

Habitat and Status   A scarce but widely distributed species, formerly found in all counties. In recent years, numbers have decreased, with the largest populations now based in eastern, south-eastern, northern and some western counties. Found along hedgerows on arable farmland, woodland edges, overgrown scrub and gorse slopes and young conifer plantations. Nests on or near the ground in overgrown bases of hedges and brambles.

Goldfinch

yellow wing patches

conspicuous red, black and white head pattern

white rump

Yellowhammer

Male

striking head pattern

unstreaked chestnut rump

white outer-tail feathers

Female

Goldfinch

Yellowhammer

Buntings

Corn Bunting 17–19cm
Emberiza calandra   Gealóg bhuachair

A large, heavily streaked, brownish bunting with a large, thick bill. **Summer adults** show a streaked brownish crown, a pale supercilium and a broad dark border to heavily streaked ear-coverts. Underparts whitish with a thick malar stripe meeting heavy streaking on the sides of the breast, and continuing onto the flanks. Upperparts greyish-brown with heavy dark streaking on the mantle, and dark centres to the wing feathers. Long brownish tail does not show white outer feathers. **Winter adults** and **immatures** appear duller, with whitish-buff underparts. Shows a very thick, pinkish bill. Legs and largish feet pinkish-orange. Usually seen perched prominently on telegraph wires and fences.

Voice and Diet   Gives a low, sharp *tikk* call. The far-carrying song is a fast, complicated jingle of rattles and chirps. The distinctive song has often been described as sounding like rattling keys. Feeds on a wide variety of seeds and cereals but will take some insects on occasion.

Habitat and Status   A very rare breeding bird of coastal farmland and open country. Formerly found in most counties at the turn of the century, the range of the Corn Bunting has diminished seriously. Breeding populations are now confined to widely scattered, isolated groups in western and north-western regions. Nests on the ground in long grass or thistles.

Reed Bunting 14–16cm
Emberiza schoeniclus   Gealóg ghiolcaí

A striking bunting with a long, white-edged tail. **Summer males** show a black head and throat contrasting with a white moustachial stripe and neck collar. Upperparts rufous with black streaking and centres to wing feathers. Underparts whitish with flank streaking. In **winter**, black on head and throat obscured by buffish tips. **Adult females** and **immatures** show a brownish crown with a thin, dark, lateral crown-stripe and buff supercilium. Ear-coverts and lores brownish, with a dark eye-stripe from behind eye forming a dark ear-covert border and a moustachial stripe meeting the bill. Creamy throat shows a malar stripe. Breast and flanks streaked. Bill greyish. Legs brownish.

Voice and Diet   Song consists of repeated, hurried *tzik-tzik-tzik-tzizzizik* notes. The song is usually delivered from the tops of reed-stems or from bushes. Most frequently heard calls include a loud, shrill *tswee* and a harsh *chink*. Feeds on a wide range of insects and larvae in summer, taking mostly seeds in winter.

Habitat and Status   A common, resident, widely distributed species present in all counties. Found in a wide range of habitats, including reed-beds, marshes, hedgerows, sand-dunes and young conifer plantations. Nests on or near the ground in tussocks, rank vegetation or bushes. In winter, are altitudinal migrants, leaving more mountainous regions in favour of low-lying or coastal habitat. Can also be found on farmlands in winter.

Corn Bunting

large, heavily-streaked bunting

thick, pale bill

lacks white on tail

Reed Bunting

Female

conspicuous white moustachial stripe on black head

dark streaking on underparts

striking head pattern

Male (summer)

Corn Bunting

Reed Bunting

Buntings

Lapland Bunting 14–16cm
Calcarius lapponicus

A long-winged bunting with a short, yellowish bill. **Winter males** and **females** show a buff crown, a black lateral crown-stripe, and buff lores, ear-coverts and supercilium. Black eye-stripe forms a thick border to ear-coverts and continues as a moustachial stripe. Nape chestnut or warm buff. White tips to median and greater coverts, and chestnut greater coverts, contrasted with streaked, buff upperparts. Creamy underparts show a malar stripe and streaking on breast and flanks. **Winter males** tend to be brighter with dark blotching on the breast. **1st winters** show a dull head and nape. **Summer males** show a black head and throat with white from eye to sides of breast. Legs dark.

Voice and Diet   In flight or when flushed, gives a very distinctive, dry, rippling, rattling *trickitick* call which can often be followed by a softer, descending *teuu*. This latter call can resemble that of Snow Bunting but is softer. Moves on the ground in a low, crouched manner, feeding on a wide range of seeds. Will occasionally take insects.

Habitat and Status   A scarce but regular autumn and winter visitor. On passage, found on northern, western and south-western coastal islands and headlands, frequenting crop and stubble fields, pastures and moorland. In winter, found along coastal counties, including eastern and south-eastern areas. In winter, is normally found on coastal stubble and crop fields and saltmarshes. Can be very tame and hard to flush.

Snow Bunting 16–18cm
Plectrophenax nivalis   Gealóg shneachta

A striking, tame bunting with a yellowish bill and dark legs. **Winter males** show a warm buff crown, cheeks and breast sides and a pale buff nape. Underparts white. Dark-streaked, pale buff upperparts contrast with white inner wings and black primaries. In flight, shows white sides to black tail. **Females** show dull buff upperparts, crown, cheeks and sides of breast with streaking on nape and upperparts. Wings show brown primaries and less white, with dark bases to coverts and markings on secondaries. Underparts creamy with buff flanks. **Immatures** are very dull, showing a very small area of white on the wings. **Summer males** show a black and white plumage and a black bill.

Voice and Diet   In flight or when flushed, gives a rippling, musical *tirrirrirrip* call. Also gives a plaintive *teu* call. Feeds on the ground, taking a variety of seeds and other plant material. Will occasionally take insects.

Habitat and Status   An uncommon but regular autumn passage migrant and winter visitor. On passage, found on coastal headlands and islands, frequenting pastures and moorlands. Winters in small numbers along most coastal counties. Frequents coastal shingle banks, dunes, stubble and crop fields, piers and harbours. Can also winter inland, usually on mountain tops. Occasionally occurs in spring.

Lapland Bunting

1st winter

Summer
Male
(rare)

long wings, yellow bill

Male (winter)

Snow Bunting

Female (winter)

yellow bill, black legs

white underparts and wing
patches

Male (winter)

Lapland Bunting

Snow Bunting

Index

English

Index

Index

Latin

Index

Index